Developmental Problems of Childhood and Adolescence

Prevention, Treatment and Training

Martin Herbert

D0068185

BPS Blackwell

© 2005 by Martin Herbert
A BPS Blackwell book

BLACKWELL PUBLISHING
350 Main Street, Malden, MA 02148-5020, USA
108 Cowley Road, Oxford OX4 1JF, UK
550 Swanston Street, Carlton, Victoria 3053, Australia

The right of Martin Herbert to be identified as the Author of this Work has been
asserted in accordance with the UK Copyright, Designs, and Patents Act 1988.

First published 2005 by The British Psychological Society and Blackwell Publishing Ltd

Library of Congress Cataloging-in-Publication Data

Herbert, Martin.
    Developmental problems of childhood and adolescence prevention, treatment, and
training / Martin Herbert.—1st ed.
        p.   cm.
    Includes bibliographical references and index.
    ISBN 1–4051–1592–0 (pbk : alk. paper)
1. Developmental disabilities.   2. Abnormalities, Human.   3. Child psychopathology.
4. Adolescent psychopathology.   5. Developmentally disabled children.   6. Children
with disabilities—Development.   I. Title.
    RJ135.H56 2005
    618.92′8588—dc22   2004024917

A catalogue record for this title is available from the British Library.

Set in 10/12.5 Adobe Garamond
by SNP Best-set Typesetter Ltd, Hong Kong
Printed and bound in the United Kingdom
by TJ International, Padstow, Cornwall

The publisher's policy is to use permanent paper from mills that operate a sustainable
forestry policy, and which has been manufactured from pulp processed using acid-free
and elementary chlorine-free practices. Furthermore, the publisher ensures that the text
paper and cover board used have met acceptable environmental accreditation standards.

For further information on
BPS Blackwell, visit our website:
www.bpsblackwell.com

Developmental Problems of Childhood and Adolescence

*For my good friends and fellow musicians: Arthur,
Colin and Reg*

Contents

Preface

I very much regretted, when completing my book *Typical and Atypical Development: From Conception to Adolescence*, that I could not follow up the discussion of normal child development, and the diagnosis and causation of developmental disorders, with an account of prevention, treatment and training issues. It was not possible, in one volume, to do justice to the vast range of theories, interventions and resources available to multi-disciplinary professionals working with children and adolescents in need of help.

I hope, in the following chapters, to make good those omissions by describing the major approaches available to remedy or prevent the disorders listed below. At times my choice of where best to place the discussion of particular physical and mental health problems is somewhat arbitrary as they have their effect at various ages. I have been guided, as far as possible, by the time of life when they are first detected, become observable, or when their impact proves to be particularly disabling. Some are transient but recur; others constitute the kinds of disability that engender special needs throughout the life span. Among the disabilities included are:

- pervasive developmental disorders (e.g. autism);
- genetic disorders (e.g. Down's syndrome; Turner's syndrome);
- physical disorders and impairments (e.g. bronchial asthma, cystic fibrosis; cerebral palsy and sensory impairments);
- intellectual disabilities (learning difficulties);
- neuro-developmental disorders (e.g. epilepsy, AD/HD);
- emotional and behavioural disorders (e.g. phobic anxiety, conduct disorder, delinquency);

- attachment disorder (e.g. reactive attachment disorder);
- feeding disorders (failure-to-thrive; anorexia nervosa);
- growth disorders (congenital short stature; obesity);
- self- and body-image problems (body dysmorphia);
- educational problems (e.g. dyslexia).

■ Developmental Framework

What guides my discussion of disorders like the ones listed above is a consideration of the developmental tasks that are salient at particular stages of children's
progression towards adolescence. There are difficult physical, social, cognitive and
emotional challenges faced by all youngsters, particularly if disabled, at these
times. Among the major tasks are learning to walk and talk, and to control toileting functions. They also include the development of self-control over aggressive and sexual inclinations, the acquisition of moral attitudes and social skills,
adjustment to school life and the mastering of academic knowledge. All involve
a degree of confidence, and the development of independence and maturity of
judgement.

The issues of *competence* and *achievement* are central to these age- and stage-
related tasks. Both parents and children worry about the 'timetable' they imply.
Success tends to result in a sense of well-being; failures or delays may lead to loss
of dignity, self-esteem and the confidence needed to tackle further developmental tasks. Failure often leads to lowered self-esteem, mockery from peers, and disapproval by those in authority.

As we shall see when we come to deal with interventions, all of this (and many
other considerations) make the physical and social training, and the education of
children with disabilities, critically important. The likelihood that children and
teenagers will cope successfully with life's tasks, whatever the 'hurdles', is immeasurably increased when parental influence and professional help are committed,
authoritative and wise.

■ Individual Development

Effective work with children requires knowledge of what is typical in their physical and verbal behaviour – an empathic understanding of what they think, feel,
do and say, as they grow up. I dealt with these issues in *Typical and Atypical Development: From Conception to Adolescence*, and will therefore not dwell on them,

except (at times) briefly. What emerged from the research that informed that book is the impressive variability in outlook, activities, abilities and physical capabilities displayed by children who are developing in a *typical* manner, and also youngsters diagnosed as *atypical, disabled* or *delayed.* A consequence of such marked differences in the personalities and, indeed, within the disabilities of individual children, is the need for a particularly wide range of agencies, professions and interventions to alleviate or prevent their disorders.

■ Readership

In writing this book, I have had in mind postgraduate trainees and qualified practitioners who work in services designed to meet the needs of children with the developmental and related health problems listed above. They belong to many disciplines and voluntary services:

- clinical and educational psychology
- child psychiatry
- hospital and community paediatrics
- speech, occupational and physiotherapy
- health visiting and paediatric nursing
- social work
- Portage work
- pre-school advising and special needs teaching
- nursery nursing
- residential child-care
- volunteers in many activities (e.g. specialist associations, help-lines).

■ Organization of the Book

These disorders are discussed, after an introductory chapter on conceptual issues, in 14 chapters in Parts I to V of the book. The problem categories are considered in relation to what is relevant at the prenatal, perinatal, infancy, pre-school, school-going and early adolescent stages of development. Each disorder is discussed, as appropriate, in terms of:

- diagnosis
- relevant clinical features

- developmental features
- genetic, environmental, and psychosocial causes
- interventions (prevention, treatment, and training)
- outcomes.

Chapter 15 in Part VI describes in theoretical and practical detail, the analysis required for planning treatment and training programmes, and formulating care-plans. Chapter 16 provides information about the availability of individual, group, and general community resources that can help the families of children with physical and intellectual disabilities and mental health problems.

Appendices I–V contain details of clinical assessment, special education and 'statements of need', and information about developmental and clinical assessment and phone help-lines. There is also a guide to the delicate problem of giving parents worrying diagnostic news.

Acknowledgements

I am indebted to many researchers and clinicians for the ideas and research findings that have informed this book, particularly Alan Carr, Philip Graham, Patricia Howlin, Vicki Lewis, Michael Rutter, and Stephen Scott. My thanks go to Sarah Bird and her editorial and production team at Blackwell Publishing for their help in bringing the book to print. I am also grateful to Susan Dunsmore for her friendly guidance and expertise as copy editor.

Introduction

Each person is an idiom unto himself, an apparent violation of the syntax of the species.

(Gordon Allport, 1937)

Chapters 1–14 deal with the particular developmental problems referred to in the in the Preface. In Chapter 15 we step back somewhat in order to take a broader view of the way in which disabilities and disorders, in general, are assessed and formulated for planned individual and group interventions. This more global perspective includes an account of what assistance is available from community organizations, voluntary agencies, and governmental policies, for families in need of help for their disabled children.

■ Definitions

The terms in the title of this book require some explanation as they are not as straightforward as they look. 'Development' is typically defined as a progressive series of orderly, coherent changes leading to the goal of eventual self-sufficiency. This may be the hopeful expectation, but children's developmental progress through life is often disorderly and incoherent, and movement (when delayed or diverted by physical or psychological disabilities) is not always in a forward direction toward maturity.

▨ **Disabilities**

It has not proved easy to arrive at agreed definitions of this term. The World Health Organization's attempts have altered and 'slimmed down' over the years. In the 1980s:

- the word 'impairment' was used to indicate a deviation from normal, such as being unable to coordinate leg movements in order to kick a ball;
- 'handicap' defined a restriction in the ability to perform a normal activity of daily life which an individual of the same age is able to perform, as when a 4-year-old child has no speech; and
- 'disability' applied to the inability to achieve the normal role in society commensurate with the individual's age and social milieu.

Thus, a late teenager who is unable to read or attend to his or her purchases and hygiene is handicapped. Someone of the same age who is partially blind and unable to walk without crutches, but able to look after his or her daily living necessities and attend a mainstream school, is disabled but not handicapped.

These criteria meant that a child could be impaired but not necessarily disabled; or disabled without being handicapped. These definitions were criticized for:

- their closeness to medical disease classifications;
- their assumptions of normality based on able-bodied perspectives;
- taking environmental influence for granted;
- failing to appreciate cultural and ethnic differences.

The latest revision (World Health Organization, 2002) has dropped the term 'handicap' and retained the word 'disability' in an overarching definition, reflecting the interaction between individuals and their social and physical environment. Disability summarizes many different functional limitations occurring in any population, in any country of the world. People might be disabled by physical, intellectual or sensory impairment, by medical conditions, or mental illness.

Intellectual disability

A variety of general titles is used depending upon local preference, public confusion, insensitive prejudice and political correctness. Terms include:

- 'intellectual disability', which is now used in much of the UK and international literature, and is currently used by the International Association for Scientific Studies of Intellectual Disability and the *Journal of Intellectual Disability Research*;
- 'learning disability' is the semi-official term used by many practitioners in the UK;
- 'mental retardation' is the official term used in North America (*DSM-IV*) and in Europe (*ICD-10*);
- 'mental handicap' is a term that was used in the past in the UK;
- Terms like 'mental subnormality', 'feeble-mindedness', and 'imbecile' are now, thankfully, obsolete.

I have chosen to use the terms 'intellectual disability' and 'learning difficulties', except where another term is used as part of a formal study in the clinical literature.

The social model of disability

One of the significant theoretical developments in the field of disability is the insistence by many theoreticians and practitioners on a 'social model' of disability, which challenges the discrimination and social exclusion (e.g. segregated schools, residential homes and day-centres) suffered by disabled people. Its beginnings in 1976 emerged from a conference of the Union of the Physically Impaired Against Segregation (UPIAS). A later development in Britain was the founding of the Disabled Peoples' Movement. Members aim to enforce in legislation, their rights and responsibilities as citizens, and also highlight failures in the provision of services for disabled people.

Normality and Abnormality

The aim to *normalize* as far as possible, the lives of people with physical and intellectual disabilities begs an obvious, but awkward question. What is typical or normal development? The term 'normal' derives from the Latin word 'norma', meaning a rule or standard. With its prefix 'ab', meaning 'away from', the term 'abnormal' means a deviation from a standard. For medical practitioners, with their emphasis on pathology, specific syndromes (symptom clusters and disease patterns) or handicapping conditions (physical disabilities), abnormal phenomena involve deviations (as in the case of a cleft palate) from a structurally 'sound' standard, or (as with diabetes) a 'healthily' functioning bodily system. For psychologists, the concept of abnormality usually means a deviation from a social rule or standard, with all the room for subjectivity that criterion allows.

Labelling

A dilemma for those writing about disorders associated with childhood and adolescent development is the risk that the individual who is said to 'have' the difficulties is submerged by the diagnostic category, so that *it* becomes the 'problem' that is uppermost. In a sense, the disorder 'has' the child, whose individuality and personal strengths are overlooked or undervalued. The whole person becomes less, rather than more than the sum of his or her parts. The categorizing of a child as abnormal or disabled may convey a therapeutically pessimistic 'message' that is not intended or appropriate. By no means do children with atypical conditions necessarily display all-embracing developmental attributes that are untypical or disabling.

Terminology should reflect the desire to avoid the reductive language that diminishes the child, as when we refer to a child with Down's syndrome as a 'Down's child', or a pre-school child with learning difficulties as a 'mentally retarded pre-schooler'. These remarks about categories do not mean that they do not exist. There are continuities and discontinuities between conditions which are 'typical' and 'atypical' in physical and psychological development. As Michael Rutter (2003, p. 934) puts it, 'Both continuities and discontinuities between normality and disorder must be tested for, rather than assumed.' Nevertheless, the findings in both childhood and adulthood do indicate that a categorical distinction between psychopathology and normality can be rather artificial and misleading. As he points out:

> sub-clinical levels of symptoms have correlates and consequences that are broadly comparable with those that apply to clinically significant disorders . . . many risk and protective factors operate dimensionally with effects within the 'normal' range (statistically speaking), as well as with overt psychopathology or disorder.
>
> (***ibid.***)

It is important to bear in mind that not all children with disabling (atypical) conditions have atypical developmental patterns in all areas as they grow up. Aspects of the impaired child's development may be *normal*, developing within the range of variation reported for non-handicapped children. Among the differences between the development of disabled ('handicapped') and non-disabled ('non-handicapped') children, may be:

- *Delay*: the same stages are passed through but the atypical child may not ultimately reach the more advanced stages of development.
- *Abnormal*: there are behaviours and developments not seen in children who are not handicapped because the processes of development are different from the normal.
- *Absent*: the child fails to develop in a particular area.
- *Compensatory*: development in the atypical child follows a different path from that taken by the typical child, although the arrival point is the same.

■ Causation (Aetiology)

The complexity of developmental and psychological problems has led to much confusion in the analysis of causes. There is an all-too-human tendency to oversimplify and think of causality in linear, univariate terms: A causes B; B is the effect of A. However, there is no limit to the analysis of causes. One finds, not a single antecedent, not even a chain of antecedents, but a whole interlacing network of them. Many of the major developmental disorders, mental health conditions, psychological and psychosomatic problems to be discussed in the coming chapters, have interacting genetic, organic, biochemical, and psychological causes. The reality for developmental and clinical psychologists and psychiatrists is the complex, multivariate nature of most of the phenomena they study (see Kim-Cohen, et al. 2004; Rutter, 2003).

A further complication of concepts such as cause and effect is that they have no anchorage in *absolutes*. An event which may be formulated as an *effect* in one analysis may be perceived as a *cause* in another analysis; and what one theorist regards as a cause, another may regard as a *mediating response*. And if a child is identified as a patient at a time earlier than the circumstance immediately preceding the development (*cause*) of a disorder, the treatment is likely to be called *prevention*.

Social Ecology

The term *social ecology* is used to describe the system of psychosocial influences (benign and adverse) impinging on the child and adolescent and their environment (Bronfenbrenner, 1989). They include:

- the *microsystem*, which comprises all relationships and transactions in a particular setting, e.g. the social and physical family environment;

- the *mesosystem*, which includes the interrelationships between the major settings such as home and school where children do their growing up;
- the *macrosystem*, which contains the general beliefs, values and traditions of the culture or subculture that control the interactions between the various layers of the social system, and the tenets that reflect the meaning and value of life.

■ Treatment and Training

These terms have been differentiated in the sub-title of the book. However, the distinction between treatment (usually conducted at a Child Development Assessment Centre or Child and Adolescent Mental Health Centre) and training (often located for outreach individual or group work in the home, school or community centre) is at times indistinct. The treatment model is most appropriate to the 'acute' physical and emotional disorders of childhood (e.g. hydrocephalus or specific phobias), the training model to the longer-term problems (e.g. autism or attention deficit/hyperactivity behaviour). Behavioural methods are much in evidence with these disorders.

Behavioural Work

The generic terms 'behavioural work' (and 'behavioural methods') cover a many-sided approach to children's emotional, behavioural, developmental, and 'everyday' problems which is referred to variously (depending on the context of client or patient, training task or treatment plan) as *behaviour therapy, cognitive behavioural psychotherapy*, or *behavioural family therapy* (treatment models), *behaviour modification* (training and behaviour change models), and *behavioural consultation* (triadic model). Behavioural work is essentially about the influence of the social environment on the behaviour of human beings and of the impact of human beings on their environment. It represents elaborations of a common theoretical framework – applied learning theory – which has an impressive track record in dealing with a wide variety of the psychological problems referred to Child Development Centres and Child and Adolescent Mental Health Centres.

At a 'tactical' level – as a series of techniques for managing, and achieving relatively simple changes in behaviour – applied learning (behavioural) theory is used by most non-psychologist professionals in their work with children. The same can be said of parents (see Herbert and Wookey, 2004). At a 'strategic' level behavioural work is more than a collection of techniques to be applied recipe-style. It represents a theory (some would say a philosophy) of training and treatment rather than a technology, and is based upon a broad and empirically-based theory of normal and abnormal behaviour. Behaviour therapy methods offer the practitioner quite clear guidelines as to how to approach a wide range of children's problems with some hope of amelioration.

Behavioural work draws upon principles from learning theory, emphasizing (as it has from its beginnings) the principles of classical and operant conditioning. But it is not restricted to them, applying theories from other branches of experimental psychology such as social and developmental psychology and cognitive science. The importance of private events and the cognitive mediation of behaviour is recognized, and a major role is attributed to vicarious and symbolic learning processes such as imitation.

■ Prevention

One of the main themes of this book is the prevention of disabilities and disorders. In the 1960s, prevention was classified into three types:

- *primary programmes* designed to reduce the incidence or numbers of new cases of a disorder.
- *secondary programmes* whose aims were to reduce the prevalence of disorder by early identification and effective treatment.
- *tertiary programmes* of rehabilitation that attempted to reduce the severity of the impairment associated with an already established disorder.

More recent categories centre on who is being offered the intervention (see Offord and Bennett, 2002). Thus, we have:

- *universal programmes* where all residents in a geographical area as large as an entire country, or a smaller entity such as community or school, are offered the intervention;
- *targeted interventions* where individuals in the population are singled out for the intervention:

  1 In selective preventive interventions, the target group is made up of individuals or a population subgroup where there is an increased risk of developing a disorder.
  2 In indicated preventive interventions, the high-risk group is identified on the basis of having mild symptoms or a biological marker of an established disorder.

■ Treatment and Prevention

The Ecological Approach

Treatment and prevention activities may operate together in some interventions. An example of a targeted multilevel intervention is the *ecological approach*, which incorporates large-scale remedial (treatment) and preventive programmes. Broad spectrum problems require wide-ranging multi-systemic programmes which tackle the structural problems such as poor housing, inner-city deprivation and alienation that undermine parenting and family life, contribute to the development of mental and physical health problems, and lead to the conduct and delinquent disorders (Puckering, 2004; Yoshikawa and Knitzer, 1997). Other risk factors taken into account are poor family support, the absence of a positive school climate, and failures of community socialization.

Ecological projects are emerging in increasing numbers, despite their huge costs (e.g. Henggeler et al., 1998). An example is the Early Alliance Programme being conducted by Dumas et al. (1999): an integrated set of four preventive interventions which are delivered across multiple domains of functioning and across multiple social settings, designed to promote competence and reduce risk of early onset conduct disorder (CD) substance abuse, and school failure. This programme is of particular interest because of its linkage, within a developmental framework from pre-school influences to school attendance, of the risk and protective factors which play a major role in the developmental trajectory of CD. It also provides interventive plans (detailed in manuals), to address each of the areas of concern. The programme makes use of behavioural methods in the home and classroom. The trial involves 12 participating schools and longitudinal assessments. It represents (among other multi-system ecological programmes) a recognition that narrowly focused interventions fail for a significant number of families with a conduct disordered child.

Planning an Intervention

There is no one right way of arriving at a remedial, preventive or treatment programme. Different disciplines have designed assessment or diagnostic protocols, for example the social work Core Assessment leading to a multi-agency plan of action for a 'child in need', or the educational *statement of need* for 'special' educational provision. Two examples of assessment procedures: (i) a statutory social work protocol; and (ii) an assessment leading to a general casework formulation, are provided in Chapter 15. They illustrate the way in which a formulation is conceptualized, and the consequent selection of data describing the patient's (client's) problem, varies according to its nature, purpose, and the theoretical assumptions of the professional.

■ Conclusion

It is clear from the Preface to this book that the goals I have set myself are ambitious, and therefore somewhat daunting. Certainly, it is not possible to be as comprehensive as one would wish in the space available, nor can one deal with every developmental problem to a depth that does justice to its complexity or significance. Inevitably, my choice of what to leave out, or what to discuss less intensively, is a personal one and not infallible. I can only express my regret if the omissions are in areas where a reader hoped for more information.

Developmental Problems Before, During and After Birth

■ The Prenatal Period

Chapter 1 begins with a description of the major genetic disorders, chosen to illustrate conditions, each of which has a major impact on (*inter alia*) intellectual, physical, behavioural or sexual development. Nature plays an early 'role' in the primary prevention of severe disorders. Very many concepti are either genetically abnormal and thus fail to develop, or they implant themselves in a location incapable of sustaining them, and consequently the pregnant mother-to-be miscarries. The prevention of inherited disorders by means of advice from genetic counsellors, the use of screening methods (ranging from amniocentesis to gene tests), and the decision to terminate a pregnancy, are discussed. Ethical and moral issues with regard to termination – at the personal and policy levels – are raised as a subject of concern. The many gaps in our knowledge about genetic mechanisms in the causation of disabilities await further research on the human genome, and its underlying protein activity.

■ The Uterine Period

The first task of the newly conceived baby-to-be is to survive a potentially hazardous prenatal journey, and make the transmission from a watery existence of parasitic dependence on the mother's body, to a healthy, physiologically independent life in the outside world. In spite of all the risks described above, the vast majority of neonates are in a healthy state. Fortunately, the mother's womb is almost always a hospitable environment in which the baby-to-be can develop.

In relatively atypical circumstances there are psychological and physical influences which disrupt the development of the tenant by disturbing the host mother, notably during embryonic development. Appendix V contains a brief summary of prenatal stages of development.

Much of the evidence on the precise effects of maternal stress on her unborn child is extremely difficult to evaluate. It is clearly difficult to infer cause–effect relationships from the only possible ethical evidence – retrospective correlational studies. In addition, observations to do with the effects of prenatal influences on postnatal developments in the child are contaminated by the mother's management of her baby after birth, and by other environmental and genetic factors that cannot be controlled. Despite these difficulties and caveats there are findings of interest to suggest that home visiting and other forms of physical and emotional support can be beneficial to young mothers, and these are discussed briefly in Chapter 2 (a longer account awaits later chapters).

The term *teratogen* is applied to any disease, chemical, drug, or other environmental agent capable of harming a developing embryo by causing severely retarded growth, physical deformities, deafness, blindness, brain damage, and also death. I have chosen to describe the effects of two major potential teratogens – excessive smoking and alcohol ingestion during pregnancy – because of their near universality, and the high risk of serious damage to which they can subject the developing fetus.

The chapter ends with a diagnostic and treatment profile of two congenital disorders: fetal alcohol syndrome and hydrocephalus.

■ The Perinatal and Neonatal Periods

Chapter 3 introduces the subjects of problematic births and the diagnostic and treatment profiles in several congenital conditions. It also investigates the risks of being a very low birth weight baby, problems involving brain injury and other disabilities. Maternal stress during pregnancy, family poverty and social disadvantage are among the multiple causes (along with infections) to produce pre-term labour and low birth weight babies (e.g. Pattenden, Delk and Vrijheid, 1999). Early interventions for babies at high risk are described. The chapter describes a 'window of opportunity' in which to apply these methods (e.g. home visiting, intensive care and early stimulation) in order to mitigate short- and long-term ill-effects.

CHAPTER 1

The Prenatal Period
Genetic Disorders and Disabilities

The phenotypes that result from genetic disorders tend to be expressed in various ways (Fryers, 1984). Not all of the genetic disorders lead primarily to intellectual disabilities as is the case with the Fragile X syndrome. In some, the major impact is behavioural (e.g. Tourette's syndrome); in some the main impact is physical and medical (e.g. cystic fibrosis); in others the genetic fault leads to anomalous sexual development (as in Klinefelter's syndrome). There follows below an account of several disorders (a small sample of the many hundreds of inherited conditions) chosen *inter alia* to illustrate their particular consequences for (i) intellectual; (ii) physical; (iii) behavioural; and (iv) sexual development.

■ Impact on Intellectual Development

Fragile X Syndrome

Diagnostic history

Fragile X syndrome, also referred to as the Martin–Bell syndrome, seen in approximately one in 1,200 males and one in 2,500 females, is the next most common form of genetic intellectual disability (mental retardation) after Down's syndrome. Males with the syndrome are usually intellectually disabled and tend to exhibit characteristic behaviour patterns and physical features (Hagerman, Amery and Kronister, 1991; Hagerman and Silverman, 1991). Affected females display a similar, but generally less extreme phenotype.

The disorder had probably been present for many centuries but its first identification had to await the 1960s. This was followed, after a period of clinical 'silence', by the discovery in the late 1970s of the link between an abnormal fragile site on the X chromosome and a syndrome of intellectual disability. The next major breakthrough was the identification in 1991 of the gene which causes Fragile X (FMR1). Once the Fragile X syndrome was recognized as a distinct condition, cases began to be diagnosed in all races, world-wide.

Diagnosis

The phenotypic manifestations of Fragile X syndrome as described in the literature are not specific, and the list of associated difficulties can lead to problems of differential diagnosis. Approximately 15 to 20 per cent of those with the disorder exhibit autistic-like behaviours: difficulty in relating to people, poor eye contact, hand-flapping or odd gesture movements, hand-biting, and poor sensory skills.

Individuals with Fragile X syndrome often share a number of recognizable physical features, including:

- a high arched palate
- strabismus (lazy eye)
- large ears
- long face: coarsening of features
- macro-orchidism (large testicles) in the post-pubertal male
- hypotonia: poor muscle tone
- generalized disorder of connective tissues
- flat feet
- sometimes increased head circumference.

Clinical features

Although many individuals with Fragile X syndrome have a characteristic 'look' (long face and large ears), by no means do all have the other so-called 'typical physical features'. There is such variability in their extent (with some intellectually disabled males showing few of the physical components) that clinical diagnosis becomes difficult.

Many hospitals and laboratories perform blood tests to diagnose Fragile X syndrome. To confirm the diagnosis it is necessary to detect an alteration in the FMR1 gene (chromosomal locus Xq27.3). Changes in FMR are detected by molecular genetic testing. DNA studies have improved the accuracy of testing (usually carried out on a blood sample) for Fragile X syndrome. The tests will reliably diagnose those whose learning disabilities are caused by the disease, and identify carriers of the syndrome.

Developmental features

Fragile X syndrome is more common in males (approximately one in 1,500) than females (one in 2,500). Affected individuals have normal growth and stature, and no associated malformations. Males typically have a moderate to severe form of intellectual disability. Females may also be affected but generally have a mild form of impairment.

Behaviour problems and speech/language delay are common but variable features. The boys tend to be impulsive, over-active, easily distracted, and inattentive. Girls have similar difficulties concentrating. They tend to be extremely shy and socially withdrawn.

Causation

In the 1990s, as we saw earlier, the Fragile X gene (FMR1) was identified and found to contain an 'in tandem' repeated trinucleotide sequence (COG) near its 5' end (see Warren and Nelson, 1994). The mutation responsible for Fragile X syndrome involves expansion of this repeat segment. The normal number of CGG repeats in the FMR1 genes varies from 6 to around 50. The larger the size of a mother's premutation, the greater the risk of expansion to a full mutation in her offspring. More than 99 per cent of affected individuals have a full mutation. Males and females carrying a premutation gene are unaffected.

Male carriers are referred to as 'normal transmitting males' and they pass on the mutation, relatively unchanged in size, to all of their daughters. These daughters are unaffected, but are at risk of having children who are affected. Most, but not all, males with a full mutation are intellectually disabled and show the typical characteristics of Fragile X symptoms. Approximately one-third of females with a full mutation, are of normal intelligence; one-third are of borderline intelligence, and one-third are intellectually impaired.

Treatment

There is no specific treatment for Fragile X syndrome. Instead, effort is directed toward training and education to help affected children reach as high a level of functioning as possible. Behaviour therapy and/or mild medications are used for behaviour problems, as well as speech therapy for speech and language and sensory difficulties.

Children need to be diagnosed as early as possible so that an appropriate intervention can be planned. As families generally learn about the existence of genetic faults in their family background when their children manifest the syndrome, the issue of timing for access to genetic counselling and screening is vital. To assess this matter of timing, a survey was conducted in 2001 of 140 parents whose first child affected by the syndrome, was born and had the condition diagnosed between 1990 and 1999 (Frank Porter Graham Child Development Institute, University of North Carolina at Chapel Hill). This report indicated that approximately half of the families did not receive the diagnosis for more than a year after their first concerns about their child's development or behaviour. Half reported having subsequent pregnancies before the syndrome was diagnosed in their first child. These results underline the need for screening facilities and an early diagnosis.

Prevention

- *Genetic counselling.* Genetic counselling is provided by a professional geneticist as a means of learning about the inheritable nature of Fragile X syndrome, and the risks to future offspring, or to other relatives who may be unwitting carriers of the syndrome. To this end, families with a history of Fragile X syndrome are likely to be advised to seek genetic testing and recurrence risk counselling.
- *Screening.* Prenatal testing of a fetus is possible following a positive carrier test in the mother, by means of molecular genetic testing. When the mother is a known carrier, DNA testing can determine whether the fetus inherited the normal or mutant FMR1 gene. Chorionic villus sampling (CVS), although a standard technique for prenatal diagnosis, may still require a follow-up amniocentesis if it is necessary to resolve an ambiguous result. Detained discussion of prevention procedures is continued toward the end of the chapter.

■ Impact on Physical Development

Cystic Fibrosis

Diagnosis

Cystic fibrosis (CF) is almost always diagnosed during infancy or early childhood. It is an example of a condition in which aberrant genes cause serious life-long physical problems. The severity of this disease ranges from mild bronchial symptoms and male sterility to severe lung, pancreatic, and intestinal difficulties. Suspicion is likely to be aroused where there is a high incidence of the condition in relatives. A simple blood test can detect many, but not all of the genetic abnormalities (there are several hundred) that cause CF.

Clinical features

CF does not follow the same pattern in all patients but affects different people in different ways and to varying degrees. However, the basic problem is the same: an abnormality in the gland which produces or secretes sweat and mucus. Sweat cools the body; mucus lubricates the respiratory, digestive, and reproductive systems, and prevents tissues from drying out, protecting them from infection.

- Children with CF lose excessive amounts of salt when they sweat. This can disturb the balance of minerals in the blood, possibly causing abnormal heart rhythms. Going into shock is a risk.
- Mucus in CF patients is very thick and accumulates in the intestines and lungs. The result is malnutrition, poor growth, frequent respiratory infections, breathing difficulties, and eventually permanent lung damage.
- Lung disease is the usual cause of death in most individuals with CF.

Comorbid conditions

CF can cause various other medical problems. These include:

- abdominal pain and discomfort;
- enlargement of the right side of the heart;
- gassiness (too much gas in the intestine);
- rectal prolapse (protrusion of the rectum through the anus);
- sinusitis (inflammation of the nasal sinuses);
- nasal polyps (fleshy growths inside the nose);
- clubbing (rounding and enlargement of fingers and toes);
- pneumothorax (rupture of lung tissue and trapping of air between the lung and the chest wall);
- hemoptysis (coughing of blood).

Causation

Symptoms of CF only appear if a child has two copies of the abnormal gene that cause the disease, one from the mother and one from the father. The faulty genetic make-up affects the way chloride ions are transported across cell membranes. This combines with an increase in sodium absorption to cause excessive mucous secretion in the lungs and digestive tract, increasing the risk of infections.

If a child has only one abnormal gene then he or she is a 'carrier' – one asymptomatic person in 25 carries the CF gene. Carriers are unaffected individuals who carry one copy of a gene for a disease that requires two copies for the disease to be expressed. Thus, children of parents who have no symptoms can still have CF, but only if both parents contribute the abnormal gene to their baby. If both partners actually carry the cystic fibrosis genes, the risk of their baby having cystic fibrosis is 1 in 4 (25 per cent).

Treatment

Since CF is a genetic disease, the only way to prevent or cure it would be with gene therapy at an early age. Ideally, gene therapy could repair or replace the defective gene. Knowledge of a gene mutation alone, however, does not provide sufficient information for clinicians attempting to plan an intervention. Their first task is to understand the normal function of the gene or genes associated with particular diseases, and then determine how that function is disrupted by the mutation. The need is not only for more fundamental and clinical research, but also for the resolution of the many complex moral issues that arise from altering the basic genetic 'instructions' of individual's future lives.

An option for treatment would in theory be to give a person with CF the active form of the protein product that is scarce or missing. At present, however, neither gene therapy nor any other kind of treatment exists for the basic causes of cystic fibrosis, although several drug-based approaches are being investigated. The best that clinicians can do currently is to ease the symptoms of CF and retard the progress of the disease, so the child's quality of life is maximized. This is achieved by the use of antibiotics combined with physical strategies to clear the thick mucus from the lungs.

Therapy is tailored to the needs of each patient. CF was inevitably fatal in childhood, in the past. More effective methods of treatment developed over the past two decades have increased the average lifespan of CF patients to nearly 30 years. For patients whose disease is very advanced, lung transplantation may be an option.

Prevention

As CF is an inherited condition affecting approximately one in every 2,500 babies, prenatal testing of the fetus by means of amniocentesis, is likely to be recommended by a genetic counsellor in the light of a family history (see below).

The fluid surrounding the fetus is obtained through a needle. It contains some of the baby's cells that can then be tested for the CF genes.

The likelihood that a test will accurately identify an abnormal gene depends, in part, on the ethnic background of the person being tested. CF tests currently identify 90 per cent of CF mutations in Caucasians, 50 per cent in African Americans and Hispanics, and 30 per cent in Asian Americans.

The perinatal screening of CF babies is a controversial matter because of (*inter alia*) the stigma attached to the large numbers of children who appear to be developing normally. This is a physical disease that places a great burden on the child, and on parents who have to attend to an unending and onerous task of pulmonary care. Support for the family is crucial in protecting the emotional development of children with CF, and the morale of their parents.

■ Impact on Behaviour

Gilles de la Tourette's Syndrome

The disorder is named after Georges Gilles de la Tourette, the pioneering French neurologist who first described an 86-year-old French noblewoman, the Marquise de Dampierre, with the condition in 1825. In 1885, he reported nine cases of what came to be named Tourette's syndrome (GTS) in which the triad of multiple tics, caprolalia (swearing) and echolalia were present (see Robertson, 2004).

Diagnosis

GTS is an inherited neurological disorder characterized by repeated involuntary movements and uncontrollable vocal sounds called tics. They have to occur multiple times per day. Sometimes, the syndrome will result in the vocalization of inappropriate words and phrases. In a few cases, such tics can include obscene words and phrases. The symptoms of GTS generally appear before individuals are in their late teens. Tics must be present for at least one year. Although the symptoms range from very mild to quite severe, the majority of cases fall into the mild category. The natural course of GTS varies from child to child, adult to adult.

Clinical features

GTS is diagnosed by observing the symptoms and evaluating the family history. Which may indicate a genetic predisposition to the disorder. The first signs are usually facial tics, commonly eye blinking. With time, other motor tics may appear, such as head jerking, neck stretching, foot stamping, or body twisting and bending. Caprolalia is the best known of the vocal tics and consists of the involuntary interruption of the flow of the person's speech with various unprovoked obscenities. It is not uncommon for a person with GTS to continuously clear his or her throat, cough, sniff, grunt, shout or bark.

Children and adolescents can sometimes suppress their tics for a brief period, but eventually tension mounts to the point where the tic 'bursts out'. They may tend to touch other people inappropriately and repeat actions obsessively. A few self-harm by head banging and biting their lips and cheeks. Only a relatively small proportion of children suffering from GTS displays either remission or an exacerbation of their tics. Tics worsen in stressful situations and improve when the person relaxes or is absorbed in an activity.

GTS may be associated with:

- obsessive-compulsive symptoms
- learning disorders
- AD/HD
- social difficulties
- poor achievement at school.

Developmental features

The average age of onset of GTS (based on world studies) is around 7 years. The symptoms generally appear before the individual is 18 years old. Individuals can expect to live a normal life span. Although the disorder is generally lifelong and chronic, it is not a degenerative condition; it does not impair intelligence. Tics tend to decrease with age, enabling some patients to discontinue using medication. In a few cases, complete remission occurs after adolescence. Leckman, Zhang and Vitale (1998) suggest that there is evidence that the majority of GTS symptoms disappear in half of the patients by the age of 18 years, given:

- an early age at onset (5.6 years)
- severe tics at around 10.

Although tic symptoms tend to decrease with age, it is possible that psychological disorders such as depression, panic attacks, mood swings, and anti-social behaviours may increase in frequency and/or intensity.

The psychosocial consequences of GTS are quite likely to be self-consciousness, embarrassment, irritability and depression. On the neuro-developmental side of the equation, the children display difficulty with visual-motor and expressive language tests, suggesting a disturbance in intellectual 'performance' processes. Although autism (another neuro-developmental disorder) and GTS are distinct disorders, they share certain behavioural characteristics: obsessive-compulsive behaviours, abnormal motor behaviour, and echolalia.

Epidemiology

People of all ethnic groups are affected by the disorder, males being affected 3 to 4 times more often than females. It is estimated that its prevalence in children is approximately 1 per cent of mainstream schoolchildren between the ages of 6 and 17 years. The prevalence of GTS in children with special educational needs, and also autism, is high (Robertson, 2004).

Causation

Psychodynamic theories have not stood the test of time. Prenatal and perinatal events have been inculpated in the aetiology of GTS (Leckman, Zhang and Vitale 1998), but to date the precise causes continue to be unknown. However, it is generally considered currently, to be a neuro-psychiatric brain disorder which is determined by genetic, environmental, hormonal and other influences (see Cody and Hynde, 1999). Although there is a suggestion that the genetic disorder is transmitted via a single major gene locus with autosomal dominant inheritance, no single gene has yet been identified. As with other genetic conditions interest is being shown in, and research pursued on genome scans (e.g. the Tourette Syndrome Association International Consortium for Genetics, 1999).

Treatment

There is no cure for GTS; however, the condition in many children does tend to improve as they mature. A holistic (i.e. multilevel, multidisciplinary) approach to treatment seems the most favoured intervention (see Robertson, 2004). The majority of children require no medication, but it is available when symptoms interfere with daily functioning.

GTS medications may help to reduce specific symptoms. The treatment of choice is clonodine. This drug has been in use longest, and has enjoyed modest success for the symptoms of agitation, AD/HD, and hyperarousal (see Fonagy, Target, et al., 2002). Neuroleptic and antihypertensive drugs can have worrying long- and short-term side effects, and the use of stimulants is controversial.

Relaxation techniques and biofeedback may be useful in alleviating stress. Behavioural techniques are of limited value. Psycho-education for the children with GTS, their parents and teachers, is a vital resource.

■ Impact on Sexual Development

▨ Klinefelter's Syndrome (47,XXY)

Klinefelter's syndrome (KS) – a sex chromosome anomaly that causes hypogonadism – was discovered in 1942. Harry Klinefelter and his co-workers at the Massachusetts General Hospital in Boston described nine men who had enlarged breasts, sparse facial and body hair, small testes, and an inability to produce sperm. Researchers discovered by the late 1950s that men with this syndrome had an extra sex chromosome – 47 chromosomes in each cell of their bodies XXY instead of the usual 46, the XY male pattern. In the early 1970s, researchers screened the chromosomes of thousands of newborn infants. The XXY chromosome pattern turned out to be one of the most common genetic abnormalities.

Although the cause of the condition (now referred to as Klinefelter's syndrome) – the extra sex chromosome – is widespread, the symptoms and features of the syndrome that may result from having the extra chromosome are an uncommon occurrence. There are many men who live out their lives never suspecting the additional chromosome in their bodies. For this reason, the term 'XXY male' is used by many clinicians in preference to 'Klinefelter syndrome'.

Diagnosis

KS is diagnosed by a medical history, physical examination, and chromosome analysis. With the increase in testing by amniocentesis or chorionic villus sampling (CVS) KS may be diagnosed prenatally, but also immediately after birth. The infant appears normal at birth, the defect usually only becoming apparent in the pre-teen years (around ages 11 to 12) when males often begin puberty.

Epidemiology

In random surveys, KS is found to appear in 1 in every 500 to 1,000 live born males. The fact that the largest percentage of these males is never diagnosed indicates that in many cases there is an under-diagnosis operating for various reasons, among them the fact that large numbers of affected individuals pursue normal lives with no particular medical or social complications.

Clinical features

The severity of symptoms may vary from one male to another depending on the number of extra X chromosomes and how many cells in the body are affected. Males with more than one extra X chromosome generally have more symptoms. Some males with KS may not fully develop secondary male sexual characteristics – such as the growth of the testicles and penis, deeper voice, and body hair. They are not able to produce enough sperm to father children. Some mild cases may go undetected, with no abnormalities present except infertility. Tall stature and abnormal body proportions (long legs, short trunk) are common.

Developmental features

It has been reported that individuals with KS are predisposed to psychiatric disorders. The combination of feminine physical features, poor motor coordination, and language and memory difficulties is likely to affect self-esteem and contributes to feelings of anxiety and insecurity, especially from adolescence onwards.

As children, they often learn to speak much later than do other children and may have difficulty learning to read and write. And while they eventually do learn to speak and converse normally, the majority tend to have some degree of difficulty with language throughout their lives. The children with KS are frequently reported to have below-average intelligence, a claim not supported by large-scale screening studies. Only about 20 per cent score lower than 90 on standardized intelligence tests. Most children with KS have average to superior intelligence.

Nevertheless, boys with the extra X chromosomes syndrome commonly have learning disabilities and tend to perform poorly in school, even when they have average or above IQs. They often achieve low verbal scores, poor short-term auditory memory, and poor data retrieval skills. The risk of AD/HD is high. In many cases, delayed or diminished speech and language skills or dyslexia add to their difficulties. Fortunately, language disabilities can be treated with speech therapy, the chances for success being greatest if begun in early childhood.

Causation

A person's sex is determined by the X and Y chromosomes. Normally, men have 46 chromosomes, the XY.male combination. The cause of KS is an extra X sex chromosome – 47 chromosomes (XXY) in each cell of their bodies. There are other, less common variations such as 48,XXYY, 48,XXXY, 49,XXXXY, and XY/XXY mosaic. All of these are considered KS variants, and are diagnosed by means of a chromosome analysis (karyotype), carried out usually on a blood sample.

Treatment

Testosterone therapy will improve the development of secondary sexual characteristics. This replacement therapy can have a positive effect on mood and behaviour, improving self-esteem and decreasing fatigue and irritability. Testosterone treatment usually starts at the beginning of puberty. Once this treatment begins, it needs to be continued for life. There is no treatment for the infertility associated KS. Testosterone therapy can increase osteroid formation and bone mineralization, but only if initiated before age 20.

Frequently, adolescent boys with KS undergo breast tissue development which continues to increase in size. This could necessitate its surgical removal. Enlarged breast tissue can be treated with plastic surgery if it is disfiguring.

Management of KS in teenage boys may require help from the school, especially for those boys who have learning difficulties. Counselling may benefit children and adolescents with emotional difficulties due to identity problems, low self-esteem, and in adolescence, sexual dysfunction.

Turner's Syndrome (Bonnevie Ullrich Syndrome; Gonadal Dysgenesis; Monosomy)

Diagnosis

Turner's syndrome (TS) was first described by Henry Turner, at the University of Oklahoma. He reported a set of common physical features in seven of his patients in an article published in 1938. The presence of the damaged or deleted X chromosome which indicates the endocrine disorder TS had to await the discovery, in the late 1950s, of the technology to perform a blood test of the chromosomes called karyotyping.

Clinical features

It should be noted that symptoms may vary widely among those affected with TS. Most affected girls can be recognized and diagnosed in early childhood by the characteristic physical features (e.g. small/short stature and absent or retarded development of secondary sexual characteristics), also health-related problems, which may include:

• reduction or absence of the ovaries;
• absence of menstruation;

- kidney abnormalities;
- abnormalities of the eyes;
- abnormal liver function;
- ear infections;
- hearing deficits;
- under-active thyroid glands;
- heart defects (e.g. coarctation/narrowing of the aorta);
- arthritis;
- skeletal disorders;
- type two diabetes.

The disorder inhibits sexual development at puberty, and causes infertility.

Developmental features

The ovaries do not develop normally because, with only the one X chromosome present in most children with TS, they do not produce adequate amounts of female hormones. The young teenager will not develop the signs of puberty – breasts and menstruation – unless these hormones are provided. Pubic and axillary hair may grow, the uterus and vagina are normal.

The faulty chromosomes do not mean that girls with TS do not have the identity of 'real life' females. A point that may need to be stressed in counselling sessions is the fact that they are girls or women who have a genetic condition that leads to under-developed ovaries and short stature. However, TS does cause physiological and psychological problems which have an impact on the child's development.

The two X chromosome combination (XX) has an influence beyond determining the sex of an individual; it also affects physiological growth and psychological development. For example, some girls may experience learning difficulties, notably with mathematics. Mental retardation is not a feature of Turner's syndrome, despite the claims published in older medical textbooks. Girls are of normal intelligence; however, the characteristic pattern of intellectual functioning involves a verbal 10 that is generally average or above, but a non-verbal IQ that may be considerably lower because of problems visualizing objects in relation to each other. It is advisable, therefore, to arrange for psychological testing if school problems become evident.

Epidemiology

TS is a rare (1 in 2,500 to 3,000 live births) chromosomal disorder of females. Approximately 800 new cases are diagnosed each year in the USA. The occurrence of the deleted or damaged X chromosome appears to be a random event. Thus, any couple can have a daughter with TS. In addition, the disorder equally affects those of different ethnic backgrounds.

Prevention

There is no known prevention for TS. Although the cause of this inherited disorder is known in a general sense (the result of an error during the division/meiosis of a parent's sex cells), the precise causal mechanisms that put a couple at risk of having a daughter with TS are not known. The means to carry out preventive interventions awaits discovery.

Treatment

Most girls and women are managed by endocrinologists because the most commonly prescribed treatments for TS involve:

- the use of *growth hormone* to improve growth speed and final adult height;
- *estrogen replacement therapy* to promote the sexual development appropriate to puberty. Estrogen therapy is also important for the development and maintenance of bones;
- *thyroid hormones* for some patients.

Clearly, it is important to identify children with TS as early as possible so that treatment can be initiated to promote normal growth and development. If the disorder is not treated in early childhood, the onset of puberty is delayed. Such a delay in sexual development may disrupt a major task of the teenage years – social development – and lead to low self-esteem. The older child (when in her teens) may feel uncertain about what, if anything, to tell her boyfriend. This concern about disclosing her disorder is likely to arise in other situations and with others in her life, at any time.

Discussing this issue with a trusted and supportive person may assist the youngster to cope with these problems. It is very important that the parents and the girl herself are provided with useful information. A good understanding of GTS and its implications, as well as any treatment plan arrived at in partnership with the assessment team, are vital. Psychological treatment – family and child counselling at the different stages of childhood and adolescent development – may be needed, and should prove helpful.

■ Prevention of Inherited Conditions

Eugenics

The word 'eugenics' (meaning 'good birth') was coined by Sir Francis Galton (1822–1911) in the nineteenth century, but the practice is age-old. This subject is a distasteful one to mention, nevertheless the use of sterilization as policy in the West (and I'm not referring to the grotesque murders of intellectually disabled people in the name of Aryan 'purity') was commonplace until the 1940s and 1950s.

In the USA compulsory sterilization was applied over 30 states (1907–31) to 12,000 so-called 'inferior' or 'imbecilic' people. This policy of sterilization was continued until 1942. By 1930, 68,000 intellectually disabled people were institutionalized as part of a eugenics policy with little or no regard for human dignity and rights. Sterilization continues to take place to this day in legally circumscribed situations. These issues are discussed by Field and Sanchez (1999) and McGaw (2004).

Genetic Counselling

The following discussion is designed to cover the prevention strategies that apply to all of the conditions described above. The health service comes into play in a secondary-level preventive role by applying what are called 'selective' and 'indicated' targeted interventions. There are two procedures available to prevent or detect abnormalities, with the aim of mitigating their adverse consequences.

First, genetic counselling is the profession of specialists (still relatively few in number) from a medical or nursing background who have an advanced training in genetics and personal counselling. The counselling interview is designed to meet would-be parents' needs for individual information and advice (Harper, 1998). Following an initial session, counsellors usually draw a family tree with the help of the prospective parent to gather information about both sides of the family, and identify problems that may be pertinent. Genetic counsellors provide them with:

- factual information about the risks of passing on hereditary conditions;
- options and reasons for screening genetic disease before conception;
- advice about tests conducted (*in utero*) such as ultrasonography, amniocentesis, and fetoscopy, which determine after conception the condition (e.g. identifying genetic defects) of the fetus.

Genetic counselling is not only a technically complex task; it is also a psychologically delicate one. A discussion of the risks and their implications may be necessary:

- if a mother or father has a family history of hereditary disorders;
- if the mother is in an older age-bracket, has had one or more pregnancies terminated; or has previously given birth to a baby who suffers from an abnormality.

Parents often ask the counsellor: 'Dare I try again?', 'Why did it happen to me?', 'Is there something wrong in my or his family … something inherited?' They may blame themselves for their child's disability, and feel relieved to know that there is no need to feel guilty as it was not within their powers (unless they endangered the pregnancy with avoidable teratogens such as excessive alcohol and nicotine), to prevent it happening. The counsellor is also likely to be asked: 'What tests are there, if I try again?' As the level of risk (base rate) varies for different disabling conditions, the diagnosis of a present or past condition should be accurate in order to make informed predictions about likely outcomes. Clearly, genetic diagnosis has progressed from investigating family trees for inheritable weaknesses, to the detection of fetal genetic abnormalities and the existence of carriers in conditions like haemophilia. This is a good example with which to illustrate several of the issues raised by genetic diagnosis.

The decision about whether to continue, or terminate a risky pregnancy may follow a genetic diagnosis. It is now possible to determine the sex of a fetus from a dense, stainable structure (called a 'Barr body' after its discoverer), allowing a pregnant woman with a family history of X-linked diseases such as haemophilia, to choose an abortion if she is bearing a male fetus. This bald statement about 'choosing' to terminate a risky pregnancy does no justice to the painful personal issues that have to be resolved. Such decisions cannot be 'prescribed' for prospective mothers and fathers. However, clear information about the chances of giving birth to a baby son with haemophilia, or some other disorder, may at least add an objective (factual) element to the highly subjective emotional and moral issues that make deciding so difficult.

Termination of a pregnancy

The World Medical Association offers advice to practitioners about the ethical and moral reservations they may have on this, and other contentious subjects. It suggests that physicians who consider contraception, sterilization and abortion to be in conflict with their values, may choose not to provide these medical services. However, they should not impose their personal principles on prospective parents, but are obliged to alert them when a potential genetic problem is discovered.

Ante-natal Screening

Ultrasound scanning

Throughout pregnancy, tests are available to ensure that both mother and baby are in good health. Ultrasound scanning utilizes sound waves to form a picture of the baby in the womb. It is often used between the 12th and 16th week of the pregnancy to confirm the age of the baby and to determine the presence of twins. In order to detect serious abnormalities scans need to be conducted between about 18 and 20 weeks.

The Advisory Committee on Genetic Testing (ACGT), part of the UK government's Human Genetics Commission, suggested in a consultation document submitted to health authorities across the country, that a large proportion, if not all, pregnant women could be tested to identify their unborn babies at high risk for developing genetic diseases. They would be offered diagnostic ultrasound in order to screen for the likelihood of Down's syndrome (DS). It may also detect other neurological abnormalities such as spina bifida and anencephaly (failure of the brain to develop).

The nuchal translucency ultrasound screening

This test is not diagnostic but indicates the need for further tests. The ultrasound measures the thickness of the fold at the back of the baby's neck. Babies with DS have increased fluid in the fold and a thicker fold.

The AFB blood test

This is a blood test known also as the Bart's double or triple test, which is performed (with no risk to mother or baby) between the 16th and 18th weeks of pregnancy. A small amount of blood from woman's arm is tested to measure three substances: the level of alpha fetoprotein, and two other hormone levels (the unconjugated oestral and the human chorionic gonadotropin). The constituents of the woman's blood are compared with her age. High levels may indicate the presence of a neural tube defect, for example, spina bifida; low levels possibly indicate the presence of DS. Because of uncertainties – possible alternative explanations for high or low levels – other confirmatory tests are required.

Amniocentesis

This test (carried out usually between the 16th and 20th weeks of pregnancy, under local anaesthesia) withdraws a small amount of amniotic fluid surrounding the fetus with a fine needle. The fetal cells and fluid are separated in a centrifuge and the cells are cultured for a variety of tests (e.g. for sex determination and for biochemical and enzymatic investigations). The risk of a miscarriage due to the procedure is around 1 in 100 pregnancies, and is thought too high for routine use. Laboratory tests investigate the presence of DS, Turner's syndrome, Tay–Sachs disease, neural tube defects and other structural abnormalities, also certain sex-linked conditions.

Chorionic villus sampling – CVS

This technique is carried out to diagnose conditions that would not be detectable until approximately 16 weeks of pregnancy by amniocentesis (*not* including spina bifida or neural tube abnormalities). It is not a routine procedure, but highly specialized. A tiny fragment from the edge of the chorionic tissue is withdrawn with a hollow needle, for testing.

Strep B test

Group B streptococcus in pregnant women (between 10 and 30 per cent unknowingly have the organism) is a leading cause of illness and death among newborn babies, something reputedly more common in the USA than the UK. Pregnant women can be screened for Group B Strep, two to four weeks before labour begins. Antibiotics are administered. In the UK midwives tend to act conservatively and without set protocols. They generally adopt a 'wait and see' policy, monitoring baby and mother for symptoms of illness which then lead to antibiotic treatment. In the USA, a prophylactic use of antibiotics for the mother during labour, and the baby at birth, is more common.

Gene Tests

The Human Genome Project has made it possible, in a way that was unavailable a relatively short time ago, for scientists and clinicians to identify genetic faults that contribute to, or cause many diseases. Advances in gene testing have also provided the diagnostic methods and prognostic knowledge that help them select the most appropriate interventions. Gene tests (also called DNA-based tests) have had, within a relatively short time, a dramatic impact on many people's lives, allowing families to avoid the risk of giving birth to children with devastating disorders. All diseases have some genetic component, whether inherited directly or the outcome of environmental threats to the predisposed body (e.g. from viruses or toxins). Mutation tests often search for only the most common (currently about 70) mutations. Some diseases, it needs to be remembered, occur disproportionately in certain ethnic groups (see Chapter 3), for example:

- *sickle cell anaemia* (in African Americans and Hispanics);
- *cystic fibrosis* (in Caucasians);
- *Tay–Sachs* and *Canavan disease* (in Ashkenazi Jews).

Several thousand diseases are linked to mutations in single genes that are inherited from one or both parents. Most are very rare, accounting for about 3 per cent of all disease in the general population.

Clinical sensitivity

It is critical, given the critical objectives and implications of genetic testing, to consider the clinical sensitivity of specific gene tests: i.e. the proportion of people with particular clinical conditions they successfully detect. For example, reliable gene tests are required for:

- carrier screening;
- prenatal diagnostic testing;
- newborn screening;
- pre-symptomatic testing to predict adult-onset disorders;
- confirming diagnoses of symptomatic individuals;
- forensic identity testing.

Methodology

In gene tests, scientists directly examine a *DNA sample* (obtained from any tissue, including blood) for mutated sequences; they design short pieces of DNA called probes whose sequences are complementary to the mutated sequences. These probes will seek their complement among some three billion base pairs of an individual's genome. If the mutated sequence is present in the patient's genome, the probe will bind to it and indicate the mutation. Genetic tests might also involve microscopic examination of stained or fluorescent chromosomes, as well as biochemical investigations of gene products such as enzymes and other proteins.

Many different genetic mutations can cause the same disease. The discovery of the genetic causation of cystic fibrosis (CF) is a good example of the value of gene testing, as it is now feasible to determine whether a particular pregnancy carries a normal fetus, a carrier, or a fetus with CF.

National Policy

The Advisory Committee on Genetic Testing (ACGT), mentioned earlier, stated at the conclusion of its study, that women found to have an abnormal fetus should be provided with advice on having an abortion, within legal guidelines. It commented that:

> those who undergo prenatal diagnosis have the wish to have a healthy child. Thus, when a fetus is found to have a genetic, chromosomal or structural abnormality, some may, when provided with information on the effects of the abnormality, choose to seek a termination of the pregnancy.

The draft document stresses the importance of consent from the mother, and the need for procedures and their implications to be explained with clarity. Support would have to be provided once a decision is made.

Not surprisingly, anti-abortion campaigners have criticized the suggestion of large-scale testing, asserting that it amounts to a conspiracy to 'filter out' disabled children before they are born, denying their human rights.

CHAPTER 2

The Uterine Period
Before, During and After Birth

■ Psychological Stressors

Although the uterine environment is usually a 'friendly' environment within which to develop, there are adverse influences (e.g. teratogens), as we saw earlier, which disrupt the development of the infant-to-be by affecting the mother psychologically and/or physically. I shall begin with the adverse effects of exposure of the mother and her child to psychological stress.

▤ Maternal Stress

In the folklore of all human societies there has existed the persistent belief that a mother's emotions can influence a child before it is born. In contemporary psychological language, the emotional bond between mother and unborn infant is the medium whereby maternal activity, fatigue, emotionality and personality are postulated to influence the activity level, irritability and autonomic functioning of the fetus. When a mother becomes emotionally aroused, her glands secrete powerful activating hormones such as adrenaline that cross the placental barrier, entering the fetal bloodstream, and accelerating the fetus's motor activity. Stress hormones divert blood flow to the large muscles and impede the flow or oxygen and nutrients to the fetus, possibly contributing to the stunting of its growth. Stress may undermine the mother's immune system, making her and her fetus vulnerable to infectious diseases (Cohen and Williamson, 1991).

A longitudinal study by O'Connor, Heron and Glover (2002) generated data that indicated a strong and significant association between extreme anxiety at

32 weeks gestation and behavioural and/or emotional problems in children (10 per cent) at the age of 4 years. Mothers who are victims of domestic violence are four times more likely to have low birth-weight babies than mothers who are not subjected to such prolonged stress (Browne and Herbert, 1997).

The conclusion of several decades of research is that stressful periods of short duration such as an argument, a frightening experience or a fall, have few if any harmful consequences for the mother or her unborn child. However, severe and prolonged emotional stress is associated with premature delivery, low birth weight, stunted prenatal growth, and birth complications (see review by Brockington, 1996). The common accompaniment to chronic distress is a poor appetite and a need to smoke, drink alcohol and use drugs, all of which have an influence on growth retardation and low birth weight (see Chapter 3).

Rosenblith (1992) is of the opinion that if one takes into consideration both the relatively well-controlled experimental animal research and the human studies (not forgetting the methodological minefield this area of study represents), it seems most likely that the offspring of women who are tense/anxious/stressed during pregnancy are affected adversely. Precisely how is difficult to tell.

There are many mothers who are able, because of their personal resources (notably an ability to mobilize stress management skills), to overcome their unhappy circumstances and resist adverse influences (Chapter 16 deals with the concept of resilience).

■ Biological Adversity: Smoking and Alcohol in Pregnancy

Our next concern is the adverse effect of exposing the developing embryonic or fetal brain to two nearly universal teratogens: nicotine and alcohol. The term *teratogen* refers any environmental agent capable of damaging a developing embryo.

- Mothers smoking more than six cigarettes daily during pregnancy have been shown to be more at risk of having children who later develop clinically significant behaviour problems (and more generally, the likelihood of conduct disorders in boys) than non-smokers (Wakschlag, Lahey and Loeber, 1997).
- Alcohol consumed to excess in pregnancy, compared with all the other addictive substances (e.g. tobacco, heroin, cocaine, and marijuana) can have the most adverse neuro-behavioural effects on the fetus, resulting in permanent disorders of memory function, impulse control and judgement.

Smoking

Symptoms

Among the symptoms that often follow antenatal exposure to smoking are:

- cognitive difficulties (reasoning and understanding)
- behaviour problems
- impulsivity
- attention difficulties.

Causation

Adverse changes to the infant's neural functioning are thought to be responsible for the symptoms above. Although developmental problems in children have been demonstrated through prospective studies to be associated with maternal substance use (Streissguth, 1997), these problems are often not acknowledged except in the most extreme cases. Because of the difficulty in their identification, as well as various confounding environmental influences, learning problems and aberrant behaviours can be attributed to causes other than antenatal smoking. As a result, many affected individuals do not receive correct diagnosis or treatment for their alcohol-related disabilities.

Developmental features

A prospective investigation by Brennan, Grekin and Mednick (1999) of mothers who smoked during their pregnancies (4,000 boys involved) found a close relationship between different levels of antenatal smoking and arrests in adulthood for both violent and non-violent crime.

Treatment/prevention

This will be discussed later in the chapter.

Fetal Alcohol Syndrome (FAS)

Diagnosis

According to the 'special report' of the 8th National Institute on Alcohol Abuse and Alcoholism (NIH Publication No. 94-3699), FAS is the most common non-hereditary cause of intellectual impairment ('mental retardation') in Western societies. FAS resulting from alcohol consumption during pregnancy has consequences for the offspring that are commonly life-long and devastating. It may present with a number of neurophysical attributes. Children with this condition can be recognized by growth deficiency and a characteristic set of facial traits visible at birth which tend to normalize as the child matures. Although many of these physical anomalies are less pronounced after puberty, most devastating are the lifelong effects of alcohol-induced *in utero* damage, to the central nervous system.

The behavioural outcomes of the structural brain damage that is sustained include:

- cognitive dysfunctions;
- motor dysfunction;
- mental health difficulties;
- psycho-social problems.

The boundaries of the diagnosis, as well as the markers that should be used to delineate those boundaries, are somewhat controversial. Difficulties in obtaining an adequate history of alcohol intake from the parent contribute to the complexity of this issue.

Clinical features

Although most children affected by alcohol exposure before birth do not have the characteristic facial abnormalities and growth retardation identified with FAS, they do tend to have brain and other impairments which are even more disabling.

These children (by no means all) tend to suffer deficits in general intellectual functioning. They have difficulties with learning, memory, attention, problem solving, and social interactions. If the prenatal brain damage remains undetected and emergent behavioural problems fail to be understood, the developing child is quite likely to develop debilitating secondary disabilities' (depression, suicidal threats and attempts, attention deficit problems, panic attacks and auditory and visual hallucinations) (Streissguth and Kanter, 1997).

A study carried out at the University of Washington School of Medicine (see Streissguth, Barr, Kogan and Bookstein, 1996) focused on the presence of these secondary disabilities in 415 patients with FAS and Fetal Alcohol Effects (FAS/FAE). The participants ranged in age from 6 to 51 years (median age

14.2 years), Data, obtained by interviewing parents or caregivers, revealed that over 90 per cent had mental health problems that require referral to psychiatrists, psychologists, or social workers, at some point in their lives.

Developmental features

Among children with FAS up to age 15, the social maturation process (as reported in the alcohol research journal *Alcohol Clinical Experimental Research*, vol. 22, no. 2, April 1998), may be stunted at the level of a 6-year-old child. Fewer than 10 per cent of individuals with FAS are able to achieve success in living and working independently.

Causation

Alcohol is a particularly dangerous teratogen for pregnant women because:

1 *when a mother drinks alcohol,* the alcohol enters her bloodstream and then, through the placenta, enters the blood supply of the growing baby. Clearly, it is unlikely that a single mechanism can explain all of the deleterious effects that result from alcohol exposure during pregnancy. It exerts its influence through multiple actions at different sites in the brain, interfering with the development, function, migration, and survival of nerve cells. Also, alcohol exposure at critical stages of development induces premature cell death in the embryonic cell layer that develops into the bones and cartilage of the head and face. This is thought to be linked to the facial defects sometimes observed in FAS.

2 *whether a woman abuses alcohol,* and whether she becomes pregnant and continues to drink throughout pregnancy (resulting in FAS) involve a complicated set of psychosocial factors. Other factors that influence exposure are the woman's vulnerability to adverse fetal effects at a given level of exposure.

Prenatal alcohol use does not always result in FAS. This does not offer a 'let-out' for committed drinkers, as there is no known safe level of alcohol consumption during pregnancy.

Streissguth is of the opinion that it is better to begin treatment by investigating fraught areas in the environment than to initiate the use of medication too promptly. There are often complex family dynamics that contribute to psychopathological processes in the child.

Treatment

Streissguth and her colleagues observe that appreciation of the links between the primary disabilities in FAS and the secondary mental health problems (all of which except attention deficits increase with age), are important first steps in effective treatment. (see Streissguth, Barr, Kogan and Bookstein, 1996; Streissguth and Kanter, 1997) The trouble is that many women who abuse alcohol do not receive the assistance they so badly require, either because they do not have access to the health care or social services system, because some health care professionals or social workers are uncomfortable speaking to clients about substance abuse problems, or because the women themselves are embarrassed about the stigma that attaches to females who have drinking problems.

Treatment requires a multi-modal approach including (possibly) family therapy, special education, cognitive testing and psycho-pharmacological therapy.

Alcohol-Related Neuro-Developmental Disorder (ARND)

Diagnosis

ARND describes the functional or mental impairments linked to prenatal alcohol exposure. Children with significant prenatal alcohol exposure can lack the characteristic facial defects and growth deficiency of FAS, but still have alcohol-induced mental impairments that are just as serious, if not more so. The term (ARND) was introduced to describe this condition.

ARND affects one out of one hundred babies in North America, making alcohol the leading present-day cause of brain damage (*Teratology*, November 1997; 56 (5): 317–26).

Alcohol-Related Birth Defects (ARBD)

ARBD describes malformations in the skeletal and major organ systems. Prenatally exposed children without FAS facial features can have other alcohol-related physical abnormalities of the skeleton and certain organ systems; these are known as alcohol-related birth defects (ARBD).

Diagnosis

Despite the apparently large number of affected individuals who are born each year, FAS, ARBD, and ARND are rarely diagnosed. However, ARND and ARBD affect more newborns every year than Down's syndrome, cystic fibrosis, spina bifida and sudden infant death syndrome combined.

■ Prevention of Tobacco and Alcohol Use in Pregnancy

For obvious reasons, the focus of prevention efforts has been on the prevention of maternal tobacco and alcohol use in pregnancy or (in the case of intractable alcoholism) on the prevention of pregnancy itself. The logic has been that support and/or treatment programmes that help women give up smoking and significant alcohol consumption during pregnancy offer most hope of being cost-effective and having the greatest benefit for both mother and offspring.

FAS can be prevented, first of all, at a 'tactical' level. Given its unquestioned association with alcohol consumption during pregnancy, it can be completely eliminated. If pregnant women abstain from drinking at that critical time, there would be no such disease.

One can imagine the challenge this offers to anti-smoking and anti-alcohol lobbies, and national health policy-makers. Public awareness, education, and access to prenatal health counselling are possibly the keys to prevention at the 'strategic' level. Another preventive strategy is to screen women of reproductive age who have smoking and alcohol problems, and provide treatment to eliminate smoking and drinking before conception.

As yet, there are few signs of success in these areas to engender much hope of radical changes in alcohol addiction and the associated protection of unborn babies. Despite researchers' best efforts (see the reviews by Coughlan, Doyle and Carr, 2002, and MacKillop and Lisman, et al., 2003, on educational programmes), neither universal prevention nor more targeted activities have had a very strong impact on those persons most at risk, and many children continue to be affected by teratogenic exposure. Only 39 per cent of women of child-bearing age in the USA know what FAS is about (*National Institute of Health Report*, 1993), and over 50 per cent of women of child-bearing age drink alcohol. Women in the UK at highest risk of drinking during pregnancy include:

- women who smoke
- who are single
- who are in college or have a degree
- women in households with above average incomes.

(*Obstetrics and Gynecology*, vol. 92, pp. 187–92, August 1998)

About 20 per cent of women, knowing they are pregnant, continue to drink. The incidence of drinking during pregnancy has increased substantially in the past several years. Binge drinking in the USA is still common; and there has been a fourfold increase in frequency and quantity of drinking during pregnancy (US Center for Disease Control and Prevention).

■ Congenital Conditions

Hydrocephalus

Diagnosis

Hydrocephalus is a congenital condition and the term congenital means that hydrocephalus is present at birth; it does not imply that the condition is hereditary. In early infancy, hydrocephalus is usually detected by the family or a paediatrician because of the baby's rapidly enlarging head. In the first six to twelve months of life, the diagnosis can often be made with an ultrasound scan of the brain. After the skull fuses the diagnosis is best made with MRI or CT.

Causation

The precise cause cannot always be determined. In hydrocephalus (water on the brain), there is a blockage of the watery fluid known as cerebrospinal fluid or CSF, which circulates through connected chambers (known as ventricles), and around the brain and spinal cord. Eventually it is reabsorbed over the surface of the brain into large veins which carry the fluid back to the heart. This orderly cycle of spinal fluid production, flow and absorption maintains a protective environment for the nervous system.

Hydrocephalus is that state in which something has occurred to prevent this orderly procession of events. If the drainage pathways are blocked, the fluid accumulates in the ventricles causing them to swell. In babies and infants, the head will enlarge. The build-up of spinal fluid in the brain can lead to injury or even death if not treated. A child's prognosis is not so much based on the hydrocephalus *per se*, which as we shall see is treatable, but rather the actual *cause* of the hydrocephalus.

While many cases have no clear cause, the following conditions have been associated with the development of hydrocephalus:

- bleeding
- infection

- trauma
- tumours
- vascular problems
- structural problems.

Some of these difficulties occur during pregnancy and others after birth. In addition, a small number can be transmitted genetically.

Treatment

Hydrocephalus itself can be treated; however, the underlying cause of the condition may not have a good prognosis. It may involve irreversible damage to the brain. Most forms of hydrocephalus require surgical treatment. If a definable mass is causing the obstruction of CF flow, it may be possible to remove the mass and allow for normal flow and resolution of the hydrocephalus. More often than not, however, the blockage cannot be removed and the fluid has to be found a way to bypass the normal circulation.

Most surgeons use a shunt to channel the fluid from the ventricles to other sites in the body The shunting device is a system of tubes with a valve to control the rate of drainage and prevent back-flow; it is inserted surgically so that the upper end is in a ventricle of the brain and the lower end leads either into the heart (ventriculo-atrial) or into the abdomen (ventriculo-peritoneal). The most commonly used site is the abdominal cavity. Here the spinal fluid is absorbed onto the surface of the bowels to be returned to the blood stream along with the vital salts and other products it contains.

This does not represent a cure. The shunt controls the pressure by draining excess CSF, thus preventing the condition becoming worse. Symptoms caused by raised pressure usually improve but other problems (damage to the brain tissue) will remain. In addition to these operations, certain types of hydrocephalus can be treated by making a tiny hole internally in the ventricle to re-establish normal flow. This procedure, called a ventriculostomy, is growing in popularity due to improved surgical instruments and imaging techniques. However, for the foreseeable future the treatment of choice for most types of hydrocephalus will be the placement of a shunt.

Risk Factors for Hydrocephalus

- *Prematurity.* Babies born prematurely are at risk of developing hydrocephalus. A baby born early is far more vulnerable than one which goes to full term because its blood vessels are very fragile and can be easily burst if the baby suffers too large a swing in blood pressure or becomes severely ill from other causes. If these complications do occur, then the baby is at risk of developing a haemorrhage from the rupture of the fragile vessels; this can lead, in turn, to a blood clot developing, which could be big enough to break through the wall of the ventricle. Should the clot block the flow of CSF, the baby will develop hydrocephalus. The blockage may be temporary or permanent.

- *Meningitis.* Meningitis is an infection of the membranes covering the brain. The inflammation and debris from this infection block the drainage pathways resulting in hydrocephalus. Meningitis is most common in children. The incidence of one form, haemophilus meningitis, has been drastically reduced by the HIB vaccine.
- *Tumours.* Tumours of the brain cause compression and swelling of surrounding tissues, resulting in poor drainage of CSF. In the treatment of brain tumours, it is often necessary to include measures to control the hydrocephalus, which might, in the case of a successful outcome, be temporary.
- *Seizures.* Patients with hydrocephalus sometimes have seizures (fits) which are not due to the hydrocephalus itself, but are usually associated with an underlying cause (meningitis, abnormal development of the brain, neonatal haemorrhage, etc.).

Developmental features

The learning difficulties that are associated with hydrocephalus include problems with concentration, reasoning and short-term memory. Hydrocephalus can also result in subtle effects involving impairments in co-ordination, motivation and organizational skills. Visual problems, or an early onset of puberty in children, may also occur. Many of these effects can be overcome or reduced by means of teaching strategies or treatment.

Prognosis

As mentioned earlier, the prognosis for the successful management of the hydrocephalus, *per se*, is excellent. The overall outcome depends ultimately on the underlying causes in particular individuals.

CHAPTER 3

The Perinatal and Neonatal Periods

■ Birth

▩ Congenital Abnormalities

Diagnosis

The clearest diagnosable type of disability at birth is a congenital abnormality of structure. Among the signs in a newborn are:

- paleness;
- jaundice (yellow skin and eyes) that begins within 24 hours after delivery;
- unexplained bruising or blood spots under the skin;
- tissue swelling (oedema);
- breathing difficulty;
- fits;
- lack of normal movement.

Outstanding acoustic characteristics of the newborn cry seem to be related to nervous system difficulties. High-risk infants with more shrill and high-pitched cries tend to have significantly lower IQ scores at five years of age.

Assessment of the neonate

In the first minutes of life, a baby takes her/his first test, the Apgar test, named after Virginia Apgar (1953), who developed it. It is designed to evaluate the health and status of the baby. A doctor or nurse checks the infant's physical condition

Table 3.1   Apgar scores

Identification		Description		Score
Pulse/heart rate	–	strength and regularity		
		100 beats per minute	–	Score 2
		below 100 beats per minute	–	Score 1
		no pulse	–	Score 0
Breathing	–	maturity and health of the lungs		
		regular breathing	–	Score 2
		slow, irregular breathing	–	Score 1
		none	–	Score 0
Movements	–	muscle tone		
		active movement	–	Score 2
		some movement/limited flexion	–	Score 1
		limp/flabby	–	Score 0
Skin colour	–	effective oxygenation of the blood		
		pink skin all over	–	Score 2
		bluish extremities (arms/legs)	–	Score 1
		totally blue skin	–	Score 0
Reflexes	–	response to stimuli		
		crying	–	Score 2
		whimpering/grimace	–	Score 1
		silence/no response	–	Score 0

by looking at five standard characteristics which are rated from 0 to 2, recorded on a chart, and totalled – giving a range of from 0 to 10 (see Table 3.1).

Apgar scoring

Most infants score between 7 and 10. It is quite common for neonates to have scores lower than 10 in the first round, since babies usually have blue fingers and toes on arrival. At the five-minute evaluation, the majority of babies score 9 and 10; 7 or better indicates that the infant is not at risk. A score of 4–6 indicates that the infant requires assistance in establishing normal breathing patterns. Scores lower than 4 indicate that the baby is in a critical condition and often requires an active intervention (probably intensive care) in order to survive.

A low Apgar score signals that the baby is quite likely to have a developmental disability; more than 1 in 10 with ratings lower than 4 (at five minutes) develop conditions such as cerebral palsy, intellectual impairment and seizures. Fortunately, infants with low ratings are by no means always denied normal development.

Infant reflexes

Reflexes are the names given to newborn infants' ability to respond motorically to sensory stimulation of particular kinds, in predetermined (i.e. canalized) ways. Their possession of a repertoire of instinctive survival reflexes helps them to adapt to their new surroundings and to satisfy basic needs. They indicate (with other signs and symptoms) the preparedness of infants for their journey through life. There are several adaptive reflexes, some having more obvious survival value than others. The Babinski reflex is a response to stroking the sole of the foot from the toes toward the heel; the big toe extends and the smaller toes spread out. The reflex disappears by the first year's end. It may not be present in newborns with lower spinal cord damage.

So-called 'primitive reflexes', like the swimming reflex and the grasping reflex, may have useful functions. They are controlled by the lower sub-cortical areas of the brain and are lost once the higher centres of the cerebral cortex begin to guide voluntary behaviours. If these or other reflexes are not present at birth, or if they continue for too long in infancy, there would be reason to be concerned about a possible congenital (neurological) difficulty.

The Neonatal Behavioural Assessment Scale (NBAS), administered a few days after birth, was designed in the United States by T. Berry Brazelton in order to assess the strength of 20 inborn reflexes, changes in the infant's state, and also reactions to comforting and other social stimuli (Brazelton, 1984; 1995). The instrument has far wider applications and usefulness. It has been used to encourage strong parent–infant relationships by helping parents to be aware of their infant's physical and social signals and cues. It is also used by clinicians to construct infant profiles which serve as a basis for care-giving and attachment-enhancing plans. For successful examples of these and other applications, see Parker et al. (1992).

Birth Complications

Calling birth the most hazardous single event in a person's life (as is common in the literature) may be an exaggeration, but the process of giving birth is certainly one of the most memorable life-events for women.

Potential physical complications

A child can be harmed during the process of birth:

- by a particularly difficult delivery (e.g. abnormal positioning of the baby) Neonates who are breech babies have a raised incidence of congenital hip dislocation, club foot and scoliosis, and are more likely to have cervicothoracic spinal trauma.
- in the event of mother–child Rh factor incompatibility;
- by medical instruments: forceps and vacuum extraction can be traumatic if improperly applied;
- in the aftermath of an accident, for example, direct trauma to the brain and consequent haemorrhaging.

Causal link with brain disorders

Obstetric and neonatal complications are common but are generally innocuous. Robert Goodman (2002) cautions that when it comes to an aetiological link between birth complications and 'brain damage' (a term he prefers to replace with the words 'brain disorder'), neurological theories about causation are prone to error. The received wisdom that cerebral palsy, mental retardation and epilepsy are commonly due to perinatal complications 'is almost certainly false'. In his opinion, if birth complications are not common causes of overt brain disorders such as cerebral palsy, it is even less likely that they commonly result in minimal brain damage manifesting solely in behavioural or learning difficulties.

In a large-scale study by Jacobsen and Kenney (1980) more than 60 per cent of all pregnancies experienced at least one complication, but that most of these complications caused no problems. He makes the point that it is possible that perinatal complications compound whatever damage has already occurred prenatally. Since the fetus is an active participant in the delivery process, and not simply a passive passenger that is expelled when its time has come, it is not surprising that an abnormal fetus should be particularly liable to an abnormal birth.

Lawrence Impey, on the basis of a study of 8,580 women, carried out with colleagues at the National Maternity Hospital in Dublin, concluded in *The Lancet* that babies can be damaged during delivery but it is in pregnancy that most damage is done (study cited by Thomas Stuttaford: 'Medical briefing', *The Times*, Friday, 7 March, 2003, p. 12).

■ Congenital Brain Injuries

Given the extraordinary complexity of the brain, the symptoms resulting from different types of cerebral injury, *whatever its origins*, are very varied. The range of brain injuries (both open and closed) seen in children include:

- trauma
- cerebral haemorrhage
- infection
- tumours
- aneurysms
- hydrocephalus (disruption of normal spinal fluid absorption in the brain)
- oxygen deprivation (hypoxia).

The concept of 'brain damage' is a popular explanatory notion for hyperactive, conduct-disordered patterns of behaviour. And it is a good example of the misuse of a medical explanation. Being tautologies or renamings in most instances, they tell us very little about the child and only too often are therapeutically pessimistic. For example, parents and teachers are sometimes told that a particular child's difficulties at home and at school are a result of brain damage, suffered perhaps as early as at birth. This is no more helpful than for a general practitioner to tell a mother her child is physically ill when she takes him along for a diagnosis of a bodily malaise.

Certainly no programme of rehabilitation, either remedial teaching or treatment, could be planned on the basis of such a vague diagnosis as 'brain damage'. What is required, in assessing referred children, is not a meaningless label but precise information, with practical implications, about their specific physical and intellectual problems, and also about any emotional and social difficulties that have a bearing on their ability to learn and adapt to life's challenges (Herbert, 1964).

A complicating factor, particularly in early childhood, is the brain's plasticity. This plasticity is the brain's bonus of compensatory capacity which allows it to circumvent emergencies, sometimes including disease or damage to brain tissue. The superfluous number of functional units in its construction provides a latent reserve, so that certain brain centres can undergo a dynamic readjustment of their function, and take over from other damaged parts (see Battro, 2001; Herbert and Kemp 1969).

The brain injuries described above give rise to many medical complications that involve various levels of care:

- seizures;
- hydrocephalus;
- subdural haematoma (blood clots);
- spasticity (abnormal increase in muscle tone);
- pneumonia (respiratory complications);

- incontinence (loss of bladder or bowel control);
- dysphagia (difficulty swallowing);
- mood disorders (depression, agitation);
- sleep disorders;
- infections.

Treatment

It is the complexity and indefinite nature of brain injuries that make treatment (requiring a multidisciplinary team) unique for each patient.

The Care Team might include
- physicians specializing in physical medicine and rehabilitation;
- occupational therapist;
- physiotherapist;
- speech and language therapists/pathologists;
- rehabilitation nurse;
- neuro- and clinical psychologists;
- dietician.

Interventions

Among the interventions are the following:

- medical (e.g. medication, nutrition and respiratory care);
- cognitive retraining (learning aids and educational input);
- cognitive, emotional and behavioural evaluation;
- behaviour therapy;
- sensory stimulation: 'stimulation therapy';
- mobility: (e.g. mobility devices where required);
- therapeutic recreation: aquatic therapy, creative therapy, adaptive play and sports;
- special educational services: helping children to return to school;
- family and child/adolescent counselling/psycho-education;
- special educational services: helping children to return to school;
- preparation for the return from hospital to home: interacting and socializing with other people; simulating a 'typical day' to practise daily routines of medication, school, play and other life activities.

Rh Incompatiblity

Diagnosis

Rhesus (Rh) incompatibility occurs when a woman is Rh-negative, but her fetus has inherited Rh-positive blood from the father. It rarely occurs in a woman's first pregnancy. She only becomes sensitized to the fetus's Rh-positive blood once she comes in contact with it. This is usually not until very late in pregnancy or during childbirth. This can also occur during a miscarriage or if the fetus is aborted.

Symptoms

Symptoms and complications only affect the fetus and/or newborn. They occur when standard preventive measures are not taken and can vary from mild to very serious. The mother's health is not affected. Symptoms of the newborn baby include:

- anaemia;
- swelling of the body (which may be associated with heart failure and respiratory problems);
- kernicterus (a neurological syndrome).

Clinical features

A woman is unable on her own, to detect from physical symptoms whether she is Rh incompatible, in any given pregnancy. When she is pregnant, the standard procedure is for her doctor to arrange a blood test that will determine whether she is Rh positive or Rh negative. If the blood test indicates that she has developed Rh antibodies, her blood will be monitored regularly to assess the level of antibodies it contains. If the levels are high, an amniocentesis is suggested to determine the extent of the impact on the fetus. The risk factors that increase a woman's chance of suffering this condition:

- being pregnant with Rh-negative blood, and a history of a prior pregnancy involving a fetus that was Rh positive;
- being pregnant with a history of prior blood transfusion or amniocentesis.

Epidemiology

Most people – about 85 per cent – are Rh positive. But if a woman who is Rh negative conceives from a man who is Rh positive, there is the potential for incompatibility. The baby may have Rh-positive blood, inherited from the father. At least 50 per cent of the children born to an Rh-negative mother and Rh-positive father will be Rh positive.

Treatment

Since rhesus disease is almost completely preventable by the application of simple precautionary steps and the use of Immune Globulin Injection of RhoGAM, prevention remains the best treatment. Routine prenatal care should help identify, manage, and treat any complications of Rh incompatibility. Mothers need to be monitored carefully by their doctor during pregnancy. If the father of the infant is Rh positive, the mother is given an injection of RhoGAM at week 28 of the pregnancy. This desensitizes her blood to Rh-positive blood. She will also have another injection of immune globulin within 72 hours after delivery (or miscarriage or abortion). This further desensitizes her blood for future pregnancies.

Treatment of a pregnancy or newborn depends on the severity of the condition. It could range from:

* aggressive hydration and phototherapy using bilirubin lights;
* early induction of labour;
* a direct transfusion of packed red blood cells (compatible with the infant's blood), to exchange transfusion of the newborn to rid the blood of the maternal antibodies that are destroying the red blood cells.

Developmental features

Full recovery is expected where Rh incompatibility is mild. In severe cases, long-term problems can result (e.g. hydrops fetalis which has a high mortality rate, and kernicterus). Other problems include cognitive delays, movement disorders, hearing loss, and seizures.

■ Genetic Disorders Remediable after Birth

▒ Haemophilia

Diagnosis

Haemophilia is a disorder in which there is an absence of the blood clotting factor FVIII which causes profuse bleeding from any external or internal injury.

Clinical features

A diagnosis can be made from a sample of fetal blood at 18 to 20 weeks of the pregnancy. Haemophilia may be dominant across the generations before it makes its appearance to the surprise of the family.

Causation

The condition is caused by a mutant gene located on the X chromosome of the 23 pairs – the sex chromosomes. The defect would be masked if a normal X chromosome is present and in such a case, not show itself. Since females have two chromosomes the defective X acts like a recessive gene in the female but like a dominant one in the male. For heterozygous females, the unmutated copy of the gene will provide all the factor FVIII they require. Heterozygous females are called 'carriers' because although they have no symptoms of haemophilia, they pass the gene on to approximately half their sons, who develop the disease, and half their daughters, who also become carriers.

In males, who have a Y chromosome instead of a second X chromosome, the disease will express itself. Males, with only a single X chromosome, who inherit the defective gene (invariably from their mother) will be unable to produce factor FVIII and will suffer episodes of bleeding.

Treatment and prevention

The usual treatment is infusion of factor FVIII concentrates to replace the defective clotting factor. Parents can administer them at home when they first see signs of their child bleeding. The amount infused depends upon the severity of bleeding, the site of the bleeding, and the child's size.

Depending on the severity of the disease, factor FVIII concentrate may be given prior to dental extractions and surgery to prevent bleeding. Children with severe forms of the disease may need regular prophylactic infusions.

Kernicterus

Diagnosis

The chances of jaundice in newborn infants being harmful are fortunately low. However, a small percentage of infants with jaundice do develop a severe form of brain disorder called 'kernicterus'. The yellow skin colour, a feature of jaundice, is caused by high blood levels of bilirubin leading to bilirubin toxicity that can damage areas in the brain in various ways.

Clinical features

Kernicterus may cause complications of brain functioning, leading to problems with vision, hearing loss, and dental development. It can cause intellectual disability, although many children with kernicterus have normal or superior intelligence. They are disabled by bodies whose movements they cannot control (athetoid cerebral palsy) and the hearing difficulties referred to above. Implants in the inner ear (cochlear implants) have proved successful in treating the hearing difficulties.

Causation

In some newborn babies, the liver produces too much of bilirubin, leading to jaundice. Babies who are more likely to suffer from jaundice than others, are those with a sibling who has had jaundice, or those who have bruises at birth. When a bruise begins to heal red blood cells die; bilirubin is produced when red blood cells break down. The healing of large bruises may cause high levels of bilirubin and the baby may become jaundiced. When this occurs the skin and whites of the infant's eyes turn yellow. This 'jaundice' usually disappears spontaneously. However, the jaundice in a few babies, if not treated, gives rise to levels of bilirubin that can damage the brain and lead to kernicterus.

Risk factors

Preterm babies (born before 37 weeks of pregnancy) become jaundiced because their liver may not be fully developed, and the immature liver may not be able to get rid of an excess of bilirubin. Babies who do not eat much are more likely to get jaundice. A baby born to an East Asian or Mediterranean family is at a higher than usual risk of becoming very jaundiced.

Treatment and prevention

A baby's jaundice can be treated and brain damage prevented. In the case of excessive jaundice he or she can be treated with phototherapy. The baby is placed under blue lights most of the day. The blue lights do not distress the baby. If the baby gets extremely jaundiced an exchange transfusion can be arranged.

Phenylketonuria

Diagnosis

Phenylketonuria (PKU) is a rare hereditary condition which is caused by the lack of a liver enzyme required to digest phenylalanine. The genetic abnormality involves a missing enzyme which means that phenylalanine cannot be used in a normal fashion.

Clinical features

Phenylalanine is one of eight essential amino acids in protein-containing foods such as meat, cow's milk, over-the-counter infant formulas and breast milk. As a result of not being properly metabolized, high levels of phenylalanine and two closely related phenylalanine derivatives build up in the body. These compounds are toxic to the central nervous system, and cause brain damage. This, in turn, leads to severe intellectual impairment by the end of the first year of life if proteins are not scrupulously avoided. Older children may develop movement disorders if not treated.

Because phenylalanine is involved indirectly in the production of melanin, the pigment responsible for skin and hair colour, children with phenylketonuria often have lighter complexions than their unaffected siblings. Nearly 90 per cent have blond hair and blue eyes. Other signs include skeletal features such as a small head, short stature, and flat feet. PKU sufferers may also have the skin disorder eczema.

There is a characteristic musty odour in children suffering from undiagnosed PKU. This smell in the urine and sweat results from the accumulation of phenylacetic acid, which occurs if the condition has not been treated immediately from birth, or if foods containing phenylalanine are consumed. If treatment is begun late (after 3 years of age), or if the disorder remains untreated, brain damage is inevitable.

Causation

The faulty gene, which is inherited as an autosomal recessive trait, only emerges when two carriers have children together and pass it on to their offspring.

Epidemiology

One out of every 10,000 live births will suffer from PKU.

Treatment

PKU, fortunately, is treatable. A heel-stick blood sample from the infant is used for the screening. In the UK every baby is seen at home within 14 days of birth by a health visitor who tests those who were not born in hospital, or who left hospital prior to 7 days of age. The infant with PKU is put on a low phenylalanine diet, but not so low that it stunts growth. Careful ongoing monitoring is required. Where there would have been severe impairing of intellect, IQ seems reasonably protected, although there may be some behaviour problems. If dietary treatment is followed closely, beginning shortly after the child's birth, he or she should live a reasonably normal, healthy life.

Prevention

Genetic counselling is recommended for prospective parents with a family history of PKU. It is a disease that can be easily detected by a simple blood test prenatally. Tests include:

- an enzyme assay to detect the carrier state (of would-be parents);
- a chorionic villus sample to detect fetal PKU (prenatal diagnosis).

Adult women who have PKU, and who plan to become pregnant need to adhere to a strict low-phenylalanine diet both before and during pregnancy. Babies of women with PKU who are not on the diet during pregnancy, can be severely malformed and intellectually impaired. However, females who are on the diet give birth to normal, healthy infants.

■ Fatal Postnatal Disorders

Tay–Sachs Disease

Diagnosis

Tay–Sachs disease (TSD) is a fatal genetic disorder, most commonly occurring in children, resulting in progressive destruction of the nervous system. A baby with Tay–Sachs disease appears normal until about five or six months of age when its development slows. By about two years of age, most children experience recurrent seizures and diminishing mental function. The infant gradually regresses, and is eventually unable to crawl, turn over, sit or reach out. Eventually, the child becomes blind, mentally retarded, paralyzed and non-responsive.

Clinical features

A simple blood test can identify Tay–Sachs carriers. Blood samples are analysed by either enzyme assay or DNA studies. The enzyme assay is a biochemical test that measures the level of Hex-A in a person's blood. Carriers have less Hex-A in their body fluid and cells than non-carriers. Prenatal testing for Tay–Sachs can be done around the 11th week of pregnancy using CVS (chorionic villi sampling). This involves removing a tiny piece of the placenta. Or the fetus can be tested with amniocentesis around the 16th week of pregnancy. In this procedure, a needle is used to take a sample of the fluid surrounding the baby in order to test it.

Carriers of Tay–Sachs – people who have one copy of the inactive gene along with one copy of the active gene – are healthy. They do not have Tay–Sachs disease but they may pass on the faulty gene to their children. Carriers have a 50 per cent chance of passing on the defective gene to their children. A child who inherits one inactive gene is a Tay–Sachs carrier like the parent. If both parents are carriers and their child inherits the defective TSD gene from each of them, the child will have Tay–Sachs disease.

When both parents are carriers of the defective Tay–Sachs gene, each child has a 25 per cent chance of having Tay–Sachs disease and a 50 per cent chance of being a carrier. Both parents must be carriers in order to have an affected child. When both parents are found to carry a genetic mutation in hexosaminidase A, there is a 25 per cent chance with each pregnancy that the child will be affected with Tay–Sachs disease. Prenatal monitoring of pregnancies is available if desired.

Epidemiology

While anyone can be a carrier of Tay–Sachs, the incidence of the disease is significantly higher among people of eastern European (Ashkenazi) Jewish descent. Non-Jewish French Canadians living near the St Lawrence River and in the Cajun community of Louisiana also have a higher incidence of Tay–Sachs disease.

Causation

Tay–Sachs disease is controlled by a pair of genes on chromosome 15 which code for production of the enzyme Hex-A. If either or both Hex-A genes are active, the body produces enough of the enzyme to prevent the abnormal build-up of the GM2 ganglioside lipid. The disease is caused by the absence of a vital enzyme called hexosaminidase-A (Hex-A). Without Hex-A, a fatty substance, or lipid, called GM2 ganglioside accumulates abnormally in cells, especially in the nerve cells of the brain. As nerve cells become distended with fatty material, a relentless deterioration of mental and physical abilities occurs.

In children, the destructive process begins in the fetus early in pregnancy, although the disease is not clinically apparent until infants are several months old. By the time children with Tay–Sachs are three or four years old, the nervous system is so badly affected they become blind, deaf, and unable to swallow. Muscles begin to atrophy and paralysis sets in with rapid and progressive deterioration. This condition is life shortening with death usually occurring by the age of 5 or 6 years.

Treatment

There is no cure or effective treatment for Tay–Sachs disease. However, researchers are pursuing several approaches in the hope of finding a cure. For example, scientists are exploring enzyme replacement therapy to provide the Hex-A which is lacking in babies with Tay–Sachs. Bone marrow transplantation has been attempted also, but to date has not been successful in reversing or slowing damage to the central nervous system in babies with the disease. Another avenue of research is gene therapy in which scientists transfer a normal gene into cells to replace an abnormal gene. This approach holds great promise for curing Tay–Sachs, but that goal is not yet in sight.

Genetic counselling

If both parents are carriers, they are likely to consult a genetic counsellor for help in deciding whether to conceive, or whether to have a fetus tested for Tay–Sachs.disease. Extensive carrier testing of Ashkenazi Jews has significantly reduced the number of their children with the disease. Today, most cases of Tay–Sachs disease occur in populations not thought to be at highest risk.

Assisted reproductive therapy is an option for carriers who do not wish to risk giving birth to a child with Tay–Sachs. A new technique used in conjunction with in-vitro fertilization enables parents who are Tay–Sachs carriers to give birth to healthy babies. Embryos created in-vitro are tested for Tay–Sachs genetic mutations before being implanted into the mother, allowing only healthy embryos to be selected.

Canavan Disease

Diagnosis

Canavan disease (CD), a condition first described in 1931, is a rare hereditary and neurological disorder characterized by spongy degeneration of the brain, in which the white matter is replaced by microscopic fluid-filled spaces.

- the disease usually begins in infancy (at around three to nine months) with subtle changes such as visual inattentiveness or an inability to perform motor tasks;
- one of the earliest signs is low muscle tone (overall);
- there is a lack of head control.

Clinical and developmental features

As the child grows, motor skills and mental functioning deteriorate. The child eventually goes blind, although hearing remains acute. Difficulties which arise as the child gets older, include stiffness, weakness of the muscles, seizures, and feeding problems. The presentation and progression of illness vary from child to child. Affected children continue to recognize and respond to the voices of their main caregivers.

Epidemiology

Although CD may occur in any ethnic group, it particularly affects persons of Eastern European (Ashkenazi) Jewish ancestry. DNA testing of Ashkenazi Jewish couples can tell with over 95 per cent certainty, whether either or both parents are carriers. If neither or only one parent carries a mutation in the aspartoacylase gene, the couple is not at risk for having a child with CD. If both parents are carriers, there is a 25 per cent chance with each pregnancy that their child will have the disease.

Causation

CD is one of a group of genetic disorders called the leukodystrophies that affect growth of the myelin sheath of the nerve fibres in the brain. The myelin sheath's function is to protect nerves and allow messages to be sent to and from the brain. In CD, myelin deteriorates because affected children have a deficiency of the enzyme aspartoacylase. This leads to the accumulation in the brain of a chemical N-acetyl-aspartic acid (NAA) which destroys myelin.

Treatment and prevention

Treatment is symptomatic for the movement disorders, seizures, and feeding problems. It has also to be supportive, as there is no cure for CD. Genetic counselling and DNA-based prenatal testing (using samples obtained through CVS or amniocentesis), can assist family planning for couples who both carry identified mutations.

Recent developments in the understanding of the genetic defect involved in CD (an autosomal recessive trait), have increased the accuracy of carrier screening and prenatal detection.

Sudden Infant Death Syndrome (SIDS)

Diagnosis

SIDS, commonly referred to as 'cot death' is defined as the sudden death of an infant or young child which is unexpected by history and in which a thorough post-mortem fails to demonstrate an adequate cause of death. Sudden and unexpected deaths have been mentioned in the Old Testament, in Roman records, and in medical reports going back to the twelfth century.

Causation

No sufficient or necessary causes have emerged from the many investigations dating from the 1950s. Studies (see Coughlan, Carr and Fitzgerald, 2000) indicate that SIDS has serious and prolonged psychological effects on parents and siblings.

Prevention

SIDS is poorly understood so that despite reports of several environmental associations (e.g. overnight temperature, sleeping position, climate) and biological correlations (e.g. centrally determined sleep apnoea), no preventive strategies taking them into account have proved to be effective.

■ Premature Birth

Complications due to Low Birth Weight

If the birth of a baby is early, it puts him or her at risk of having a lower birth weight than the normal population.

Clinical criteria

Operational definitions used to describe low birth weight categories, are as follows:

- *Low birth weight (LBW)* or *amall for date babies* are small for gestational age. Babies are classified as LBW if less than 2,500 grams or about 5 1/2 pounds at birth. Some 7 per cent of newborns in the West are LBW. Babies who are of low weight for their gestational age (more than two standard deviations below the mean) are at risk of having abnormalities of the nervous system. About 10 per cent develop a major disabling condition such as moderate or severe intellectual impairment, cerebral palsy, blindness and deafness.
- *Very low birth weight (VLBW)* is the category used if, at birth, babies weigh less than 1,500 grams or about 3 1/2 pounds. 1 per cent of newborns in the West are VLBW. These infants have experienced slow growth as fetuses and are seriously under-weight. Even when born close to their normal due date these infants are below the 10th percentile of full-term babies' weight at birth. This means they weigh less than 2000 grams. More than 20 per cent develop a major disabling condition such as moderate or severe intellectual impairment, cerebral palsy, blindness and deafness.
- *Extremely low birth weight (ELBW)* babies weighing 1,000 grams or less, are clearly at most risk of adverse developmental consequences.

Mortality rates

The survival of babies at 25 weeks of gestation (and beyond) is problematic but fairly routine. The viability limit of preterm babies is at about 23–4 weeks or about 500–600 grams in weight. Despite the skilled efforts of intensive care staff and the intense longings of parents, the chances of survival beyond the first few days of life, when babies are this premature, are low and the likelihood of disability high. Babies who are younger than 20 weeks gestational age are very rarely born alive or survive for long.

Michael Kramer and his colleagues (2000) report (in the 16 August 2000 issue of the *Journal of the American Medical Association*) that infants born at 32–6 weeks of gestational age were six times more likely to die within the first year of life; and those born at 34–6 weeks of gestational age were three times more likely to die in the first year of life, than were full-term infants. The usual causes of death were infection, problems with breathing, various birth defects and developmental disorders, and sudden infant death syndrome.

Clinical features

When newborn babies are very immature they constitute a different organism to a full-term baby. The problems they have affect almost every organ they possess. The systems that must support their functions at birth (e.g. muscles and nervous system) are not yet sufficiently developed. The small-for-date babies are more likely than preterm infants to remain small in stature throughout childhood, to experience learning difficulties and behaviour problems at school, and to perform poorly on IQ tests (Goldenberg, 1995).

Infants with lbw are at high risk of neurological impairment and cognitive problems as demonstrated by Sykes, Hay, et al. (1997) who tracked 243 premature babies (1500 g) and found that primary schoolchildren who were born prematurely were rated less well adjusted than full-term controls. Other disadvantageous outcomes are: health and educational difficulties, behaviour disorders and hyperactivity (see Middle et al., 1996; Pharoah et al., 1994).

Nicholas Wood and his associates (2000) reported a prospective study of nervous system disability after extremely pre-term birth (25 or less weeks of intrauterine age). All surviving children born between 20–5 weeks of intrauterine life (gestational age) in the United Kingdom and Ireland from March through December 1995 were studied. 811 were admitted to intensive care; 314 survived to go home. Overall, 49 per cent of the 283 children who were eventually assessed at 30 months, suffered significant nervous system disabilities, including 23 per cent who had severe disabilities. It was concluded that neurological disability (particularly severe disability) is common in surviving infants born very prematurely. The disabilities included impairment of motor function (movement), sensory acuity (vision, hearing), communication (speech) and/or mental disabilities. Some 75 of the children with disabilities had cerebral palsy. At six years of age, 40 per cent of the surviving children had moderate to severe learning disabilities compared to 2 per cent of their classmates.

There is evidence from a study of 439 newly diagnosed children with visual defects throughout Britain in 2000, led by Jugnoo Rahi at the Institute of Child Health, that an increase in the number of premature babies who survive, has led to more children becoming visually impaired or blind (Rahi et al., *The Lancet*, October, 24, 2003). The risk of blindness was inversely related to birth weight. Rahi concludes that 'severe visual impairment and blindness in childhood is more common, appears more frequently, and has greater associated mortality, than previously assumed.'

Feeding

Tube feeding and parenteral feeding are commonly used with premature infants who are at the highest risk for oral feeding if they have required prolonged assistance on a ventilator, have chronic lung disease, or a history of central nervous system damage. As they recover, the transition to oral feeding begins, an exercise requiring delicacy and caution as the child has difficulties in integrating breathing into the suck–swallow cycle, and may thus experience physiological instability (e.g. hypoxia, bradycardia). If children are not to develop mistrust in their oral abilities, they need opportunities to have some feeding experiences by mouth during the 6 to 10 months 'sensitive period' for the development of oral feeding. This should help them to learn control and coordination and trust in the mechanisms of feeding.

Causation of preterm birth

In about a third of pregnancies preterm birth occurs because there is some infective process. There are organisms in the vagina that become pathogenic, and make their way up into the uterus causing problems in the fetal membranes. Contractions occur to remove the fetus from possibly terminal danger – a protective outcome for baby and possibly the mother as well. In a further 20 per cent of pregnancies the health of the fetus or the mother makes it imperative that the baby be born prematurely. In the remaining 50 per cent it is not known why there is an early entry into life.

There are many poorly understood correlations reported between different circumstances and prematurity. For example, women who change partner between having their first two children have an increased risk of premature birth, low birthweight and infant mortality. A research team at the Norwegian University of Science and Technology in Trondheim (with Lars Vatten in the lead) compared the medical records of 450,000 women who had the same partner for both births, with those of almost 32,000 women who had changed partner (study reported in *The Times*, Friday, 14 November 2003). Women whose second babies were conceived with different men were more than twice as likely to give birth prematurely, three times more likely to have a child of low birth-weight and 1.6 times more likely to have a miscarriage. The risk of infant mortality was also raised.

The researchers speculated that the figures might be explained by social and lifestyle factors. They suggested that women who changed partner had a 'higher prevalence of risk-taking behaviour, such as heavier smoking and alcohol consumption and poorer nutrition'. According to Lars Vatten (2003), their observations covering more than 30 years show that child-bearing with different partners is increasingly more common. He commented that:

> Women who change partner may be a selected group with characteristics that increase risk, or they may change their lifestyle or behaviour in ways that are unfavourable on pregnancy outcomes. But we can only speculate on the causes because we don't have any definite answers.

Another unsolved mystery (at least in its entirety) is the association between prematurity and brain damage. Certainly, the skull of the premature infant does not provide as effective a protection to brain-tissue as is provided in the case of an infant born at full term, and is thus more likely to show serious nervous system injuries. Pressure during birth may cause the fracture of bones. Should this happen in the vicinity of nerve centres, there may be temporary or permanent injury to some of them, or to the sense organs, particularly the ears and eyes. However, it is also very likely that the factors that caused the premature delivery may also have led (in the first place) to brain injury of the fetus or infant.

Whatever the cause of a premature birth, it is considered that the very immature brain does not develop well outside the uterine environment, despite the advanced technology of neonatal special care units.

Developmental features

Although the life expectancy of children born prematurely has improved dramatically, if they are born early, they will continue to develop as if they were still in the womb. Experiencing the outside world prematurely will not accelerate the normal progression of development. Most prematurely born babies and many full-term infants who have neonatal problems, will experience at least temporary delays in their development. *Developmental delay* is a term used to indicate that development is proceeding more slowly than would be associated with a normally developing child. It does not imply anything about whether or not the child can be expected eventually to 'catch up' or attain a normal rate of development. Because neonatologists have developed new skills and technology over the years, it is thought that the chances of immature babies escaping from adverse developmental effects have increased. Despite this optimism, the risks to very premature babies remain high. The evidence suggests that extreme prematurity is an important contributory cause of developmental brain disorders, particularly cerebral palsy.

'Catching up'

There are no simple answers to parents' anxious queries about developmental delay. The age by which children born prematurely should have 'caught up' remains controversial. As prematurity is not a homogeneous 'entity', there is no simple formulaic answer. Premature babies are initially retarded in many areas of growth and development, but most (depending on the extent of the prematurity and LBW) do eventually catch up.

It takes the best part of nine months for all systems in an infant's body to be at the point of maturity associated with a full-term newborn. Catching-up growth is attained at:

- approximately age 18 months for head circumference;
- age 24 months for weight;
- age 40 months for height.

If a child is born early s/he will continue to develop as if s/he were still in the uterus. A baby who is 4 weeks premature and is 4 weeks behind developmentally is not 'delayed' or 'retarded'. If it is 6 weeks behind developmentally but is 4 weeks premature, such a developmental lag suggests a disability. However, developmental lags are difficult to detect in very young infants; furthermore they may be temporary. In some premature babies with very low birth-weight, catching-up growth does not occur until early school age.

Growth in premature infants

When plotting growth charts for premature babies, a 'corrected age' is required – calculated by subtracting the number of weeks of prematurity from the post-natal age. Special growth charts based on gestational age rather than chronological age have been developed for infants beginning at 26 weeks' gestational age; they may not be completely reliable.

Outcomes

Many babies remain hospitalized or are dependent on technology until their first birthday or later. Social, economic, and emotional support is crucial. Children in less stable, deprived homes, experience more emotional problems and manifest long-term intellectual and academic deficits. Women from ethnic minority groups and low-income sections of the community are particularly at risk because of dietary inadequacies and less than satisfactory antenatal care (e.g. Kopp and Kaler, 1989).

Outcomes tend to be positive when mothers are sensitive to the factors that promote and stimulate healthy development (Caughy, 1996). However, this can be difficult to achieve for mothers who resist the offer of parent training, or who find the requirement for regular attendance too demanding. Mothers who drink heavily and use drugs (often, consequently, malnourished when pregnant) are likely to deliver undersized babies. Their lifestyle may make regular attendance at parenting courses difficult to manage. Twenty per cent of all premature infants are born to adolescent girls (Goldberg and Craig, 1983) who often find the responsibilities and trials of parenthood too much for them.

Later school performance

It is school performance for children who were LBW babies that seems to be more affected than IQ, as such. Many are in special education settings, and have learning difficulties. Language development seems to be especially affected. In a study by Largo, Molinari et al. (1986), LBW babies (compared with full-term babies at age 5), were delayed in language development which was negatively correlated with both birth weight and gestational age, even for premature infants who were not neurologically impaired. Where there is some evidence of later improvement for a LBW group, this is not the case for the VLBW children.

Prevention and risk

Clearly, the first line of defence against the risks for pre-maturity is vigilant medical monitoring and care. Various illnesses and conditions may predispose women to premature delivery and birth complications:

- *Hypertension.* Pregnant women sometimes suffer from high blood pressure in the second half of pregnancy. If combined with oedema (accumulation of fluid in issues) and/or protein in the urine it may result in toxaemia in pregnancy or pre-eclampsia. The condition will persist until after delivery, and carries a significant risk of prematurity and intrauterine growth retardation.
- *Diabetes.* Here the foetal pancreas produces excess insulin which results in blood sugar levels that are abnormally low (hypoglycaemia). If not treated, it results in brain damage in the infant.
- *Herpes.* This active viral infection can be transmitted from the mother to the relatively immune deficient infant during delivery. It may precipitate premature labour or lead to infection or fetal deformities. The condition causes death in a majority of infected infants and significant neurological damage in half of the survivors.
- *Structural abnormalities.* The mother's pelvis may put her at risk if it is too small to allow the passage of the baby's head (cephalopelvic disproportion) or it may dilate too early (incompetent cervix), which can result in premature delivery or miscarriage.
- *Uterine contractions.* If the uterus contracts too forcefully, it can interfere with fetal circulation, causing oxygen deprivation or bleeding in the brain.

- *Placenta praevia.* This is another adverse condition that puts a pregnancy at risk. Normally the placenta attaches itself high on the uterine wall, away from the cervix. The placenta covers the cervix partially or completely. Any change in the cervix, such as the softening and dilating that occurs close to the time of delivery, can cause the placenta to separate from the uterus and bleed. This may be life-threatening to the unborn child. Placenta praevia occurs to some degree in 1 out of 200 pregnancies. The problem shows itself as sudden painless bleeding during the second or third trimester of pregnancy, especially the last 13 weeks.

Intensive care

Low and very low birth-weight babies require intensive medical care. It takes advanced technology in intensive care units, to provide the life-support the uterus would have been responsible for, and specialist neonatal nursing and medical expertise to monitor and intervene as necessary. Procedures in a Special Care Baby Unit (SCBU) might include:

- being placed under a radiant heater for the control of temperature;
- monitoring of humidity and oxygen levels;
- monitoring of heart rate;
- feeding (possibly) through nasogastric tubes;
- using fortified breast milk or special formula food;
- monitoring of respiration: the present-day effectiveness in treating respiratory distress syndrome is responsible for much of the improvement in survival rates of premature babies.

The constant light in a SCBU and the noise of the life-support apparatus result in a lack of patterned sensory experience for premature infants. Potential sensory deprivation may be pre-empted by handling, stroking and rocking where this is feasible. More formal early stimulation programmes are implemented in some hospitals (see below). Because very low birth-weight infants are placed in high-technology SCBU beds, the opportunities for mothers and their infants to interact intimately or frequently in the early days following birth, are less than those born at term. There was a time when no contact was allowed. Premature babies are often delivered by Caesarean section because there is less of a risk to an infant already under some degree of stress. In the case of placenta praevia a Caesarean section is also performed as soon as possible. The advantages and disadvantages of Caesarean operations, and the criteria for carrying them out, are argued fiercely.

▨   Early Interventions

Prematurity and associated low birth-weight place babies at risk for (*inter alia*) developmental delay in growth, motor development, and cognitive functioning (Drillien, 1964). Several preventive programmes, notably in the United States, have been designed to mitigate these problems. There are three main approaches: child-focused; parent-focused; and multisystemic.

Child-focused interventions

Sensory stimulation and enrichment involve:

- tactile stimulation (e.g. regular handling, rubbing, massaging, stroking, holding, rocking);
- kinaesthetic stimulation (e.g. flexing and extending the baby's arms and legs);
- visual stimulation (e.g. brightly coloured mobiles, coloured patterns);
- auditory stimulation (e.g. talking, singing during periods of interaction).

Examples of these programmes are published by Field et al. (1986), Powell (1974) and Leib, Benfield and Guidubaldi (1980), among others.

Parent-focused interventions

Parent education and training programmes are concerned with:

- education to provide an understanding of the needs of their biologically vulnerable infants;
- providing them with the confidence and skills to put this understanding into effect;
- helping them learn how to interpret infant behaviour;
- teaching them about infant development;
- encouraging mother–infant interaction;
- facilitating parent–child mutual attachments;
- the provision of support to meet parents' needs.

Examples of these programmes can be found in the studies of Rauh, Achenbach et al. (1988) and Meyer et al. (1994), among others.

Multisystemic interventions

Multisystemic parent-focused and child-focused interventions involve (i) infant stimulation; (ii) home visits; and (iii) parent training. Examples of such multiple inputs have been published by Barrera, Rosenbaum and Cunningham (1986). All three approaches, of which the above represent only a small sample, have a positive impact on child development in general and cognitive development in particular. Infantile outcomes measured have included:

- accelerated growth;
- weight gain;
- motor behaviour;
- psychosocial development.

Also, the parents' attitudes, knowledge and skills should be encouraged.

Sensory stimulation and parent education programmes designed to prevent developmental delays in LBW babies have been gratifyingly successful as demonstrated in a detailed review by O'Sullivan and Carr (2002, pp. 19–20). Their database was derived from experimentally sound evaluative studies published between 1967 and 1988 and involved 1,600 North American families (782 cases in prevention programmes and 818 in routine medical-management control groups). The authors conclude that it is important to do the following:

- begin infant stimulation and parent education while the premature baby is in a neonatal care unit;
- initiate home-visiting;
- plan community-based outpatient and pre-school follow-up sessions.

It is advisable to carry on the programme through the pre-school and early school-going years, until the child's development falls within normal limits. Of course, 'normal limits' may not be attainable by biologically vulnerable children with neurological and other impairments.

II

Developmental Disorders of Infancy and Toddlerhood

■ Infancy: Early Attachments

The most crucial social task during the first 12 to 18 months of life, is the development of mutually secure attachments between the baby and his/her mother, and significant others. At the heart of attachment theory is an emphasis on the security, warmth and affection that one or both parents give their offspring. At the other end of the 'emotional bonding' equation is the infant's first attachments to the parent/s (usually the mother) – a strong disposition to seek proximity to, and contact with her when frightened, tired, ill, or in need of company or comfort.

John Bowlby (1969; 1973; 1988) in his seminal writings on attachment theory, described the survival value to infants, of five innate behavioural signals (crying, smiling, sucking, following and clinging) that ensure close proximity and contact during a long period of immaturity between them and their caregiver. Not only is the baby's attachment behaviour 'in-built', but the mother as a member of the same species, is presumed to be genetically programmed to respond to the child's proximity-seeking repertoire. A child's lasting sense of security, confidence or optimism (as opposed to distrust, insecurity, inadequacy or pessimism) is thought to be based upon the mother's responsiveness, involving:

- stimulating interactions;
- affectionate communication;
- continuity of care-giving;
- prompt satisfaction of the infant's needs.

These crucial social and emotional 'ingredients' are not always available, leading to a potentially devastating disruption of the emotional bonds that should be forming between parent and child. A group of dysfunctional attachments – failures and distortions – are described below, with examples of disorders that illustrate possible outcomes.

Dysfunctional attachments

- *failed attachments*: autism;
- *physically disturbed attachments*: organic failure-to-thrive;
- *delayed attachments*: Down's syndrome;
- *inappropriate attachments*: the parentified child;
- *insecure attachments*: separation anxiety disorder.

Dysfunctional parenting

- *rejecting parents*: non-organic failure-to-thrive: reactive attachment disorder;
- *depressed parenting*: anxiety states;
- *overprotective/restrictive parenting*: insecurity, hostility.

An early intervention is important in cases like these. The nature of the help, and where to get it, are not straightforward issues, as we see in Chapter 4. The therapeutic task is formidable. Put simply, the basic purpose of attachment therapies is likely to be helping the child create or 'restore' a dysfunctional attachment. Among the goals in such an agenda would be:

- helping the child bond to the parents;
- a gain in self-esteem;
- developing a liking for him/herself and others;
- developing or regaining a trust in relationships (e.g. to resolve their fear of giving and receiving love and affection).

Chapter 4 describes 'reactive attachment disorders' using the term generically, to cover different patterns of interpersonal interaction, distorted emotional bonds, or dysfunctional 'mind-sets'. Diagnostic and treatment issues in connection 'attachment therapy' are critically evaluated.

Another potential attachment problem 'non-organic failure-to-thrive' is also dealt with in this chapter.

■ Toddlerhood

The toddler stage of development confronts children with many tasks: physical, social and psychological. They need to achieve a sense of competence by learning skills such as locomotion, speech (see Chapter 5), how to behave 'appropriately', and eventually physical control over their bladder and bowels (see Chapter 6). Young children find many of these tasks sufficiently challenging, without also having to contend with disabilities which make their achievement difficult, sometimes impossible. Visual and hearing impairments are particularly limiting for children who have an overwhelming inclination to 'try things out' for themselves, and at a peak stage of activity and curiosity.

After infancy it becomes difficult to pinpoint developmental milestones precisely, as the range of age-related attainments is even broader than the diverse tasks of the earlier period. This is particularly true of toddlerhood, largely as a result of the growing influence of culture and experience, and the rapidity of maturational change. There are many 'don'ts' (too many or too few in some families) to conform to for curious and active children. They have to begin exerting self-control, learning to hold in check or modify their angry, aggressive, acquisitive and sexual impulses. These issues are about the child's dawning comprehension of what is socially appropriate and what is not. Not surprisingly, they challenge many of the prohibitions – some children with so-called 'oppositional defiant disorders', to an extreme degree.

Among the developmental problems of children in toddlerhood and the early pre-school years (overlapping with problems in Part III) are the following:

- atypical motor development (Chapter 5);
- problems connected with social training (socialization): (i) toilet training problems; (ii) oppositional defiant behaviour (Chapter 6).

▨ Atypical Motor Development

Motor development is the most readily observable domain in the first year of the child's life. The *basic* stages of motor development have generally taken place as infancy nears its end: a sequence proceeding from lying, to sitting, to standing. Because of their curiosity about their world and increased mobility, toddlers and later 'pre-schoolers' earn the reputation of being 'great explorers'. Clearly, restricted bodily movements severely frustrate them and, indeed, all children's activities, and for that reason are important subjects to consider in Chapter 5.

Four movement disorders are described there: *developmental dyspraxia, Duchenne muscular dystrophy, spina bifida,* and *cerebral palsy.*

Social Training Problems

At around the ages of 2 to 4 years children are at the cusp between dependent infancy and increasingly independent childhood. There are many social rules for them to learn: the subtle distinction between 'do as I say, not as I do', and the sometimes confusing difference between what is allowed and what is forbidden.

Toddlerhood and the pre-school years are sensitive times for social training (socialization) to take root, or to fail. The existence of serious (e.g. oppositional-defiant) behaviour problems are becoming easier to identify, as they stabilize at around the age of 3. There are vital physical skills to master during this period of development, notably the control of bladder and bowel functions.

Toileting Problems

The appropriate use of the toilet, an item on the training agenda which parents get very concerned about, may be a formidable task for any child, but particularly one who suffers from physical disabilities. There are several stages on the way to successful toilet training. The skills include:

- having words for urine and faeces, and for the place they are deposited in;
- going to the toilet (e.g. indicating need to caregiver, going unaided);
- sitting on the toilet;
- managing clothing/wiping, at the toilet;
- having control (continence).

Bladder control

There are significant individual differences in children's readiness for managing these tasks. In the case of bladder training, most children at 18 months of age are physically mature enough to hold their urine for between one and two hours without much leakage. The coordination to be able to sit comfortably on the potty or toilet is another sign of readiness. So is their ability to understand simple instructions. It is the fervent hope of parents and teachers alike that children will achieve bladder control during the day by the time they start school.

Bowel control

The control of elimination via the bowels and rectum means the inhibiting of processes which are, at first, completely involuntary. The baby's muscles must mature until they are strong enough and coordinated enough to hold back the waste products that are trying to emerge from his or her body. Of all the muscles in the trunk region, those which control the organs of elimination are the slowest to come under voluntary control. The total time required to complete bowel training has been found to be less (only about five months being required) when it is initiated relatively late, at 20 months or older.

Oppositional Behaviour

The early pre-school years are a notorious period for the development of oppositional defiant problems. For children with sensory or motor impairments, temper tantrums and oppositional behaviour are easily triggered when their speech and hearing problems make it difficult to make their needs understood, or limitations of movement hinder them from getting around and reaching interesting objects.

More serious are the extreme *oppositional defiant disorders* (ODDs) that take root in some children, at this stage of life. They emerge because of the inability of parents for a variety of reasons (socio-economic, emotional or social), to confront their children's coercive behaviour in a manner that will move them on into the vital later stages of moral development and impulse control (see Herbert and Wookey, 2004). The longer-term ramifications of past failures of the emotional bonding (attachment) process, expressed through anti-social aggressive and defiant behaviour, are by now having a powerful impact at home and the nursery school.

While disobedience and defiance are fairly common problems as children grow up, and their consequences frustrating for caregivers, if they persist and intensify as happens with ODDs, the provocation they represent can prove dangerous in homes where there is a risk of child abuse. There is *danger* in another sense of the word. A reasonable degree of compliance to certain parental requests and instructions is crucial if the child is going to learn essential social, intellectual and physical skills, also the need for safety. The child has to learn to avoid dangers, a difficult task for children who are hyperactive. The desire to enjoy harmony within the family is undermined by uncontrolled, destructive children who are not welcome visitors, and contribute to the social isolation of their parents and themselves. Failure of social training is clearly costly to family life.

In the long run, the persistence, from as early as 2 or 3 years of age, of the undisciplined, uncontrollable behaviour of children with ODD, ensures a doubtful future for them. They are unable and/or unwilling to comply with the rules that operate at all levels in society, and begin to descend (in many cases) a slippery slope that ends with the diagnosis 'conduct disorder' or 'delinquent' (see Sutton, Utting and Farrington, 2004, also Chapter 14).

Parent education and training (using intervention manuals based on the 'Consultation Model') are touched on briefly in Chapter 6, as an introduction to a detailed account of the treatment of the conduct disorders and delinquency – the subject of Chapter 14. They are aimed directly at the parents of aggressive/anti-social children rather than at (or in addition to) the children themselves; the aim being to change the child's behaviour by changing the parents' behaviour. The rationale for this approach is anchored in research findings that indicate that parents of dysfunctional children themselves have deficits in certain fundamental parenting skills.

One of the major strategies successfully followed in attempting to reduce behaviour problems among children involves training the parents to alter the attitudes and actions that support the anti-social behaviour of their children.

CHAPTER 4

Attachment Difficulties and Disorders

■ Introduction

Babies and young children who are developing normally possess innate proactive behaviours and responses which facilitate their early orientation to human communication and the social world. Among the indicators of typical social development are:

- eye-to-eye signalling (mutual attention);
- the use of social or emotional gestures;
- reciprocity in social interactions;
- language that develops on time.

Displays of attachment behaviours include:

- the ability to use parents as a secure base;
- an interest in peer relationships;
- empathic behaviour;
- an interest in sharing positive emotions;
- crying for attention.

Several childhood disorders are described below in order to illustrate several of these types of attachment that fail to take place, or are dysfunctional in some way. Problematic types of parenting that adversely affect the development of emotional bonds in the child are also described.

■ Failed Attachments

▨ Autism

Diagnosis

There are very early signs in a relatively small number of children that may be indicative, because of the absence of attachment or relationship-related activities, of a serious developmental disorder. Formal diagnosis of autism used to be postponed until the middle years of childhood, as the first year of life does not provide definitive criteria of the presence or future likelihood of the disorder. However, many parents begin to worry at that early stage of their child's life, and a majority identify what turns out to be autism when the child is around 18 months of age (Baird, Charman et al., 2000).

The developmental omissions that cause their parents particular concern include the following observations.

From birth to 6 months: the baby

- makes no anticipatory social responses;
- has no smiling response or it is delayed;
- makes no or poor eye-contact;
- fails to respond to mother's attention;
- fails to respond to toys.

From 6 to 12 months: the baby

- fails to show affection;
- is difficult to engage in baby games;
- shows no interest in toys;
- does not wave bye-bye;
- pushes objects away.

From 12 to 24 months: the baby

- displays no distress on separation;
- shows unusual use of toys (e.g. lines up objects).

The autistic (spectrum) disorders are considered in Chapter 12.

■ Delayed Attachments

▨ Down's Syndrome

Clinical features

Babies with Down's syndrome (DS) make very little eye contact with their mother until about 3 months of age. When it appears later, it is of less contact duration than babies with typical development (TD). They also show less attention to the talk of others, and other things going on around them than TD babies. Crying is one of the earliest social signals, and the evidence is that the cries of infants with DS are different from those of TD babies in the first year of life, both in quantity and quality. They cry less frequently when in pain, take longer to cry, and differ from TD babies in the intensity and pitch of their cries. Altogether, they present weaker proximity-seeking signals (as perceived by others) than TD children (see Lewis, 1987; 2002). Down's syndrome is discussed in Chapter 9.

■ Inappropriate Attachments

▨ The Parentified Child

Diagnosis

The term 'parental' or 'parentified' child is used to describe a child who, by virtue of having a cross-generation coalition with one parent, is permitted (usually inappropriately) to have parental authority over siblings. The term 'parentification' has been used to describe the expectation that one or more children will fulfil the parental role in the family system.

Clinical features

Clearly, these are generally unsatisfactory burdens for a child to assume although sometimes invaluable to a parent who has been abandoned, or is struggling to cope with a severely disabled sibling, a restrictive mental health problem (e.g. agoraphobia or depression), or an unresolved bereavement. Nevertheless, a child who assumes, unprompted often, many of the adult responsibilities and worries of family life and attempts to provide emotional support to his or her parent/s, is in a role-reversal that might be thought of as deprivation, perhaps even abuse.

Developmental features

Barnett and Parker (1998) point out that it is not surprising that the professional literature tends to emphasize the pathological aspects of 'parentification'. But they suggest that the issue is not wholly clear-cut. For some individuals (depending on a host of mediating variables), parentification experiences may involve some advantageous compensatory adaptation, positively enhancing their competence for coping with life. The concept of resilience is discussed in Chapter 16.

■ Insecure Attachments

▨ Separation Anxiety Disorder

Diagnosis

Separation anxiety disorder (SAD) is severe, persistent anxiety of an intensity going beyond that expected of the child's developmental level, about being away from home or attachment figures. The anxiety must be severe enough to cause not only significant distress, but also to interfere adversely with normal activities such as social, academic and other important areas of functioning. School phobia is an example of a separation anxiety disorder to be described in Chapter 12.

Clinical features

The child:

- shows particular distress when separated from parents;
- worries that the parents may suffer harm when away from home;
- may have nightmares and sleep problems when separated from them;
- at times has physical symptoms such as nausea, headaches and abdominal pains before or during a separation. These tend to remit rapidly when the separation is cancelled or is over.

The perennial problem for clinicians is determining what constitutes dysfunctional anxiety as opposed to normal anxiety (see Chapter 10).

Developmental features

Separation experiments with infants (see Ainsworth et al., 1978) have categorized children into four types:

- securely attached;
- insecurely attached 'avoidant';
- insecurely attached 'ambivalent';
- insecurely attached 'disorganized'.

When followed up at a later age, 'insecure' children have been found to have more serious problems than 'securely' attached children; the 'insecure avoidant' and 'insecure disorganized' children being the most likely to develop aggressive behaviour (Greenberg, Kusche and Mihalic, 1998; Lyons-Ruth and Jacobwitz, 1999).

Determinants

Maccoby (1980) is of the opinion that the parents' contribution to attachment can be identified by one of four styles of care-giving. A parent may demonstrate:

- *sensitivity* – meshes his/her responses to the infant's signals and communications to form a cyclic turn-taking pattern of interaction, whereas the *insensitive* parent intervenes arbitrarily, and these intrusions reflect his/her own wishes and mood;
- *acceptance* – acknowledges in general his or her responsibility for child-care, demonstrating few signs of irritation with the child. The *rejecting* parent, on the other hand, has feelings of anger and resentment that eclipse his/her affection for the child, often finding the child irritating and resorting to punitive control;
- *co-operation* – respects the child's autonomy and rarely exerts direct control. The *interfering* parent imposes his/her wishes on the child with little concern for the child's current mood or activity;
- *accessibility* – is familiar with her or his child's communications and notices them at some distance, hence s/he is easily distracted by the child. The *ignoring* parent is preoccupied with her or his own activities and thoughts. S/he often fails to notice the child's communications unless they are obvious through intensification. S/he may even forget about the child outside the scheduled times for care-giving.

The adverse features of parenting: insensitivity, interference, rejection and unavailability appear in the examples of dysfunctional attachments described below.

■ Dysfunctional Parenthood

▨ Rejecting Parenting: Failure to Thrive

Diagnosis

Failure to thrive (FTT), as a generic term, lacks a precise definition because it describes in part, an ongoing condition, rather than a specific disease. Thus, we have a generalized diagnosis which has many possible causes. Three categories of causation identify FTT in children:

1   *Organic FTT* is a term applied to growth failure resulting from an acute or chronic disorder known to interfere with normal nutrient intake, absorption, metabolism, or excretion, or to result in increased energy requirements to sustain or promote growth. This disorder is discussed in Chapter 7.
2   *Non-organic FTT* usually refers to growth failure resulting (in the absence of a physiological disorder that accounts for the failure) from a variety of adverse environmental and psychosocial influences, notably an abnormal relationship between the caregiver and infant/child (see Iwaniec, Herbert and Sluckin, 2002; Raynor and Rudolf, 1996).
3   *Mixed organic and non-organic FTT* refers to a multidimensional definition of FTT.

Common to all cases of FTT whatever the aetiology, is what is observable: the infant's failure to grow as expected. The physiological basis of FTT is inadequate nutrition for adequate weight gain to take place.

▨ Non-Organic Failure to Thrive (NOFTT)

Diagnosis

Non-organic failure to thrive (NOFTT) was previously known as 'marasmus' more recently as 'maternal deprivation syndrome' or 'growth failure'. Failure of normal physical growth is usually detected in infants through their unsatisfactory weight gain.

Clinical features

For children with organic FTT (OFTT) the onset may be at any age depending on the underlying disorder; most children with NOFTT manifest growth failure before 1 year of age, and many by the age of 6 months. Children who fail to thrive are commonly born prematurely.

Children who fail to thrive tend to be withdrawn, depressed, lethargic, anxious, whiny and tearful. The infant/child frequently refuses food, or struggles against the mother's attempts to feed him or her. Admission to hospital, in severe cases, allows for close observation of mother–child interactions and feeding patterns, also the restoration of eating and weight gain as the child generally accepts food from other people (e.g. nurses). This tendency understandably dismays and demoralizes the parent.

The consequence of persistent failure to thrive may be:

- retarded growth (see Chapter 3);
- deficits in cognitive development;
- poor academic attainments;
- emotional instability;
- feeding difficulties.

Developmental features

Attachment theorists emphasize the importance of feeding among other early social activities, because to become attached (bonded) mother and baby have to get to know each other. The mother's exposure to her baby, with its many attractive ways, contributes towards the development of a mutual bond between her and the baby.

There is evidence that attraction to, and liking for others, is initially a direct function of familiarity learning, certainly a feature of the successful mother and baby feeding experience (Herbert, Sluckin and Sluckin, 1982). Mothers commonly gaze and talk to their baby, and smile if it smiles; and pick it up when they hear crying. It is the many encounters of this kind (the reinforcing consequences of the infant's signals) that gradually attach social meaning to his or her actions. Parents and child develop mutual attachments in the course of these interactions.

The stresses and strains in their relationships which cause the child to balk at feeding (resulting in NOFTT) may stem from:

- the demoralizing effect on parents of the extremely difficult temperament possessed by their young child;
- their child's persistent feeding problems, which may have originated earlier in his or her swallowing difficulties: a consequence of the pain arising from organic disorders such as oesophageal stricture and pyloric stenosis;
- the child's anxiety or depression – reactions to adverse (perhaps abusive) relationships within the family.

When there is little or no predictable outcome – an absence of synchrony – in the mother–child relationship, a sense of helplessness eventually develops in the infant, and he or she learns that responding in general does not matter. Experiences of helplessness, if repeated over and over, lead to an absence of response initiation, a negative frame of mind (cognitive set) anxiety and depression. All of this is disastrous for the infant because what is developing is foundational – the base of the infant's 'pyramid' of emotional and motivational structures.

Causation

As we have seen above, FTT has traditionally been thought to be the result, in large part, of maternal rejection. It is suggested that the problems are frequently the outward physical signs of failures or distortions of the attachment process associated with emotional abuse and/or neglect (see Iwaniec, Herbert and Sluckin, 1988; 2002). Skuse (1989) believes that there is a too ready emphasis (often in the absence of direct evidence of neglect) on parental culpability as the cause of NOFTT. He suggests that among influences affecting the symptomatic infant might be:

- inadequacy of nutrition caused by both a failure of adequate provision of food and by inadequate intake;
- a vicious circle of maladaptive behavioural interactions between caregiver and infant, sustained by high emotional tensions.

Skuse suggests that clinicians inquire about more than simply the nutrition children receive. He found behaviour at meals and psychosocial issues to be an important variable, affecting whether children obtain sufficient energy. Poor parenting and family dysfunction can also negatively affect a child's energy intake.

Families characterized by less adaptive relationships, higher levels of family conflict, and less emotional support for the mother have an increased percentage of children with NOFTT. Stimulation for the child may be inadequate because the caregiver (usually, the mother in such cases):

- is depressed or apathetic;
- has poor parenting skills;
- has lacked preparation for parenthood;
- is unhappy with her parenting role;
- feels alienated from and hostile toward the child;
- has a severely temperamentally difficult, emotionally disturbed, or chronically ill/disabled child, whose care is too much for her;

- is coping with real or perceived external stresses (e.g. demands of other children, a delinquent partner; a bereavement, marital conflict, divorce, poor housing, financial difficulties);
- suffers from a psychiatric disorder.

Treatment

Case management is best provided by a multidisciplinary team. The goal of treatment, following a physical examination, is to provide sufficient resources – health and environmental – to facilitate the child's weight gain and the parent's capacity to manage. Interventions are based ideally on direct observation of the parent and child relationship and interactions in different environmental contexts, particularly the feeding situation.

Interventions may take place with the child:

- attending the clinic with his or her parent/s as outpatients;
- hospitalized in a tertiary care unit;
- in extreme cases of feeding failure, placed in foster care.

The treatments need to be formulated and planned as multilevel interventions. For example, the following strategies may be relevant:

- use of a day-nursery or family centre;
- parent training in groups (see Chapter 16);
- informal and formal dynamic/social group-work to reduce social isolation;
- individual work on feeding and other interactions;
- provision of emotional support for the parent/s as well as developmental counselling: awareness training with regard to children's development and needs (Davis, 1998; Davis, Day et al., 2003; Egeland and Erickson, 2003);
- personal counselling;
- information about welfare rights, housing, etc.;
- attachment therapy (see below);
- clinic and home-based (or combined) cognitive behaviour therapy.

Attachment programmes

We saw earlier how vital parental responsiveness is in providing growth-enhancing sustenance to a baby. Typically, feeding times need to be relaxed and adapted to the cycles of hunger and satisfaction of the infant. The mother needs to be alert to changing needs for nourishment as the child matures, by altering his/her diet. The MAW programme was designed to facilitate these processes.

Mutual Attachment Work (MAW) 1

This programme was developed and evaluated at the Centre for Behavioural Work at Leicester University and the Paediatric Assessment Centre at the Royal Infirmary (Leicester) (Iwaniec, Herbert and McNeish, 1988). It combined developmental counselling, cognitive behavioural family therapy, and paediatric care. The objective was to restore mutual attachments in general, a calmer feeding routine for mother and children, and consequent weight gain in particular. It proved successful in all those objectives when applied to a series of 17 infants who were failing to thrive. A behaviour management programme was also included.

Essentially, the task with the feeding difficulties was to 'disentangle' an intractable approach-avoidance conflict that functioned on one or both sides of mother–child dyadic interactions. It was often the task (with methods akin to systematic desensitization) to reduce very gradually the infant's/young child's fearful avoidance of the mother's feeding routine (and sometimes other attentions), while encouraging (by means of gradual exposure training) the approach of an anxious, alienated or hostile mother towards gentle feeding/nursing, and other nurturant activities.

See Iwaniec, Herbert and Mc Neish (1988) and Iwaniec, Herbert and Sluckin, 2002, pp. 255–7, for details of this technique, and a brief description below of more broadly conceived strategies designed to initiate or restore mutual bonds between parent and child.

The behaviour problems and child management issues (which are commonplace in NOFTT) were tackled individually or in behavioural parent training (BPT) groups. Cognitive restructuring is an important component of these Cognitive-Behavioural Therapy (CBT)-based programmes. One example is the issue of 'loving' and 'liking' – a matter of some potential confusion to child and mother alike. Frequently older children express the belief that they are unloved, when the evidence from the way the parent perseveres with them against all odds, is that she loves her child, but dislikes him/her. Or rather (a matter for correction for both of them), she dislikes his/her behaviour.

Given the abstract and largely invisible nature of maternal love, her dislike (expressed in harsh words, nagging and endless criticism) impacts on the child more strongly than any concept of an essentially committed, loving but bitterly resentful/angry/frustrated mother. What comes across is someone who says she 'dislikes him/her' which seems to the young child the same as 'she doesn't love me'. These are matters for debate in groups. Clearly these distinctions do not apply to many parents whose rejection is based on repugnance and even hatred for the child (Browne and Herbert, 1997).

Reactive Attachment Disorder (RAD)

Diagnosis

The older child is described in the literature as:

- superficially charming, acts cute to get what he/she wants;
- indiscriminately affectionate with unfamiliar adults, lacking in genuine affection with primary caregivers (especially mother);
- controlling, bossy, manipulative, defiant, argumentative, demanding, impulsive;
- preoccupied with fire, death, blood, or gore;
- cruel to animals, destruction of property, aggression toward others or self;
- destructive, accident-prone;
- having rages or lengthy temper tantrums, especially in response to adult authority;
- displaying poor eye contact, except when lying;
- blaming others for his/her problems;
- lacking self-control;
- poor at cause/effect thinking;
- prone to lying or stealing, and shows no remorse, no conscience, defiant;
- hoarding or sneaking food, strange eating habits;
- having difficulty maintaining friendships;
- under-achieving at school;
- displaying a grandiose sense of self, lacking trust in others to care for him/her.

One could be excused for thinking these criteria were being applied to describe a psychopathic child (see McCord and McCord, 1964).

Treatment

Because children's early attachment relationships influence other relationships throughout life, an effective early intervention could reduce the adverse long-term effects of attachment difficulties.

Mutual Attachment Work (MAW) 2

The purpose of the Mutual Attachment Work programme (MAW) is more broadly conceived here, than in the FTT situation described above. Its aim is ambitious and therefore daunting: to produce or restore a generalized bond of affection between child and caregiver. It is hoped that if this emotional attachment is formed, the child will develop a sense of safety and trust and a level of conformity which will counteract his/her anti-social alienation, and reduce in turn their disruptive behaviours.

All of this requires the development of dependent attitudes in a hostile or fearful (avoidant) child – behaviourally/operationally defined as increases in:

- proximity-seeking to the mother;
- help-seeking from the mother;
- approach to the mother for comforting and affection;
- initiation of affectionate verbal and non-verbal actions (e.g. hand-holding, cuddling, kissing, conversing).

With regard to the work with the parents which is essential, emotional bonding might be indicated by:

- proximity seeking to the child;
- providing prompt and appropriate help when needed;
- proactive, consistent and predictable caring;
- conversing with the child;
- playing with him or her;
- stimulating and teaching (socializing) the child;
- supervising and protecting him or her from harm;
- showing evidence of love and 'belonging';
- being available.

Among the many ways in which children with attachment disorders can have their emotional bonds to the parents encouraged or strengthened, is the programming of gentle and warm social 'messages' on the part of the mother/father, These are carried out in the course of

- feeding;
- bathing;
- changing;

- dressing;
- playing with the child.

These activities require an awareness of the child's communications (listening with the 'third ear'); providing warm affection, and cool patience at all times (see Herbert and Wookey, 2004). Play and story telling are ideal 'special/quality times' for reciprocal activities and for engaging in tender displays of caring. Physical contact (holding, hugging, kissing) may have to progress slowly when there has been a history of one-sided or mutual aversion. Carefully planned 'systematic desensitisation' and 'exposure training' are likely be the therapeutic effective bonding strategies of choice.

Baby massage (touch therapy)

There are many claims for the benefits of touch therapy with infants and older individuals. Facilitating bonding with infants at risk is a particular claim of Tiffany Field's research team at the Touch Research Institute of the University of Miami. It is suggested that the benefits of massage extend to pregnant women, and include increased blood circulation, thus providing more oxygen and nutrients to both mother and fetus. This means greater vitality for the mother and better nourishment for the unborn child. It is suggested that once the baby arrives, he or she will continue to benefit from regular gentle touches, soothing voices, and a calm environment.

In 1985, Field divided a sample of 40 healthy premature babies in a neonatal intensive care unit into stimulation and control groups to test the effect of massage. The results of the massage group were a 47 per cent weight gain, greater responsiveness, and a 6-day earlier discharge from the hospital at substantial cost savings per baby. Follow-up studies eight months later showed a continued advantage in weight as well as in mental and motor development. Comparable results also have appeared in studies with cocaine-exposed and HIV-exposed newborns.

The baby massage technique was as follows: three 15-minute massage sessions, three times a day, for 10 days duration of the programme. There were marked improvements in weight gain compared with a control group. Other outcomes in Field's studies (see review in Field, 2000), have been reductions in the infants' crying and cortisol levels, better sleep habits, less fussiness, and overall behaviour improvement. There were associated falls in the mothers' anxiety and depression levels.

Further research is required in order to tease out the particular therapeutic components of touch therapy, and additionally its effectiveness outside hospital and clinic settings.

Attachment therapy (AT)

There is a paucity of hard data to support what is called 'attachment therapy' (AT). It is barely mentioned in the burgeoning ('what works?') review literature on rigorously designed evaluation studies. This absence reflects the lack of validational investigations. The problem is exacerbated by the lack of clarity about the conceptual boundaries of AT. Questions that come to mind are: 'Is it psychodynamic; family therapy; behavioural work; counselling; or an eclectic synthesis of approaches? Or is it simply a poorly integrated collection of *ad hoc* techniques?'

Many therapeutic modalities have been described under the rubric of attachment therapy, among them

- 're-parenting';
- parent holding (i.e. parents holding the child while being supervised by the therapist);
- role-playing;
- modelling of appropriate behaviours;
- behaviour shaping;
- cognitive restructuring;
- gestalt therapy;
- psychodrama;
- family therapy.

Given the current popularity of attachment therapy, it is perhaps worth describing one well-known model in some detail. Attachment therapy (AT) as practised at the Attachment Center at Evergreen, Colorado, now known as The Institute for Attachment and Child Development (IACD) (Levy and Orlans, 1995), is a two-week intensive intervention model. The referred child, his/her parent(s) or referring agency (if the child has no parents), the treating therapist in the child's home town, the IACD therapist, and the primary IACD therapeutic foster parent (usually the mother) are all present for 30 hours of therapy over a two-week period.

The therapy is broken down into 10 three-hour sessions that take place daily for 10 consecutive working days. Each family entering treatment is assigned to a therapeutic treatment family trained by IACD, and the child lives with that therapeutic family throughout the two-week intensive period. The child's parents spend time in the therapeutic foster home learning the parenting tactics required to successfully parent a child with RAD. Otherwise they have minimal contact with their child in this phase. The treatment team also provides at least an hour each day working with the parents to help them learn needed parenting skills.

Attachment therapy includes four basic therapeutic techniques:

- *cognitive restructuring* (helping the child to recognize the cognitive errors in his/her thinking and to learn more healthy ways of thinking about him/herself and about others);
- *psychodrama* (taking the child through early life events that are acted out by others in the room so that he/she can find better solutions for dealing with the trauma of those events and so have less need to act-out against others);
- *'healing the inner child'* (i.e. helping the child to find ways to give voice and support to the severely wounded inner child);
- *nurturing and re-parenting* (i.e. where the foster/adoptive parents hold the child on their laps and work with him/her, to learn that they will not abuse him/her as other parents have done).

The parents, home town therapist, therapeutic foster parent(s), and IACD therapist (the treatment team) meet together every day to discuss the child's history, current behaviours, and progress since attachment therapy began. After the treatment team has met, the remainder of each session is spent with the child being held on someone's lap, usually by the therapist, but occasionally by both the therapist and therapeutic foster parent, or by the child's parents. The child has his/her head resting on a pillow, allowing for close proximity between the child and the therapist, for good eye contact to be maintained by the child, and for easy management of his/her aggressive behaviour.

The therapist has a contract with the child to obtain agreement about which problems the child is experiencing, and what he/she is willing to do to resolve them. Later, the therapist focuses on helping the child bond to the parents – the basis for coming therapeutic efforts. Psychodrama, cognitive restructuring, healing the inner child, and other nurturing techniques are used as appropriate, to help the child work through unresolved issues from his/her earlier history. The therapist also works with the family to increase understanding of how early maltreatment affects perceptual, emotional, and cognitive functioning, and how the child's world-view needs to change to a trust in others to meet his/her needs.

The child's home town therapist is an active participant in attachment therapy, as he/she will need to help the family continue to work on issues once they return home. If the child is going to stay for long-term treatment at IACD, the treatment team will contact the home town therapist prior to the child's discharge from the long-term programme to plan for post-discharge therapy.

Although two studies carried out at IACD have shown statistically significant reductions in a variety of behaviour problems as a result of attachment therapy, both have methodological limitations, primarily due to selection criteria issues, the small group size, and the absence of a control group.

Developmental features

Children lacking adequate care in the earliest few years of life suffer from excessively high levels of stress hormones, with consequent effects on crucial aspects of brain and body development that are adverse. Conscience development, dependent upon brain development and appropriate emotional bonding is disrupted. Moral and social development, in turn, are likely to be compromised (Herbert, 1987a). The children go on to display aggressive, disruptive and anti-social behaviours (see Chapter 14).

Prevention

Parental responsiveness is a major element in preventing the alienation of young children. The quality of parenting is a complex and many-sided phenomenon, but there are at least three different elements which make for what one might assess to be sensitive responsiveness: the tendency to react promptly, consistently, and appropriately, to their offspring's needs. These include:

- physical care and protection;
- affection and approval;
- stimulation and teaching;
- discipline and controls that are consistent and appropriate to the child's age and development;
- opportunity and encouragement to acquire gradual autonomy, that is, for the child to take gradual control over his or her own life.

Available evidence suggests that what is important in child rearing is the general social climate in the home, for example, the attitudes and feelings of the parents, which form a background to the application of specific methods and interactions of child rearing (Herbert, 1998; 2004). Crucial is a rich supply of positive reinforcement for positive behaviour 'fuelled' by a strong attachment to a caregiver with whom a child can therefore identify. Parents make firm moral demands of their offspring; they use sanctions consistently – techniques of punishment that are psychological rather than physical (i.e. methods that signify or threaten withdrawal of approval).

■ Depressed Parenting

Postnatal Depression

Diagnosis

Postnatal depression (PD) is obviously not of itself an insecure attachment disorder; however, the children of mothers who suffer from postnatal depression (PD) tend to have insecure attachments still present at 18 months of age. The disturbed mother–infant relationship also has an adverse impact on the course of children's cognitive and emotional development; boys show a high level of behavioural disturbance at 5 years (Cooper and Murray, 1997).

Assessment

Primary care teams (e.g. health visitors) often fail to detect PD (see Seeley, Murray and Cooper, 1996). The Edinburgh Postnatal Depression Scale (EPDS), developed as a screening device, should make an early diagnosis more possible (see Cox, Holden and Sagovsky, 1987).

Clinical features

Risk factors (see Cooper and Murray, 1997) include:

- a psychiatric history;
- a history of depressive episodes;
- obstetric complications;
- social adversity;
- the absence of social support.

Developmental features

Most examinations of infant attachment following postnatal depression have reported a significant rate of insecure attachments (e.g. Lyons-Ruth, Zoll et al., 1986). There is evidence that these emotional problems persist. Infants are disrupted by the blank face of a depressed mother when interacting with her, also by her mistiming of those interactions. Several studies of families living in conditions of severe adversity have found consistent associations between postnatal depression and significant impairments in maternal responsiveness to the infant, hostile and intrusive interactions, also disengaged and withdrawn behaviour (Herbert, 2003).

The occurrence of inconsistent, harsh parenting has been found to be associated with persistent early-onset anti-social behaviour (Herbert, 1987a). PDs (e.g. maternal mood disorders) may adversely affect children's cognitive development especially males. Socio-economically disadvantaged children are particularly vulnerable to the impact of PD in their mothers (see Murray and Cooper, 1997; Murray, 1992; Murray, Fiori-Cowley, Hooper et al., 1996).

Epidemiology

Postnatal depression affects about 10 per cent of women in the early weeks post partum, with episodes typically lasting two to six months The duration of postnatal depression is similar to that of depressions arising at other times. Episodes typically remit spontaneously within two to six months (O'Hara, 1997). Some depressive symptoms remain up to a year after delivery.

Treatment

Given the adverse outcome of PD for children's security of attachment – events taking place during the early post-partum days or weeks – early detection is vital. Treatment and preventive interventions by primary care teams are most effective. The provision of individual, home-based support, conducted weekly over the first few months after birth (around six to ten sessions), is the intervention of choice for improving maternal mood (Appleby, Warner et al., 1997; Cooper and Murray, 1997; 1998). There is a beneficial 'spin-off' for the offspring, This counselling and supportive role is one for which health visitors are particularly well placed.

Over-Protective Dominating Parenting

Over-protective, restrictive and authoritarian parents attempt to dominate, shape, control, and judge the attitudes and behaviour of their children according to absolute rules of conduct, standards often motivated by theological considerations.

Profile of the child

The dominating form of overprotection may lead to children who:

*   are excessively dependent, passive, and submissive in their actions;
*   are easily discouraged from acting independently, exploring, and experimenting;

- tend to adopt timid, awkward, apprehensive and generally self-deprecating behaviours;
- lack self-reliance and the ability to cope realistically with their problems;
- are apt to be uncritically obedient;
- prefer to withdraw from situations they find daunting.

They also tend often as adults, not to 'leave behind' their parents psychologically, and in many cases, never vacate physically their childhood homes as well.

Determinants

Obedience is valued by dominant parents as a virtue, and punitive measures are used to curb self-will when the child's or teenager's actions conflict with what the parents believe is appropriate conduct. They believe in intimidating, as opposed to educating their children into having 'proper respect' for traditional (e.g. conservative) values. Verbal give-and-take in the form of arguing or debating social or moral issues is discouraged or forbidden. Children are allowed no voice of their own. Physical punishment is often applied as a means of discipline.

Outcomes

Clearly we are not talking about illness entities resulting from extremes of restrictively over-protective behaviour that is rigid and punitive in its underlying ideology. But there are certainly risks of the development of maladaptive patterns of behaviour. Moral and social development in turn are likely to be compromised. For example, the combination of physical maltreatment with a background of hostile, rejecting parenting is particularly invidious. The victims are at risk of going on to display aggressive, disruptive and anti-social behaviours (see Herbert, 1987a, b).

CHAPTER 5

Atypical Motor Development

■ Muscular Dystrophies

▨ Duchenne Muscular Dystrophy (DMD)

Diagnosis

DMD was first described by a French neurologist in the 1860s. It is one of the most prevalent, among several types, of genetic muscular dystrophy characterized by rapid progression of muscle degeneration early in life.

Clinical and developmental features

Boys (an estimated 1 in 3500 worldwide; in girls it is rare) begin to show signs of muscle weakness as early as three years of age. The wasting and weakness begin with microscopic changes in the muscles. The disease gradually weakens the skeletal or voluntary muscles – those in the arms, legs and trunk. As they degenerate over time, sufferers' muscle strength declines and they lose the ability to walk. They are usually confined to a wheelchair for their relatively short lives. By early adolescence, sometimes earlier, the heart and respiratory muscles may also be affected.

Causation

Until the late 1980s, little was known about the cause of muscular dystrophy. Researchers have now discovered that DMD occurs when a particular gene on the X chromosome fails to make the protein *dystrophin* that is needed inside muscle cells to strengthen them and provide structural support. In its absence, the cell membrane becomes permeable; extra-cellular components enter, increasing the internal pressure until the muscle cell is destroyed.

Interventions

A paediatric team has an important role with its members (special needs teacher, counsellor, educational or clinical child psychologists, and speech, occupational and physiotherapists) supporting children with this potentially demoralizing wasting disease, their parents and teachers, and preparing a plan to help the child at school and in his or her other settings. Movement and muscular disability will be treated by specialists in those fields (see cerebral palsy treatment below).

Becker Muscular Dystrophy (BMD)

Diagnosis

Becker muscular dystrophy (BMD) is named after Peter Emil Becker, who described this variant of DMD in the 1950s. BMD is a much milder version of DMD. Its onset is usually in adolescence or early adulthood, and the course is slower and far less predictable than that of DMD.

Causation

Children with BMD have some dystrophin, but it is insufficient or poor in quality. Having some dystrophin protects the muscles of those with BMD from degenerating as badly or as rapidly as those of children with the fully fledged DMD.

Cerebral Palsy (CP)

Diagnosis

The term CP refers to a disorder of movement and posture. Extreme muscular tension and rigidity with a partial loss of voluntary movement are involved, plus spasm of the affected muscles. CP, the most common motor disability, is not a homogeneous entity. Several different motor disorders are referred to under the generic term CP. In medical terms these are descriptions of the underlying disorder associated with a variety of CP syndromes and the primary cerebral pathology. In functional terms it is the way cerebral palsy 'expresses' itself in the individual child, and the consequences for his or her development throughout the stages of their lifecycle that are most significant.

No two children are alike in the combination and extent of their difficulties – an example of the diversity found in children who have a single diagnosis associated with central nervous system lesions. Although the symptoms may change over time, cerebral palsy as such is not progressive. If a child shows increased impairment later on, the problem lies somewhere other than the CP itself (see Goodman, 2002).

A definite diagnosis is not always easy, especially before the child's first birthday. It has to be remembered, however, that the problems range from severe to 'moderate' and 'mild' – qualifying words that represent subjective judgements rather than specific criteria. Uncertainty about the diagnosis may continue for years.

Clinical features

A consultant may suspect CP in a child when the following normal motor milestones are delayed:

- reaching for objects (3–4 months);
- sitting (6–7 months);
- walking (10–14 months).

Also taken into account would be:

- abnormal muscle tone;
- abnormal movements;
- abnormal reflexes (see Chapter 1).

The disorder is estimated to occur in some 2.3 babies per 1000 live births. Most children with CP can be diagnosed by 18 to 24 months of age, meaning a long and anxious wait for some parents. X-rays and blood tests are of no help unless other co-morbid conditions need to be investigated.

Developmental features

Professionals who work with children with CP often face parents who, on being informed of the diagnosis, ask: 'Will my child ever walk?' This is among the most difficult questions put to a clinician. The complexity of CP is such that there are few definitive answers to questions about the prognosis for an individual child. Any attempt to make predictions of likely long-term outcomes for an infant under six months of age, amounts to no more than guesswork; for a child under 1 year of age, a prognostication may be a little more feasible, but it continues to be something of a 'guesstimate'. After all, the child needs to be about two years of age before the paediatrician can determine with confidence, whether he or she has *hemiplegia*, *diplegia* or *quadriplegia*.

Outlook

A reasonably independent adult life in the community lies ahead for about a half of children with CP, depending on the degree of impairment, and the quality of rehabilitative work carried out from early in life.

Interventions

As the child with CP gets older, continuing attention to his or her mobility is required. For example:

- *Casts and splints* applied for 2 to 3 months in order to improve the range of movement of a joint and decrease muscle tone.
- *Mechanical aids*: a variety of helpful convenience devices and more complex mechanical aids to ease the physical restrictions. These aids range from simple Velcro shoe straps to motorized wheelchairs and computerized communication apparatus. Computers are capable of enhancing the lives of children who are unable to speak or write. They learn, fitted with a light pointer attached to a headband and a voice synthesizer, to use simple head movements in order to communicate.
- *Orthopaedic surgery* which, by lengthening muscles and tendons, can prevent spinal deformities and contractures that cause severe movement problems.
- *Gait analysis* involves the use of cameras and computers to record and analyze the child's style of walking. Muscle activity is recorded by electromyography and is used to identify problem muscles, eliminate compensation factors associated with walking, and check surgical results.
- *Stereotactic neurosurgery* may improve rigidity, choreoathetosis, and tremour. A CT scan of the head is performed to produce images of the brain. Co-ordinates of the location to be treated are moved to a stereotactic frame that is used like a map to guide an electrode to the target area in the brain. An

electrical impulse is transmitted through the electrode into the brain tissue so as to alter the brain cells.

- *Stereotaxic thalamotomy* can reduce some hemiparetic tremors. This risky procedure involves cutting parts of the thalamus, the brain's centre for relaying messages from the muscles and sensory organs.
- *Cerebellar stimulation* is a procedure that improves spasticity according to some studies (but not others) by surgically implanting electrodes on the surface of the cerebellum, which coordinates movement. The hope, by stimulating certain nerves, is to decrease spasticity and improve motor function.

Several problematic behaviours that can complicate CP may require attention. For example:

- incontinence, caused by faulty control over the bladder muscles;
- dribbling, caused by poor functioning of the muscles of the throat, mouth, and tongue;
- eating and swallowing difficulties. These may require occupational or physiotherapy to support and promote proper positioning while eating or drinking, or help extend the neck away from the body to reduce the risk of choking. Severe swallowing problems may necessitate the use of a tube to deliver food down the throat and into the stomach.

Stigma

Because children with CP may suffer from incontinence and difficulties (e.g. seizures, uncontrolled movements and communication difficulties) which arouse distress or embarrassment, they sometimes suffer cruel name-calling (such as 'spastics' and 'freaks') from peers and others. These insensitive remarks arouse feelings in them of being different from other young people. Teachers, in schools where this occurs, need firm and empathic management skills to spare children with this or other disabilities such humiliations.

Spina Bifida (SB)

Diagnosis

Spina bifida (literally a divided spine) is a defect that is present at birth. It is one of a group of neural tube defects that also includes anencephaly and encephalocele.

Clinical features

One or more of the 13 vertebrae – the bones which form the backbone – fail to form properly, leaving a gap or split in the spinal column, and causing damage to the central nervous system (CNS). SB can occur anywhere along the spinal column. The functions of the vertebrae are to:

- provide anchorage for the muscles that facilitate movement;
- provide protection to the spinal cord.

The SB types are:

- *spina bifida occulta* is a mild and common form of SB; the vertebrae do not fuse right over but the cord itself is usually undamaged; it rarely causes any disability
- *spina bifida cystica* (cyst-like). There are two forms: *meningocele* and *myelomeningocele*, the latter being the most common and most serious.

Hydrocephalus: Most babies born with spina bifida also have hydrocephalus (see Chapter 2).

Prevalence

The incidence of SB varies in the UK from one region to the other. Prior to the 1960s the majority of babies born with this condition died soon after birth. Advances in medical treatment (e.g. the discovery of antibiotics, invention of the shunt for associated hydrocephalus, and increasingly skilled surgery) have reduced the mortality rate.

Causation

At present there is no certainty about causation. When the neural tube develops incorrectly it is probably a result of both genetic and environmental factors. Among the suggested causes are:

- diabetes during pregnancy;
- alcohol;
- certain seizure drugs;
- genetic factors;
- inadequacies of diet.

Most cases of neural tube defect occur in the absence of any family history. However, once there has been an affected pregnancy, there is an increased risk of SB pregnancies. In an adult with the condition, the chances of having a baby similarly afflicted are about 1 in 35 (i.e. approximately 3 per cent).

Developmental feature: care and therapy

In all stages of growth and development the child and adolescent with SB have to work hard to reach new levels of independence. This requires practice, experience, encouragement and assistance. Help may be needed in learning skills such as:

- bathing
- dressing
- bowel and bladder control/management (e.g. self-catheterization; toilet transfers)
- gender-appropriate personal hygiene
- mobility
- grooming
- meal preparation
- medical management
- prevention and treatment of pressure sores.

Various habilitation/rehabilitation programmes exist to train these and other skills (see Chapter 6).

Public health recommendations

The US Centers for Disease Control would like every sexually active woman from puberty to menopause to take vitamin supplements with folic acid (a B-vitamin) in the daily diet, to prevent SB.

▨ Down's Syndrome

Developmental delay

Children with DS reach various motor milestones later than children with typical development (TD), and may follow a different developmental path. The average child with DS begins to walk at about 24 months of age, around 1 year later than a typically developing child. There are four main adverse influences affecting gross motor development in DS:

1 *Hypotonia*: Hypotonia (reduced muscle tone) makes it difficult for the child to acquire certain gross motor skills. Tone (controlled by the brain) refers to the tension in a muscle in its resting state. Hypotonia is clearly observed during infancy; when children with DS are picked up; they feel 'floppy'. It generally persists throughout life, although it may diminish somewhat over time. Hypotonic conditions tend to improve with age.

2 *Ligamentous laxity*: The joints of children with DS show excessive flexibility because the ligaments that hold the bones together are slack to a greater degree than is usual. When lying on their back, infants' legs will tend to be positioned with hips and knees bent and knees wide apart. Later, when standing, the feet are flat and joints unstable and it is difficult to balance.

3 *Decreased strength*: The children have reduced muscle strength and tend to compensate for their weakness by using movements that are easier in the short term, but counter-productive in the longer term (e.g. stiffening/locking their knees in order to stand).

4 *Short arms and legs*: Arms and legs are short relative to the length of their trunks. This shortness makes it more difficult to learn to sit because they cannot prop themselves on their arms unless they lean forward. Short legs also make it difficult to learn to climb, since the height of stairs and furniture present formidable obstacles.

Treatment

Gross motor movement programmes devised and supervised by occupational and physiotherapists have been demonstrated to be effective in reducing the symptoms of hypotonia. These programmes improve large body movements, such as walking, turning, sitting, standing and climbing stairs. Such interventions are recommended from between four and six weeks of age.

Physiotherapy and occupational therapy also provide parents and child with the opportunity to learn how to cooperate in overcoming the problems of gross motor development. Physical exercise becomes a fixed part of day-to-day life. These problems are discussed further in Chapter 9.)

CHAPTER 6

Problems of Social Training

■ Toilet Training Problems

Enuresis

Diagnosis

The term enuresis is applied to a child over the age of 6 (an age at which a majority of children are continent at night) who has never ceased to wet the bed, or more recently has lost his/her skill. The following diagnostic terms are also used:

- *primary enuresis* refers to a behavioural deficit: the child has never gained control of nocturnal incontinence. (i.e. bed wetting);
- *secondary enuresis* refers to the child who reverts to bedwetting after a period of being dry. The child's control may have been tenuous at best, and a period of stress may have triggered the regression.

A further distinction can also be made between children who are 'regularly' and those who are 'intermittently' enuretic. 'Diurnal enuresis' is the term used for daytime wetting.

Clinical features

The child will usually (and preferably) be examined first by a GP or paediatrician in case there is a physical cause for the bed-wetting, although organic aetiology is somewhat uncommon. Clinical psychologists have the particular behavioural skills that are effective for assessing and treating enuresis.

Epidemiology

Nocturnal bedwetting (at least once a week) occurs in approximately 13 per cent or 14 per cent of five-year-old boys and girls respectively (Rutter, Tizard and Whitmore, 1970); some estimates make the rate higher. The prevalence rate is 1 per cent to 2 per cent for youngsters over 15 and adults. Enuresis is a very common occurrence among children in residential establishments, and many cases continue (if untreated) into late adolescence or even adulthood. Daytime wetting (diurnal enuresis) is present in approximately 1 in 10 nocturnal enuretics.

Causation

A high level of skill is needed before the bladder can be controlled during sleep. It is perhaps not surprising that some children do not master it with ease, especially when disabled or under stress, or lose their new-found mastery when distressed. The causes are multiple:

- enuresis may have its origins in faulty learning;
- harsh 'pressurizing' of the child or (conversely) complacent neglect of training may lead to a failure of this development;
- emotional problems may be superimposed when the child is made to feel acute shame at his or her 'babyish' ways.

Physical causes

As many as 10 per cent of all cases of enuresis are the result of medical (physical) conditions, most commonly urinary tract infections. Approximately 1 in 20 female and 1 in 50 male enuretics have such an infection. Among other contributory causal influences are deep sleep, small functional bladder capacity, genetics, maturational factors and developmental disorders. Other uncommon physical causes are chronic renal or kidney disease, diabetes, tumours and seizures. Such potentially important causes should make an expert physical examination a matter of routine.

Emotional influences (anxiety)

A variety of psychological factors may contribute to enuresis. There is often a relationship between feeling anxious and wetting the bed; children who wet the bed may also tend to be anxious or nervous children. What is not certain is cause and effect in the relationship between anxiety and bed wetting. Undoubtedly, the child is often ridiculed by her/his brothers and sisters and perhaps even by parents. Staying at a friend's house or going on school camps is not possible. It is even very difficult to hide from neighbours. It is not surprising that the bed-wetter becomes very anxious about, and embarrassed by the problem.

Treatment

Many clinicians prefer to begin treatment with the use of incentive sticker (reward) charts adding a urine alarm if the child does not respond. The evidence for the superiority of the *urine alarm* method (with rates of remission between 80 and 90 per cent) over no-treatment and other-treatment control procedures is well documented for nocturnal enuresis, and makes it the main line of defence. Doleys's 1977 review of data (based on over 600 subjects) revealed an average relapse rate of 40 per cent; but nearly 60 per cent of these returned to continence after booster sessions.

In the Van Londen et al. (1995) study of 110 enuretic children, 97 per cent in the urine alarm programme which was supplemented with immediate contingency management (operant procedures) became continent compared with 84 per cent of the group that received delayed contingency management and 73 per cent who received a routine enuresis alarm programme. Only 8 per cent of the first group had deteriorated after two and a half years.

A meta-analysis of 78 studies by Houts, Berman and Abramson (1994), while reporting that the highest success rates for psychological programmes were those using urine alarms, also found the alarm method to be no more effective than the medical treatments (tricyclics and desmopressin) at post-treatment. However, they were significantly superior at follow-up.

Butler (1998) provides an excellent review of the advantages of the enuresis alarm, and some of the practical difficulties that can hinder the usual expectation of success. A detailed description of behavioural and combined methods of treating nocturnal and diurnal enuresis has been prepared for practitioners and parents by Herbert (1996a).

Less specific psychotherapeutic interventions such as individual or family therapy have not proved to be effective.

▪ Encopresis (Soiling)

Diagnosis

An encopretic ('soiling') child is any child over the age of 4 and under the age of 16 who regularly soils his/her underwear and/or bed.

Clinical features

Soiling is associated with:

- enuresis;
- low birth weight;
- behaviour problems (e.g. non-compliance and defiance).

A common encopretic problem is 'retention and overflow'. Normally, when stool enters the rectum, causing it to stretch, sensory nerves are stimulated. These nerves send a message to the brain telling the child he/she is full and needs to evacuate. When the child withholds stool (for whatever reason), the rectum enlarges slowly over weeks and months. Eventually it becomes so large that it can no longer be suddenly stretched by the passage of stool into the rectum. At this point the child no longer knows if the rectum is full or not. The constipation becomes so severe that it leads to a partial blockage of the bowel. Some of the motions liquefy and leak around the impacted area, soiling the child's underwear.

Children with encopresis due to rectal impaction cannot prevent themselves from soiling; they are unaware of their blockage and unable to prevent the leakage (i.e. the soiling). Sometimes (after about one to three weeks, when the rectum is so loaded that messages get through) a stool (a large hard lump of faecal matter) is let out when the child's muscle relaxes. The child usually does not realize that it is happening until it is too late. Some children, fearing ridicule or punishment, hide the evidence – the soiled clothing.

Constipation, or hard bowel movements, cause pain, irritability and a decreased appetite. This may cause the child to be afraid to go to the toilet, and to be defiant when coerced. A child's emotional state (due to stress and trauma) can affect the functioning of the bowel. Soiling may thus result from distressing life-events. The child is quite likely to be taunted, teased, and bullied at school because of the disability. Children have been suspended from school because soiling is so difficult to manage there. For the family, there are feelings of bewilderment, frustration, failure, revulsion and anger. It is one of the most common precipitants of physical abuse incidents (Claydon and Agnarsson, 1991).

Epidemiology

Encopresis is not an uncommon problem; three in every 100 children entering primary school at five years will still be soiling. Between 7 and 8 years, about two out of 100 children are soiling. At 12 years, about one in every 100 boys (and some girls) are still soiling. More boys soil than girls.

Treatment

Family therapy has not proved useful without the addition of behavioural, dietary and/or medical intervention (Walker, 1995). Individual psychotherapy has not been demonstrated to be more effective than no-therapy (e.g. Doleys, 1977). Doleys (1978) in his review of treatment studies, reported that 93 per cent of cases were successfully treated by the use of behavioural methods.

Herbert (1996a) has described the details of encopresis treatment in a manual for practitioners and parents. Combined behavioural and medical treatment (e.g. laxatives) are recommended for common 'retention with overflow' cases of encopresis. The programme involves:

- an assessment of possible fear elements (constipation may make toileting painful);
- an initial cleanout phase (usually with laxatives);
- educational input;
- scheduled toilet settings;
- reinforcement of appropriate toileting behaviour and for staying clean;
- cleanliness training;
- mild penalties for inappropriate behaviour;
- fibre intake and other dietary considerations.

Fireman and Koplewicz (1992), using this type of programme with 52 children (44 retentives) found that 84.6 per cent were symptom-free post-treatment and 78.8 per cent still so, after a 7-week phasing-out period.

■ Socialization Failures

Oppositional Defiant Disorder

Diagnosis

In the fourth edition of the psychiatric classificatory system *Diagnostic Statistical Manual* (DSM-1V), oppositional defiant disorder (ODD), is defined as a repetitive pattern of defiance and disobedience, and a negative and hostile attitude to authority figures of at least 6 months duration. To meet the criteria, four of the following behaviours must be present:

- loss of temper;
- arguments with adults;
- defiance of, or non-compliance with, adult rules and requests;
- being a deliberate source of annoyance;
- blaming others for one's own mistakes;
- being touchy and easily annoyed by others;
- frequent anger and resentment;
- spite or vindictiveness.

These behaviours must be frequent and lead to impairments of social and academic functioning.

Clinical features

ODDs occur in some 15 per cent of children during the course of their first five years of life (Scott, Knapp et al., 2001). There are two developmental pathways related to conduct disorders: the early starter (life-course persistent) versus late starter (adolescent onset) model. The early onset pathway begins with the emergence of (ODD) in early pre-school years and progresses to conduct disorder (CD) in middle childhood, and then on to the most serious aggressive anti-social activities of adolescence. By contrast, the prognosis for youngsters who become delinquent at adolescence, following a normal social and behavioural history, appears to be more benign than it is for adolescents who were early starters.

Causation

Social learning theorists suggest that children with serious anti-social problems are deviant because (*inter alia*) their early socialization has been ineffective. There is a continuing absence, as they get older, of an emotional aversion to anti-social activities, a diminished capacity to resist temptation, and a lack of feeling of remorse when they inflict harm. Not surprisingly, if unchecked, the long-term implications of such persistent and pervasive defiance and anti-social behaviour are of great concern, not only to parents but to the community as a whole. Other contributory causes are described in Herbert (1987a) and Kazdin (1998).

Developmental features

There are several investigations that have reported the continuity mentioned above, between ODD in the pre-school years and conduct disorders (aggressive, anti-social activities) in the school-going years and during adolescence (e.g. Caspi,

Moffitt et al., 1996). The adverse circumstances of early childhood can cast an even longer shadow, reaching into adulthood. Stevenson and Goodman (2001) followed up a sample of 828 children in a London borough from 1970 when the children were 3 years old, until they were around 23 years of age. The risk of having any adult conviction was found to be associated with the following behaviour at age 3:

- soiling and wetting during the day time;
- having a high activity level;
- their parents having difficulty in managing them.

Furthermore, the risk of later (adult) violent offences was associated with the 3-year-old children having serious temper tantrums which (*inter alia*) the parents had difficulty in managing.

By means of observations of family interactions in their homes, Gerald Patterson (1982) has demonstrated that a hostile response to an aggressive act serves to perpetuate the aggression. When a punitive response is part of a hostile interchange, far from bringing the provocation to an end, it tends to make things worse, and spreads outwards to involve other members of the family. The consequence of these accelerating hostile reactions is a family pattern of coercive negative interchanges.

■ Interventions

The early timing of an intervention to deal with the predisposing factors described above is critical for treating and preventing anti-social and delinquent behaviour (see Sutton, Utting and Farrington, 2004). Fortunately, effective parent education and training programmes are available.

Parent Education and Training

The agencies providing parenting courses include local education authorities, schools, health authorities and trusts, social service departments, voluntary organizations, churches and other faith groups, young offender institutions and prisons and academic institutions. The Parenting Education and Support Forum was established as a national 'umbrella' body for providers of parent education.

The two largest groups of professionals running programmes are educational psychologists and health visitors, followed by social workers and teachers. Two of the most widely available programmes – Parenting Matters and the Veritas courses – operate by training parents to become group leaders, thus extending accessibility to help. Hutchings, Gardner and Lane (2004) provide a review of parent education programmes.

Samra (1999) conducted a systematic evaluation of 550 ethnic minority parents who attended parenting education groups. The participants increased in confidence, re-appraised their child-rearing techniques, and came to the opinion that the programme served as a catalyst for personal growth (e.g. going on to further education).

Behavioural parent training (BPT)

There is an extensive literature describing the 'curricula' and theoretical principles of BPT programmes (see Scott, 2002). Manuals containing structured courses for group or individual use, by multi-disciplinary practitioners who work with birth- and foster-parents, are available (e.g. Herbert and Wookey, 2004). Interventions are generally focused directly on the caregivers of aggressive/anti-social children rather than on the child themselves. There are, however, courses designed for children (see Webster-Stratton and Dahl, 1995).

Group programmes

These programmes generally emphasize methods designed to reduce confrontations and antagonistic interactions (coercive commands and criticisms, extensive use of threats, anger, nagging and negative consequences) among family members. A vital item on the training agenda is an increase in the quantity and quality of positive interactions. In the groups, parents learn a means of understanding the consequences of their behaviour and the role it plays in maintaining their child's 'problematic' repertoire. In effect, they learn a new method of communicating, verbally and non-verbally, with their children.

Group-based programmes are more effective than individual programmes; and are more acceptable to parents when the venue is in the community rather than a clinic (Barlow, 1997). It is vital for clinical practitioners to know precisely the details of an intervention programme – a role for the training manual. There needs to be a balance of clear manual guidelines, possibilities for improvisation, and space for individual therapist differences – a challenging task (see Kazdin, 1998) (see Chapter 14 for a detailed account).

Treatment effectiveness

The various behavioural parenting training (BPT) programmes have been evaluated more intensively than any other psychological interventions. Reviews of the effectivenerss evidence have been published by Barlow, Coren and Stewart-Brown, 2002; Brestan and Eyberg, 1998; Webster-Stratton, 1991, among others.

Target and Fonagy (1996) conclude that, in the most general sense, the answer to the question 'What works for whom?' is that behavioural treatments are more effective than non-behavioural or family treatments.

Early Learning Programmes for Children

Philip Graham (1994, p. 820), on the basis of a review of the early learning literature, listed the following requirements for successful programmes:

- developmentally appropriate curriculum groups of fewer than twenty 3- to 5-year-olds, with 2 adults in each group;
- trained staff;
- supervisory support;
- in-service training;
- sensitivity to the child's non-educational needs;
- developmentally appropriate evaluation procedures;
- high-quality caregiver–child verbal instruction;
- an experimental programme director.

Home visiting

In a review by Carr (2002a) of well-designed studies published between 1965 and 1991, on mainly Afro-American families (7 home-visiting, 3 pre-school, 6 combined home-visiting and pre-school, and 2 multi-systemic), the following emerged:

- children from socially disadvantaged backgrounds were delayed in their development of cognitive abilities;
- multi-systemic programmes that attempt to do what the other programmes do and, in addition, extend support services for children and their families into middle childhood, are the most effective;
- next in effectiveness were the home-visiting programmes;
- then came the combined home-visiting and pre-school programmes;

- and last in effectiveness, were the programmes that involved pre-school enrolment alone.

The longer programmes, extending beyond five years in duration, were more successful than shorter programmes.

Multilevel intervention

Sanders (2003) devised the Triple P: the Positive Parenting Programme, an effective multilevel intervention in Australia, in order to provide parents with advice and support. Level 1, for example, includes media information designed to raise community awareness of parenting issues, and to convert the learning about child behaviour into a straightforward activity for parents. At higher levels, the interventions are more intensive to tackle more serious problems; for example Level 4 deals with diagnosed behavioural difficulties in children (e.g. different formats of parenting skills training). Level 5 provides adjunctive interventions (e.g. marital therapy, stress management) aimed at family problems which complicate children's difficulties. Much emphasis is placed on training and other aspects crucial to programme integrity.

III

Developmental Disorders of the Pre-school Years

The disorders described in Part III are among those usually diagnosed in the early and later pre-school years (see Chapters 7, 8 and 9).

■ Problems of Growth and Feeding

Problems of Growth

Failures to gain length and height are among the problems of growth discussed in this chapter, as are subjects such as obesity and organic failure to thrive. In describing these matters one has to go back in time, as very early health nutrition influences later healthy body development, and is vital for brain development. No aspect of growth in the human being is more critical than the rapid early development of the brain, which depends on adequate nutrition. At birth the infant has already reached about 25 per cent of its adult brain weight as compared with less than 5 per cent of its adult body weight. This weight advantage is imperative in order for the brain to stay ahead in its task making all the other infant developments possible.

A child should double his or her birth weight during the first $2\frac{1}{2}$ to 3 months. Although the potential for physical growth after birth is determined largely by genetic factors (i.e. maturational changes occurring regardless of practice or training), a change in physical size may be due to dietary change in nutrition, disease and emotional factors, rather than simply a maturational effect of muscle and bone growth. One of the early concerns about diet (a foretaste of society's lifetime obsession with dietary controversy) is a long-standing debate about the advantages and disadvantages of breast- and bottle-feeding.

Feeding Problems

The forerunner of many of the later feeding problems of childhood and adolescence are rooted in infant experiences. During the early weeks after birth, many of an infant's waking hours are taken up with feeding. Nearly all babies experience some weight fluctuation after birth. They might be expected to take about 3 to 4 ounces of milk or formula in around 30 minutes of feeding. Very few develop a feeding pattern right away. Even normal healthy full-term infants sometimes have early difficulties acquiring all of the reflexes required to feed well, either at the breast or on the bottle.

Breastfeeding the baby exclusively for six months (26 weeks) before introducing solid foods is now the preferred option of the UK Department of Health, but not of all mothers, because of its many health-promoting properties. This is now the policy endorsed by the World Health Organization. Clearly breastfeeding is nutritionally superior to bottle-feeding. It is initiated as soon as possible after birth (69 per cent of women in the UK do so) in order to provide the infant with the benefits of colostrum. Among other virtues breastfeeding nurtures babies who are less likely to become obese, and who suffer a lower risk of gastro-enteritis, and respiratory and ear infections.

The advantages of breastfeeding have not overcome the cultural resistances or 'inconvenience' aspects that operate in the UK where only 44 per cent of mothers were breastfeeding by the time their babies were one month old, reducing to only 23 per cent at six months. In Norway, as many as 80 per cent were continuing to breastfeed their babies at six months, and the figures are also high in other Scandinavian countries. There is no embarrassment there in feeding the baby at the breast in public and work places.

Sucking is typically the primary means by which babies meet their nutritional needs during the first six months of life. Survival of babies born prematurely or with congenital anomalies (e.g. cleft palate and lip) and complex developmental conditions (e.g. Down's syndrome) may cause concern if they are unable to obtain optimal nutrition by sucking during a critical period of growth and development.

Parental responsiveness is vital in something as basic as providing growth-enhancing sustenance to a baby. The caregiver needs to be alert to changing needs for nourishment as the child matures, by altering his/her diet. Typically, feeding times have to be adapted to the cycles of hunger and satisfaction expressed by the infant.

A feeding problem is diagnosed when a baby's or older child's continuing failure to eat causes inadequate weight gain or significant weight loss over at least a one-month period. The severity of eating difficulties described by parents can range from simple feeding problems and failure to thrive in infants to obesity and anorexia nervosa at older ages. These matters are among the subjects of Chapter 7 and later sections of the book.

■ Speech and Communication Disorders

The term 'speech' refers to the physical act of articulating speech sounds; 'language' denotes the entire system of combining elements of sound at different levels of complexity to express meaning. These skills, the essence of our humanity, are vital to social communication and of great concern when defective. Where they are located in the brain (the issue of 'functional localization') is a vexed question; however, modern brain imaging techniques have advanced our knowledge of how the brain processes both the production and reception of language. What we now know is that there is localization, but not exactly the rigid compartmentalization envisioned by earlier researchers.

The organization of the nerve cells combines specialization and flexibility. There is a degree of regional organization, The damage caused by a brain injury prior to, during, or after birth, may be in a specific location, or it may be diffused to many different parts of the brain:

- dysfunction in the frontal lobe tends to involve an inability to express language;
- dysfunctions in the temporal lobe involve difficulties in understanding spoken words;
- dysfunctions in the parietal lobes involve an inability (i) to attend to more than one object at a time; (ii) to name an object (*anomia*); (iii) to locate the words for writing (*agraphia*); and (iv) to read without difficulty.

Communication disorders are characterized by difficulties in speech or language (e.g. expressive language disorder). Delays or failures in language development combined with extreme problems of social communication are exemplified in childhood autism.

Undoubtedly, early communication difficulties lead to behaviour problems and interfere with cognitive development. Yet, as Law and Garrett (2004) point out in a review of the potential role of speech and language therapy in the Child and Adolescent Mental Health Services (CAMHSs), the relationship between behaviour and language development seems to be more widely recognized in the literature than in practice. This is reflected in under-reporting of speech and language problems in children with conduct disorder and delinquent activities, and other psychiatric disorders.

It may be that clinicians are unfamiliar with typical speech and language development. A brief summary is provided in Appendix V.

■ Intellectual Disabilities

I have chosen to use the term 'intellectual disability' in Chapter 9, except where another is used as part of a formal reference. It is now used in much of the UK and international literature. The *Diagnostic and Statistical Manual of Mental Disorders* (DSM-IV) classifies four different degrees of 'mental retardation': mild, moderate, severe, and profound. These categories are based on the level of functioning managed by the individual, a matter discussed in the chapter.

Intellectual disability (ID) applies in this chapter to children with an IQ of approximately 70 or below (when measurable). The psychometric model of ID locates a child as 'high' or 'low' or somewhere in between on IQ (intelligence quotient), the average being 100. One of the drawbacks of the psychometric model and the medical model is the tendency to classify individuals in terms of what they cannot do or what they do not have. Negative assumptions and conclusions can become recipes for pessimistic inaction. Nevertheless, both have important roles to play.

The American Association on Mental Retardation (AAMR) has developed another diagnostic classification for 'mental retardation' which focuses on the capabilities of the individual rather than on his or her limitations. The categories define the level of support required by the individual, namely, intermittent support, limited support, extensive support, and pervasive support. Intermittent support is the type of support typically required for most mildly impaired individuals. At the other end of the spectrum, pervasive support, or life-long, daily support for most adaptive areas, would be required for profoundly intellectually disabled individuals.

No matter what specific syndrome they suffer from, or what the causes may be, children with ID learn more slowly than the average child, and with a degree of difficulty that ranges from to mild to severe. Severely impaired children have difficulty in abstracting the general principles that describe their environment and which help them to plan, organize actions and solve problems of everyday life.

CHAPTER 7

Early Growth and Feeding Problems

■ Problems of Physical Growth

Constitutional Growth (Maturational) Delay

Diagnosis

Constitutional growth (maturational) delay (failure to gain length and height) is the term used to describe children who are small for their age but are growing at a normal rate. They tend to have a delayed 'bone age'; their skeletal maturation is younger (as indicated by X-rays of hand and wrist) than their chronological age, expressed as 'bone age equals height age'.

Developmental features

The natural history of a child with constitutional delay of maturation, begins with a newborn of normal size. Somewhere after 6 months they move down the growth (height) curve to the 5th percentile or below, which means that 19 out of 20 other children in the general population, will be taller. After the slowdown, the velocity picks up to a level commensurate with peers; however, they remain at around the 5th percentile. Small-for-date babies are more likely than pre-term infants to remain small in stature throughout childhood (Goldenberg, 1995).

Constitutional delay of growth, a variation of normal growth must be distinguished from FTT. Children with short stature resulting from constitutional delay often have a family history of delayed growth and puberty. They have a deceleration of growth in the first two years that can be confused with FTT, but then grow parallel to but below the 3rd percentile. Puberty is delayed, but ultimate height may be normal. A distinguishing point from genetic short stature is that bone age is delayed.

Familial (Genetic) Small/Short Stature

Diagnosis

This term applies to children who do not have any symptoms of diseases that affect growth. Between 3 and 5 children out of every 100 children will have short stature. Shorter parents tend to have shorter children.

Noonan Syndrome

Diagnostic background

Noonan syndrome, a genetic condition characterized by a series of birth defects including short stature, took its name from Jacqueline Noonan who reported 19 cases with the condition in 1968. In fact, the syndrome was reported as early as 1883.

Clinical features: symptoms

Noonan syndrome (NS) is a many-sided condition characterized by a series of birth defects (congenital malformations) including postnatal growth retardation, webbing of the neck (pterygium colli), caved-in chest bone (pectus excavatum), narrowing of the artery from the heart to the lungs (pulmonic stenosis). In boys, the testes do not descend normally into the scrotum (cryptorchidism).

It has been likened to Turner syndrome because short stature and webbed neck occur in both NS and Turner syndrome. The similar appearance of patients with Noonan and Turner syndromes led people to mistake NS as a type of Turner syndrome when, in fact, it is quite dissimilar.

Noonan syndrome is characterized by short stature. The final height approaches the lower limits of normal in late adolescence. 68 per cent of individuals with NS suffer from congenital heart defects. They have broad or webbed necks, caved-in T or pigeon chests. The facial features are also quite typical in children with NS, among them wide-spaced eyes, down-slanting eye slits, and thick hooded eyelids.

Developmental features

The face changes with age. The following attributes are fairly common: a failure to grow/thrive normally in infancy; developmental delay; learning difficulties (mild 'mental retardation' in about a third of individuals); and language delay.

Causation

NS is an inherited autosomal dominant disorder. The Noonan gene is on a non-sex (autosomal) chromosome and is transmitted from a parent with a 50 per cent probability to boy or girl. Although one dose of the Noonan gene is enough to cause the syndrome, the expression of the gene is quite variable with some persons appearing to be at most very mildly affected.

Failure to Gain Weight (Organic Failure to Thrive)

Diagnosis

Organic failure to thrive (OFTT) is a term applied to growth failure resulting from (i) an acute or chronic disorder known to interfere with normal nutrient intake, absorption, metabolism, or excretion; or (ii) lack of energy requirements to sustain or promote growth.

Failure of normal physical growth is usually detected in infants through their unsatisfactory weight gain. Experts seem to agree that only by comparing height and weight on a growth chart over time can FTT be assessed accurately.

Clinical features

For children with OFTT the onset may be at any age depending on the underlying disorder; Children who fail to thrive are commonly born prematurely. If OFTT progresses, the undernourished child may become apathetic and irritable, and fail to attain milestones such as sitting up, walking, and talking at the expected ages.

Once OFTT is identified in a particular child, the following information from the maternal history is important:

- the mother's smoking habits before and during pregnancy;
- her alcohol consumption;
- use of medication;
- any illness during gestation.

Data on parents' growth history is necessary.

Babies with chronic diarrhoea may fail to grow properly, so their dietary history, method and efficacy of feeding, and bowel habits, provide important information. Infections such as meningitis may have adverse effects on the growth potential of children.

Developmental features

Cognitive development is affected in children younger than 5 years who have OFTT. With improvement of nutritional status, these deficits may not be completely reversed.

Causation

The causes may exist in prenatal events or in the postnatal environment. Premature babies have an increased incidence of disorders that can lead to intrauterine OFTT, including renal disease, heart disease, lung disease, and disorders of the CNS (central nervous system). Most premature babies catch up to the growth of full term babies by the time they are aged 2 to 4 years.

Other causes of the prenatal onset of OFTT include:

- maternal illnesses such as hypertension, pre-eclampsia, heart disease, anaemia, and advanced diabetes mellitus, can lead to utero-placental insufficiency and, therefore, result in smaller babies;
- toxins affecting growth such as drug abuse, smoking and alcohol ingestion during pregnancy (causing placental insufficiency);
- intrauterine infection;
- placental or chromosomal abnormalities.

Postnatal causes include:

- inadequate energy intake due to mechanical problems;
- craniofacial abnormalities;
- lack of appetite;
- breathing difficulties;
- metabolic problems;
- excessive vomiting.

Mechanical problems result from a poor suck or swallow secondary to *hypotonia* or Prader–Willi syndrome, or from a neuromuscular or CNS system disease leading to lack of coordination of this process. Cleft lip and palate make eating difficult, as do craniofacial abnormalities which are commonly associated with inadequate energy intake and, therefore, lead to a failure to thrive.

Some children simply have unexplained poor appetites that are unrelated to mechanical problems or structural abnormalities. An example of one cause of inadequate intake is breathing difficulties.

Children with cystic fibrosis (CF) lack pancreatic enzymes that are required for absorption of nutrients. Unless supplemented with exogenous enzymes, children with this condition have OFTT from the inadequate use of ingested food. Illnesses that increase metabolic demands, such as hyperthyroidism, can also cause OFTT. The same may apply to children who have congenital heart disease which is characterized by both inadequate intake and increased loss of nutrients.

Obesity

The problem

The prevalence of overweight children is increasing and has been associated with Type II diabetes mellitus and the development of heart disease in adulthood. Research suggests that the roots of essential hypertension extend back to childhood. Body size is the most important determinant of blood pressure in children. And elevated blood pressure in childhood is often correlated with hypertension in early adulthood, thereby supporting the need for the monitoring of blood pressure in children by GPs.

Assessment

Details of daily nutritional intake are required, and a food diary is given to the parents to fill in each day. They are asked to keep a detailed record of what the child eats over the course of a day or if possible a week. This should include details of the amount and type of food eaten, including all snacks and drinks, as well as 'time and place'. A reliable record of the quantity of food eaten is critical.

Height and weight records are useful in assessment and treatment. They aid the practitioner in deciding on the seriousness (i.e. the health implications) of the eating problem. The Body Mass Index (BMI) is an anthropometric index of weight and height. The use of BMI-for-age is recommended for children aged 2 years and older This index correlates with clinical risk factors for cardiovascular disease including hyperlipidemia, elevated insulin and high blood pressure.

Intervention

There are many subtle nuances to this kind of work, requiring diplomacy and creative thinking in the planning of dietary interventions (Leon and Dinklage, 1989). There are many parental sensitivities and 'mythologies' around feeding offspring, so a focus on parents as well as the child is crucial. Many parents become very concerned that the child is not eating 'enough', or is 'unhappy', and they may therefore withdraw prematurely from the programme. A mixture of counselling, expert nutritional and dietary assistance, behaviour management skills training (featuring incentives, stimulus control, differential attention/the praise–ignore formula, time-out and response-cost consequences), and careful monitoring, are required. With much reassurance and practical help, parents should be able to cope with their child's new controlled feeding regime.

▧ Feeding Difficulties

Developmental features

The feeding situation is an important component of the bonding process between parent and child (see Herbert, Sluckin and Sluckin, 1982). While it is not contentious to suggest that the development of positive feeding patterns is significant to the child's well-being, the fuss made by early theorists about the long-term effects on personality of different approaches to infant feeding or weaning, proved to be unjustified (Lee and Herbert, 1970). Of course, this is not to deny that it is important to make a child's feeds as relaxed and pleasant occasions as possible.

Emotional difficulties

Stresses and strains in parent–child relationships may stem from feeding problems, some of which may have originated in, and become superimposed on, the pain associated with organic disorders such as oesophageal stricture and pyloric stenosis, early in the child's life. Anxiety, depression or reactions to adverse (perhaps abusive) relationships within the family may cause the child to stop eating, resulting in a failure to thrive.

Mealtime problems

Mealtimes are a common cause of worry for parents. Parents differ in the amounts of food they expect children to eat (or need nutritionally). Growth charts are more reliable than arbitrary labelling of the child as a 'poor' or 'finicky' eater. Almost

all children become fussy about food at some time; toddlers often show changing likes and dislikes for particular foods. At some ages, this is simply a matter
of disliking certain tastes or textures or being more interested in experimenting,
playing and talking than eating. However, some children learn to be fussy after
observing other family members who are finicky.

The child's appetite

Adults have usually been reared in a tradition of three meals a day. This is not
necessarily the schedule that best fits the young. Most young children require four
to five small meals a day: morning, mid-morning, noon, mid-afternoon and
evening. This affects food 'helping' sizes. A mid-afternoon snack may make the
substantial dinner redundant. Parents sometimes forget that children do not necessarily have the same appetite as themselves. A huge plateful may appear to the
child as an endurance test, especially if the parents fuss over leaving 'empty plates'.

A survey based on interviews of 2,000 parents of children aged 12 months to
3½ years (commissioned by *Mother & Baby* magazine with Pampers Kandoo)
found that 75 per cent are either 'faddy eaters' or 'refuse to eat'; and 51 per cent
throw their food on the floor. Among 3-year-olds, more than 10 per cent have
poor appetites or tend to be faddy. There are no sex differences in the rate of such
difficulties, but they are likely to persist for at least a year for most of them and
even continue for over five years in some. Among 5-year-olds more than a third
of the children have mild or moderate appetite or eating problems. Most tend to
be faddy eaters. Clearly, it is necessary to take account of a child's appetite, in
other words, daily levels of hunger, in any assessment of mealtime difficulties or
a child's feeding needs.

Eating behaviour

Typical difficulties, at later ages, are: 'bad table manners', refusing to eat or eating
painfully slowly, getting up from the table, finicky eating habits, faddiness,
tantrums and crying. The setting for a family should (or could) provide an important opportunity for children to enjoy family life, and learn interactive skills;
instead, it seems only too often (especially with pre-school children) to become
the occasion for open warfare.

CHAPTER 8

Atypical Speech and Communication

■ Specific Language Impairment (SLI)

Diagnosis

In SLI, language development is abnormal although development is usually normal in other areas. Problems with language structure are common (Bishop, 1992).

Clinical features

The prevalence rate is about 7 per cent. There is a high rate of undiagnosed SLI, especially among children referred to clinics for behaviour problems.

Causation

There is no obvious physical cause. However, short-term memory is poorer in SLI children than in typically developing (TD) children. Family aggregation studies reveal a strong genetic influence in SLI, possibly operating through some type of neuronal mechanism. Environmental factors may escalate the risk for SLI, eventually 'pushing' some vulnerable children into a full expression of the disorder.

Treatment

Speech and language therapists work with children who suffer from SLIs. There are sceptical views about the effectiveness of speech therapy and remedial education in producing durable and generalizable results. (e.g. Lyon and Cutting, 1998;

Maughan and Yule, 1994), but also more optimistic opinions (see Law and Garrett, 2004).

There appear to have been only three systematic reviews on speech and language interventions (see Law and Garrett, 2004). The evidence is of effective outcomes in the following areas.

1 *Phonology* (difficulty with speech sounds): parental administration of therapy is as effective as clinician-led treatment when children have expressive language difficulties. The use of trained parents in partnership with professionals is more effective than administration of treatment by clinicians alone.
2 *Syntax targeted interventions* are effective for some clients (children with purely expressive difficulties), but not others (children with both receptive language and expressive problems). Clinician and parent administered therapy are equally effective.
3 *Vocabulary*: similar findings to 2.

The results of combined investigations of speech therapy outcomes for early speech and language delays (methodologically uneven studies in an earlier review by Law, Boyle et al., 1998), produced median effect sizes of around 1.0. The average treated child might move from the 5th to the 25th percentile on a standard language test. The improvement of expressive language yielded higher effect sizes than was found for receptive difficulties (i.e. comprehension).

■ Absence or Delay of Speech

Autism

Diagnosis

One of the defining characteristics of autism is an extreme deficit in speech and language. Severely delayed and often very deviant language is commonly the presenting complaint of parents of pre-school children with autism. They may acquire some appropriate speech but this depends on receiving intensive therapy. The Childhood Autism Rating Scale (CARS) (Schopler, Reichler and Renner, 1999) gives scores on specific subscales including Verbal Communication.

Clinical features

1   *Speech and language failures and aberrations.* The language (communication) deficit is one of the key items in the triad of symptoms that are pathognomonic of autism. It should be noted that 'high-functioning' autistic children can learn to talk, but several aspects of their language have been shown to be atypical:

   (i)   *Semantic deficits.* These are aberrations in the organization of word meanings (lexicon) and the retrieval of words, in spontaneous speech, the comprehension of verbal utterances and the ability to put together a coherent discourse. Children with autistic symptoms tend to experience disturbances in the organization of perception, a failure to achieve order and meaningful structure from the incoming messages from the environment. This might explain their social withdrawal, limited attention span, violent emotional responses to certain forms of stimulation, and obsession with sameness (see Hermelin and O'Connor, 1970a, 1970b).

   (ii) *Language comprehension.* Many children who are autistic are able to answer concrete questions appropriately, tend to answer open-ended questions in a manner that is past the point. In order to gauge comprehension, it is useful to ask the child open-ended 'why', 'when', and 'how' questions. Most have fundamental difficulties in the comprehension of language.

2   *Failures of social communication.* The diagnosis of autism requires that impaired or abnormal development be present before 3 years of age, in all of the following domains: social communication; social relationships; and imagination.

   (i)   *Pragmatics.* Pragmatics is at the interface of language and sociability. The autistic child's apparent insensitivity to other persons' feelings and overtures appears before the child is 3 years old.

   (ii) *Non-verbal pragmatics.* These include the interpretation and display of facial expressions, body postures, gestures, and acoustic aspects of speech (prosody) that clarify the intent of non-verbal and verbal communications. An early sign of impaired non-verbal pragmatics is the failure of children to look up when called by name, or to point out things they want.

   (iii) *Verbal pragmatics.* Examples of verbal pragmatics include the initiation of communication, staying on topic, engaging in meaningful dialogue, using language as a tool to indicate or fulfil needs, and co-operating in appropriate turn-taking. Children with autism, who are verbal, may engage in long monologues without discernible communicative intent, or ignore expressions of boredom from those who are on the receiving end of non-stop talk. They are prone to make pronoun substitutions, such as 'you' for 'I'. Another feature is echolalia – an immediate or delayed repetition of another person's speech. There is a suggestion that the function of echolalia may be to give the child, in the face of poor spontaneous language skills, a way of entering or maintaining a conversation.

Developmental features

Approximately 50 per cent of children who are autistic never learn to talk, or they speak in only a most rudimentary manner, that is limited to a very few simple commands. Impaired comprehension and continuing absence of expressive language are associated with poor cognitive development in autism. The prognosis for significant language progress is extremely poor after the age of 6. The ability to acquire speech is also a crucial prediction of later adjustment in autistic children.

At a verbal level, autistic children who do talk, speak in a monotonous voice with a peculiar robotic rhythm, or in a high pitched singsong that can 'turn' affirmative sentences into what seem like questions. They are unlikely to look at the person they are speaking to, or use gestures to supplement speech. They also tend not to appreciate the implications of a threatening facial expression, or a raised tone of voice.

It is significant that the autistic child's apparent insensitivity to other persons' feelings and overtures appears before the child is 3 years old. The point is that the development of the child's mind fails at the time when most children begin to be extremely sensitive to and interested in other people's ideas and actions; also at a time when 'more advanced' speech is beginning. Nine to twelve months is a stage in development when:

- a baby is *normally* changing rapidly;
- there is the most intense communication;
- the baby shares different ways of doing things;
- children are expected to be insatiably curious and full of imagination about meanings in their play.

They wish to put these ideas into language. They demonstrate increases in alertness, in intelligence and curiosity, in purposeful, constructive handling of objects, in memory, and in willingness to share experiences and actions with companions.

Theory of mind

Children typically develop a theory of mind with profound effects on social life and on communication in general. Such a theory allows children to interpret overt behaviour by reference to invisible mental states. In this way they can distinguish 'really meaning it' from 'just pretending'.

There is a serious fault or failure in autism in the child's development of meta-representational ability (i.e. the ability to form second-order representations). Without a theory of mind, social nuances such as pretending, deceiving and bluffing are incomprehensible.

Interventions

Behaviour modification

The early behaviourists, seeking an objective approach to therapy and training, applied operant principles of learning to the problems of autistic and intellectually disabled patients (Ferster and De Myer, 1962). Operant behaviour (mainly under voluntary control) is maintained by its consequences: increased or strengthened (and thus shaped) by events that are rewarding (positive reinforcement), or that lead to the avoidance of, or escape from punishment (negative reinforcement).

Operant principles formed the basis for the analysis of the functional relationship between precisely defined and observed aspects of deviant behaviour (or its absence) and clearly specified environmental contingencies. This so-called functional analysis informed the modification of the child's environment in order to bring about desired changes in his or her behaviour.

Contemporary behavioural work of a more sophisticated kind (in educational programmes) has been applied to various modalities of communication (e.g. speech and language: Howlin, 1998; Howlin, Rutter, Berger et al., 1987). There have been efforts to teach autistic children non-vocal means of communicating (Kiernan, 1983). There is evidence that some very disabled children can learn to communicate needs using gesture, signed language, and 'communication boards' on which the child can point to pictures or symbols.

A disappointing development in the 1990s was designed to engage autistic children by means of *facilitated communication*. The child was aided by a facilitator's touch, to type on a keyboard. Raised hopes for this method were dashed by evaluations of the outcomes which indicated that the child's elaborate, seemingly spontaneous productions, were mainly artefacts of guidance provided unwittingly by the facilitator.

Other interventions, related to communication training, are:

- the management of challenging behaviour (e.g. Emerson and Bromley, 1995);
- responsiveness (Clark and Rutter, 1981);
- mind-tasks (Frith and Hill, 2003).

The Treatment and Education of Autistic and Related Communication-Handicapped Children (TEACCH) is a well-validated programme based at the University of North Carolina. It has as its focus the development of communication skills and personal autonomy. A wide variety of empirically-tested methods are tailored to the individual, and to improving his or her quality of life.

Home-based behavioural treatment

It would seem that home-based behavioural interventions are the preferred option in treating autistic children. The evidence for the effectiveness of alternative methods, when available, is weak. The conclusions of Fonagy, Target, et al. following their 2002 review (*What Works for Whom*, p. 275), are that 'findings strongly suggest that behavioural treatments are beneficial, although longer-term studies are required'.

Parent training

The quality of parent–child interactions is seen to be of particular importance in producing improvements in the home-based programmes (see Herbert and Wookey, 2004). Collaborative parent training is now a fairly standard component in early intervention programmes with intellectually/developmentally disabled children. For example: the Home-Based Teaching Project (HBTP) is based in the Department of Child Psychiatry at the Maudsley Hospital, London (Howlin and Rutter, 1987), and is an outreach programme for the families of young autistic children. The programmes are individually designed to foster language development, facilitate social development and treat behavioural problems (e.g. obsessional and ritualistic behaviours) that undermine learning and development.

Applied behaviour analysis (ABA)

Much controversy exists over the effectiveness of ABA. Lovaas developed his interest in autism after having the opportunity to work with a group of 20 children with autism at the UCLA Neuropsychiatric Institute. During this time, he discovered that with intensive behavioural therapy, these children improved their functioning. When the treatment ended, the gains they made continued until they returned to an institutional environment. Based on his observations, Lovaas theorized that the return to an institutional environment (and later, their return home from his newly founded Institute for Early Intervention) caused a regression. He hypothesized that if they could live in a more therapeutically supportive environment, they would maintain their newly developed behavioural skills. In order to continue the positive outcomes of their treatment, he began to train the parents to offer the same support structure that his Institute (the Ivar Lovaas Institute for Early Intervention) provided.

Lovaas incorporated the concept of a total learning environment into his treatment programme, on the premise that the 'normal' child is exposed constantly (and on a daily basis) to his or her learning environment. They do not attend classes for eight hours a day and then stop the learning process. When school is over, they continue to learn, during all of their waking hours. Lovaas's teaching regime was to provide a learning environment as intensive as the naturalistic one. He also arranged for learning activities to end on a positive, successful note each day. He observed that subsequent learning became easier as suggested by the aphorism: 'success builds on success, and failure breeds more failure.'

Lovaas formulated a comprehensive therapeutic and educational plan of applied behavioural analysis (ABA). This involves discrete trial teaching in which skills are broken down into minute components and systematically taught to children on a one-to-one basis. For example, since many autistic children lack imitation, ABA first teaches imitation of objects, then of body movements to finally following the leader as a way for them to naturally imitate from others. A detailed presentation of the treatment programme, based on operant conditioning theory and research on its application to autistic children, can be found in Lovaas and Leaf (1981).

Two of the major sources of evidence of the effectiveness of the ABA approach appear in randomized controlled trials by Lovaas (1987) and McEachin, Smith and Lovaas (1993) respectively. In 1987 Lovaas conducted a study on the effects of ABA (his Young Autism Project) on autistic children under the age of 4 with IQ scores falling in the mild to retarded category. The experimental group of 19 children received 40 hours a week of one-to-one intensive behavioural treatment for 2 or more years, plus parent training. The first control group of 19 children received only 10 hours a week of one-to-one behavioural treatment in their homes, plus a variety of other interventions (e.g. parent training and especial education classes). The second control group did not receive intensive behavioural treatment.

His short-term goals consisted of teaching compliance, imitation and appropriate toy play that many autistic children lack, generalizing treatment in the community, and reducing self-stimulatory behaviours such as hand-flapping. Long-term goals that were emphasized in years two and three of therapy consisted of teaching receptive and expressive language, playing with peers, teaching emotions, pre-academic skills such as reading and writing, and observational learning.

The participants in the study were followed up at a mean age of 7 years. The data revealed that children in the experimental group gained an average of 20 IQ points, and were higher than both control groups in school achievement and intellectual functioning. Of the children in the experimental group, 47 per cent achieved average intellectual functioning (normal or above average IQ scores) and normal educational functioning (going on to mainstream first grade), and were indistinguishable from their peers. Some 40 per cent were assigned to classes for the language-delayed, and 10 per cent were put in classrooms for the 'mentally retarded'.

In contrast, of the children who received the normally available services, only 2 per cent achieved normal educational and intellectual function, 45 per cent were put in language-delayed classes, and 53 per cent were put in classrooms for the retarded. Children in both control groups had IQ scores that remained stable over time.

McEachin, Smith and Lovaas (1993) went on to evaluate the long-term outcome of children in Lovaas's 1987 study at a mean age of 11½ (13 years for the experimental group; 10.for the controls). Some 44 per cent had higher scores than the control groups on adaptive behaviour and personality. They were indistinguishable from average children on tests of intelligence and adaptive behaviour, and were categorized as 'recovered' from autism. In contrast, the children in the control group did not gain such an outcome. Only 17 per cent of the control group obtained full scale IQs of at least 80, as compared with 58 per cent of the experimental group. The controls fared poorly in a way that parallels, it is suggested, the poor prognosis of autistic children if no early intervention was administered (e.g. McEachin, Smith and Lovaas, 1993; Rutter, 1985b).

Lovaas's acolytes believe he has revolutionized the way we think about autism, to the extent that autism should no longer be viewed as a severe, lifelong disability, but rather as a temporary halt in development which ABA can change, by assisting children with autism to learn from their environment. McEachin, Smith and Lovaas (ibid.) state that there is reason to believe that alterations in neurological structures are possible as a result of change in the environment in the first few years of life for young children with autism, based on past studies on laboratory animals.

Rutter (1985b) has reported that only 1 out of 64 autistic children improves without treatment. But, is ABA the answer to the treatment of autism? This is still a topic of debate, as it was in the 1960s when the plan was first implemented. It certainly has not escaped criticism (Fonagy, Target et al., 2002). A common conclusion is that the approach is 'very promising' but flawed by an overstatement of its curative powers, and an understatement of the costs in terms of time (40-hours-a-week interventions) and funding. Further research is required on the most effective ingredients of the programme: its integrity with respect to training, outcome measures, and the hours required in teaching the child. What is known is that ABA improves the lives of a proportion of the children treated (notably increases in IQ); and is most effective when initiated early in life.

Applied social learning theory

There is an important theoretical (perhaps ethical) issue for behavioural psychologists who use operant technology on autistic children. Crucially (as is recognized by social learning therapists), rewards and punishments are not simply the impersonal consequences of behaviour. They are mediated by people functioning within attachment and social systems. Children do not simply respond to stimuli; they interpret them. They are relating to, interacting with, and learning from people who have meaning and value for them. They may feel hostile to some (indifferent or antipathetic, in the case of autistic children), and therefore find them valueless, even aversive. Others are attached to people by respect and/or affection (in this case relatively few autistic children), and are thus likely to find an encouraging word positively reinforcing.

Contingent experiences create expectations rather than stimulus–response connections (Bandura, 1977). Stimuli influence the likelihood of particular behaviours because of their predictive function. Thus, the failure to comprehend meanings (a common difficulty for children with autism, semantic-pragmatic disorder or Asperger's syndrome), can have a devastating effect, and implications for the design of treatment programmes that necessitate very careful thought.

CHAPTER 9

Intellectual Disabilities

■ Introduction to Intellectual Disabilities

Diagnosis

A reliable diagnosis of intellectual disability (ID) may not be possible at birth. The first indications of an intellectual disability may be the presence of developmental delays. A toddler with moderate intellectual disability may have normal motor development but delayed language development. The extent of any developmental delay depends on the severity of the condition, some mild cases missing a diagnosis until the child enters school. By that time s/he typically has difficulties with social, communication, and functional academic skills.

Assessment

ID has its onset in childhood or adolescence before the age of 18. The level of cognitive functioning is well below average; an IQ score below 70 is the conventional threshold at which ID is diagnosed. In infants this is assessed by clinical judgement. Beyond infancy it is usually assessed by means of an individually administered intelligence test. Additional criteria require there to be significant limitations in two or more adaptive skills needed for daily life. They include the ability to produce and understand language (communication); home-living skills; use of community resources; health, safety, leisure, self-care, and social skills; self-direction; and functional academic skills.

Clinical features

The learning disabilities at the core of ID, are disorders that affect the child's ability to understand or use spoken or written language (reading and writing), carry out arithmetical and mathematical calculations, coordinate movements, or focus attention.

The onset of ID depends on the cause of the disability. Intellectual impairment may be suspected before birth through amniocentesis (e.g. Down's syndrome), or in a young infant with congenital abnormalities, or from an abnormal screening of a condition in the neonate, associated with learning disability (for example, trisomy 13, kernicterus, Prader–Willi syndrome and tuberous sclerosis). If intellectual impairment is the result of chromosomal or other genetic disorders, it is often apparent from infancy. Symptoms may appear later in childhood. For example, children who have a neurological disorder or illness such as encephalitis or meningitis may show signs of cognitive impairment and adaptive difficulties quite suddenly. The likelihood that children with ID will be suffering from additional physical and sensory impairments which affect their early learning and later education, increases with the severity of the intellectual disability.

Epidemiology

Intellectual disability (ID) occurs in 2 to 3 per cent of the general population.

Developmental features

Children with ID reach developmental milestones such as walking and talking significantly later (if at all) than is expected according to the typical timetable. In most cases, impairment continues throughout adulthood. When an infant has an intellectual disability there is usually a dawning realization that something is 'not quite right'. The awareness of developmental 'differences' may be so gradual that parents cannot say when they first came to be really concerned.

Adjusting to the fact of a child's intellectual disability may continue over many years, depending to some extent on whether the problem was apparent (obvious at birth) or more subtle – only becoming clear at a later age. Much depends upon whether the parents are informed honestly, and several times, about the nature of their child's impairment (see Appendix II for further discussion).

Causation

In about 35 per cent of cases, the cause of ID cannot be discovered. Dykens (2000) reports that there are at least 750 genetic causes of ID. This indicates an extremely heterogeneous diagnostic category. The focus on impairment of function is important for secondary prevention, limiting consequent disability, and

controlling concurrent complications such as epilepsy. A multidisciplinary paediatric team is required to plan and initiate a programme (possibly facilitated in
large part by Portage workers) that is geared to the special needs and positive qualities of the individual child.

Treatment

Emerson (1995) states that in general, approaches to intervention can be divided
into one of two categories:

1   A pathological approach which concentrates on the elimination of behaviour
    (e.g. self-harm, obsessional rituals) or states (e.g. anxiety, hostility).
2   A constructional approach, a perspective in which the solution to problems
    is the construction of repertoires (their reinstatement or transfer to new situa-
    tions) rather than their elimination.

Social skills programmes have been conducted on developmentally delayed and
intellectually impaired children. Most studies of children with IDs have concen-
trated on aspects of their:

*   poor interpersonal communication;
*   passivity;
*   excessive aggression;
*   social isolation/withdrawal (e.g. Herbert, 1998).

A variety of intervention methods is available, chosen according to the influences
responsible for the child's social or other life skill difficulties, and ability to con-
ceptualize verbally. These include:

*   communication training;
*   relaxation skills and exposure training (for coping with social anxiety);
*   assertiveness training;
*   social skills training;
*   social perception skills training;
*   use of self-instruction to guide behaviour;
*   problem-solving skills training;
*   modification of negative thoughts with positive thoughts;
*   modification of negative attributions (cognitive structuring/reframing).

Prevention

Sensible prenatal care contributes to the prevention of ID. The effects of smoking and drinking, and the need to achieve healthy nutrition during pregnancy, are key risk items (see Chapter 2). Immunization against diseases such as measles and Hib prevents many of the illnesses that can cause ID. Tests such as amniocentesis and ultrasonography can identify, as we have seen, whether a fetus is developing normally in the womb.

There are several potential disabilities in which environmental interventions based on significant advances in scientific research, have ensured the prevention of intellectual and other disabilities for untold numbers of infants. The preventive procedures involve:

• screening newborns for phenylketonuria (PKU), followed by (in the case of positive identification) dietary treatment;
• screening newborns for congenital hypothyroidism followed up by thyroid hormone replacement therapy;
• treating jaundice in newborns with phototherapy (see Chapter 3);
• preventing rubella during pregnancy by means of the rubella vaccine;
• pre-empting measles encephalitis by means of the measles vaccine;
• using child safety seats and bicycle and skateboard helmets to reduce *head trauma.*

Early Intervention Programmes

There are several early learning programmes using infant stimulation and parent education, designed to enhance the attainments of disabled and socially disadvantaged children. Some of these are described below. They follow a discussion of Down's syndrome which, as the most common identifiable cause of learning disability, deserves a more than usually detailed account, in order to illustrate and elaborate points made above, about pervasive intellectual disability.

Down's Syndrome

Background

In *The Journal of Mental Science* of 1866–67, John Langdon Down – a superintendent of an asylum for 'mentally retarded' children in Surrey – published a treatise in which he described a group of children who shared features which distinguished them from other inmates. This is generally credited as the earliest clinical description of what he called *mongoloid idiocy*. Down made a distinction between children who were *cretins* (later found to be a hypothyroid condition) and *mongoloids* – so-called because of his belief that they had Mongolian features. This ethnic group was widely believed (given the ignorance of the times) to suffer from arrested development. The original essay was reprinted in *Mental Retardation* in February 1995. Down elaborated his views at much greater length in a later book entitled *Mental Affections of Children and Youth* (1887).

In the early 1960s this racist attribution was strongly criticized by Asian geneticists. Nevertheless, the racially and personally offensive terms 'mongoloid' and 'mongolism' continued to be widely used, well into the 1980s, before being dropped from clinical usage and replaced by *Down* or *Down's syndrome* (in the USA and UK respectively).

Diagnosis

Children with Down's syndrome (DS) exhibit wide variations in intellectual disability ranging from the mild to severe. DS is recognized at birth or soon after, because of the visibility of the child's physical attributes:

- small features and head size;
- a face that is broad and flat, with slanting eyes and a short nose;
- a tongue that tends to protrude;
- upwardly slanted eyes that have folds of skin at their inner corners;
- ears that are small and low set;
- hands that are short and broad, with a single crease across the palm;
- low muscle tone that affect the baby's movement and strength, fine hair and skin.

The child with DS is typically impaired intellectually to an extent that ranges from 'moderate' to 'severe' (IQs 30 to 70). DS occurs in about 1 in 700 births. The diagnosis of the syndrome can often be made before birth, and screening is generally recommended for pregnant women over the age of 35. Low levels of alpha-fetoprotein in the mother's blood indicate an increased risk of DS in the fetus; a sample of amniotic fluid can then be taken by amniocentesis for analysis to confirm the diagnosis. Using ultrasound scanning, a doctor can often identify physical abnormalities in the fetus. At birth, the infant with DS tend to be passive, and have somewhat limp muscles. A doctor confirms the diagnosis by testing the infant's blood for trisomy 21.

Clinical features

DS is the most widely known of the chromosomal anomalies. The first specula-
tions that DS might be due to chromosomal abnormalities were made public in
the 1930s. The empirical confirmation emerged in 1959 when Jerome Lejeune
and Patricia Jacobs, working independently, determined the cause to be trisomy
(triplication) of the 21st chromosome. The quantum leap forward in the understanding of these processes came with the publication in 2000 of the DNA
sequence of human chromosome 21.

Pathology associated with the brain of children with DS includes:

- a slightly smaller brain size for age;
- a shorter diameter for the anterior–posterior brain measurement;
- an unusually steep slope to the posterior portions of the brain;
- an insufficiently developed superior temporal gyrus (see Lott, 1995).

Developmental features

Following birth, children with DS show an atypical timescale for the emergence
and disappearance of certain reflexes. The question of whether these and other
developmental differences between DS and TD (typical development) are due to
delays or qualitative differences is unresolved, and some would say, a pointless
issue (Lewis, 2002).

Motor delays

Children with DS reach various motor milestones later than children with typical
development (TD), and may follow a different developmental path. The average
child with DS begins to walk at about 24 months of age, around 1 year later than
a typically developing child. This problem in discussed with other motor problems in Chapter 5.

Atlantoaxial dislocation

Atlantoaxial dislocation is a weakness of neck muscles that affects approximately
10 to 20 per cent of children with DS. It is a problem caused by hypotonia. The
individual is at risk of spinal chord compression and injury. Cervical spine instability occurs in 10 to 20 per cent of children with DS. If instability is present,
but there are no symptoms, the appropriate precaution is to be cautious about
activities (e.g. high-jumping, diving, gymnastics, and trampoline) which might
put an excessive strain on the neck.

Growth

As babies, children with DS may have difficulty sucking and chewing. Their growth, therefore, needs to be monitored and compared with DS growth charts.

Sleep disorders

Sleep disorders that interfere with having a restful night's sleep are common. Among the causes is sleep apnea (i.e. short periods of not breathing during sleep) which occurs frequently. Children with DS have small, often 'floppy' airways, which sometimes become completely or partially blocked during sleep; they have to wake up briefly to resume breathing.

Attachment/social development

See Chapter 4 on other attachment difficulties.

Visual development

Children with DS under 1 year of age, look at objects and people for longer than typically developing (TD) children of similar developmental level, before responding. This suggests the need for a longer time to process information. Their eventual reactions tend to be similar. Some 60 per cent suffer from ophthalmic disorders that may require treatment and regular eye checks. Near- and far-sightedness, as well as cataracts and strabismus (lazy eye), are commonplace.

Tactile development

The peripheral tactile abilities are slower than, and different from (not as good as) children with TD.

Language development

See Chapter 8 on communication.

Intellectual disability

The average IQ (intelligence quotient) in children with DS is reported to be around 50, compared with the general population average IQ of 100, as measured on intelligence tests. These instruments are far from satisfactory indicators of the functional status of people with DS. For example, children and adolescents with DS may have difficulty at school with syntax in grammar lessons, yet possess a good-sized personal vocabulary and converse intelligibly with their peers.

Many children with DS may attain IQs above 70 in their first year of life, however they decline as the youngster gets older, not as a result of a failure to develop, but because the rate of development does not keep up with their chronological age (see Lewis, 2002). Very many, nevertheless, will be integrated in mainstream schools (see Chapter 10). Schools will need to be aware of some difficulties the child with DS will have in the classroom.

Hearing problems

These occur frequently; there tend to be middle ear structural abnormalities that lead to hearing loss ranging from mild to moderate loss in 68 per cent of the children. Ear infections are particularly common. It is the role of an Ear Nose and Throat (ENT) specialist to manage treatable causes of hearing loss. Annual screening of hearing is recommended until the child is three years of age, and every other year after that age.

Attention problems

Attention Deficit/Hyperactivity Disorder (AD/HD) is a quite likely to be diagnosed as children with DS frequently suffer from reduced attention span, unfocused (non-directed) motor activity, impulsive behaviour, and excessive fidgeting. Dianne McBrien (1998) cautions against a 'too rapid' assumption that these symptoms necessarily indicate hyperactivity, as there are potentially misleading medical (e.g. overactive thyroid activity), communication and emotional problems to which these children are prone.

Where AD/HD has been diagnosed, the most common medication used to treat the condition is *Ritalin* (generic name *Methylphenidate*). Ritalin is generally not recommended when a child has a seizure disorder, Tourette syndrome or tics, or has poor gains in height and weight.

Emotional problems

The circumstances that typically cause children distress, such as loss and separation or frustration and anger resulting from personal limitations and social prejudice, may lead to disruptive behaviour at home and/or school.

Causation

Trisomy 21 is responsible for about 95 per cent of the cases of Down's syndrome, resulting from chromosomal non-disjunction. The most common trisomy in a newborn is trisomy 21, although other trisomies can also occur. The most common DS genotype is non-familial. In a small minority of cases the disorder

Table 9.1   Age of mother and risk of giving birth to DS baby

Age in years	Risk (%)
29	0.098
35	0.26
49	0.89
45	3.57
50	16.7

results from a translocation of a portion of chromosome 21 to other chromosomes. The translocation may be inherited.

Most chromosomal aberrations arise as a result of a disturbance in meiotic divisions known as non-disjunctive (failure to disjoin) and can occur in male and female alike. Chromosomal trisomy in DS is a result of this accident. The most frequent aberration occurs on the 21st chromosome; the resulting fertilized egg carries an extra third chromosome, hence the scientific term trisomy 21. The extra chromosome 21 comes from the father rather than from the mother in one fourth to one third of the cases. What is known is the existence of a definite link with maternal age. However, the cause of the non-disjunction error is unknown.

Risk

The risk of giving birth to a baby with DS varies with the mother's age, rising with advancing age in the mother-to-be, as illustrated in Table 9.1.

More than 20 per cent of the infants with DS are born to mothers over age 35, yet older mothers bear only 7 to 8 per cent of all children.

Environmental influences

The causal influence of environmental factors has been estimated to be between 0.7 and 11.2 per cent for individuals with severe ID and between 8.2 and 8.8 per cent for those with mild disabilities (McLaren and Bryson, 1987). The adverse influences include:

1   Maternal malnutrition.
2   Exposure to ingestion of drugs; by the mother.
3   Exposure to alcohol ingested by the mother (see Chapter 2 on fetal alcohol syndrome).
4   Maternal diseases during pregnancy (see McLaren and Bryson, 1987)

The most common maternal diseases during pregnancy are:

- neonatal herpes, which can affect the central nervous system;
- bacterial meningitis;
- toxoplasmosis, which destroys brain tissue, among other adverse effects;
- rubella;
- cytomegalovirus (CMV), a common virus with worldwide distribution is transmitted vertically (from mother to infant before, during, and after birth). It commonly causes infection (inflammation of brain tissue) during the perinatal period and during childhood. CMV differs from other well-known causes of fetal infection, such as rubella and toxoplasmosis, because they produce congenital infection only if the mother acquires the infection immediately before or during pregnancy.
- some 10 per cent of cases of severe intellectual disability are caused by perinatal influences, notably asphyxia (lack of oxygen), extreme low birthweight (prematurity), and abnormalities of the birth process (see Chapter 3).

Prognosis

Most children with DS survive to adulthood. Heart abnormalities are often treatable with drugs or surgery. Heart disease, respiratory diseases, and leukemia account for most deaths among children with DS. Although death can occur early, there are DS individuals who live long lives. Life expectancy for a child with mild or moderate retardation is 55 years; with profound mental retardation it is 45 years.

Seizures are no more common in young children with DS than in the general population. However, beginning at age 20 to 30 years, their incidence rises substantially in the DS population. There is speculation as to whether the increased frequency is related to the ageing of the brain. There is a suggestion that DS represents a systemic acceleration of the ageing process such that pathological changes which take four and more decades to develop in typically developing people, occur at young ages in individuals with the genetic disorder. Many have progressively worsening mental functioning.

Treatment

It is generally agreed that interventions to prevent and treat DS-related problems should be initiated at an early age, before overt symptoms become manifest or deteriorate. Issues of prevention are discussed on page 27.

Multidisciplinary Interventions

Certainly, when babies are identified as having DS, they are usually given a prompt multidisciplinary examination, assessing them across several physical, psychological, and social domains. This evaluation leads on to the formulation of a care plan and early intervention programme (see Kumin, 1986; Kumin, Goodman and Councill, 1991, 1996).

Medical input

- Neurology is important in the clinical care and treatment. Among the most common involvements of the nervous system, which is always affected in DS, are developmental disabilities such as retardation in intellectual and motor development (incomplete mastery of physical coordination), hypotonia, atlantoaxial dislocation and seizures (see below).
- There are no specific surgical or pharmaceutical treatments for DS. Regular medical care to treat the chronic health problems associated with DS is a priority. As we have seen, children with DS are predisposed to several bodily and medical problems. These require regular monitoring, along with vision and hearing testing. Their families benefit from advice on the medical implications of DS.

Strengthening exercises

Children with DS are thought to benefit from therapy involving exercising of muscles and faculties associated with motor skills and brain activity respectively. It is hoped that they will increase developmental ability. The available evidence suggests that initial short-term gains from such programmes have not translated into long-term improvement, notably cognitive gains (see Carr, 1992). Wishart (1991) states that our incomplete knowledge of the learning processes of children with DS undermines the design and planning of effective intervention programmes.

Physiotherapy

Gross motor movement programmes devised and supervised by occupational and physiotherapists are described in Chapter 5. Early intervention with physiotherapy, begun shortly after birth, has the most beneficial impact on a child with DS. For example, it can help strengthen muscles needed for basic motor skills. The purpose is not to accelerate the rate at which children with DS achieve their gross motor milestones; it is about assisting them to avoid, by learning optimal movement patterns proactively, the *abnormal* movements commonly used to compensate for their physical problems. If not corrected, these abnormal patterns may result in orthopaedic problems by adolescence which impair physical functioning.

Participation in community recreation programmes such as special physical education classes, dancing, and gymnastics are encouraged as they help children to develop social and physical skills, and self-confidence. Relations with the opposite sex are discussed in Chapter 13.

Occupational therapy (OT)

OTs may become involved in programmes:

- facilitating motor coordination by promoting arm and hand movements that are foundational for the later development of fine motor skills;
- encouraging the development of further fine motor skills – a vital and challenging stage because of the low muscle tone, decreased strength and joint ligament laxity referred to earlier;
- practising fine motor skill development for the classroom – providing programmes to teach them to print, write by hand, cut out, etc.;
- guiding the young child on how to play appropriately with toys and interact with other children; helping develop self-help skills at home and at school.

Speech therapy

Speech therapists may deal with problems associated with feeding. Hypotonia and weakness of the muscles of the cheeks, tongue and lips, make feeding difficult for some infants. They assist with oral-motor feeding problems by suggesting positioning and feeding techniques.

Psychosocial training

- *Clinical psychology:* although there is no cure for DS, children born with the condition can learn to lead productive lives. Basic knowledge of applied learning theory is essential for parents and professionals alike (see Chapter 4). Infants with the syndrome are able to learn basic skills like other children: sitting, walking, talking, self-care (such as toilet training and bathing), and self-control. But they tend to do so at a delayed pace. Parents are likely to find behavioural management courses helpful (see Herbert and Wookey, 2004).

- *Portage work*: Portage Workers have an important role in training parents and children how to develop (cooperatively) self-help and social skills. These are described in Chapter 16. The Plymouth (UK) group, under the direction of Jenny Wookey and Diane Davis, have trained parents (using the *Child-Wise Parenting Skills Manual*) to manage, more effectively, the noncompliant and other challenging behaviours displayed by disabled children (Herbert and Wookey, 2004).

Education

The Special Educational Needs and Disability Act (2001) reinforces the right of children in England and Wales and parts of Scotland who have physical or behavioural problems, to be educated in mainstream schools. Children with DS nowadays attend mainstream schools in growing numbers. This is not to say that they do not have special difficulties to overcome; for example, they have a wide range of learning styles. If material is presented in a way that is incompatible with a child's learning style – for example, oral lectures for a pupil who needs visual aids and prompts – he or she may become bored and fidgety.

The child's teachers may have to try out several methods of presenting material. Content, too, is critical. Learning becomes problematic if he or she is presented with concepts that are beyond their cognitive level. Children with DS (like other pupils) become bored if the learning material is incomprehensible, boring, or too simple, and may 'switch off' becoming inattentive or disruptive (see Howlin, 1994).

The Special Educational Needs and Disability Act makes it illegal to treat disabled pupils 'less favourably' than other pupils and requires schools to make 'reasonable adjustments' (for which funding was promised) so that disabled pupils are not put at a 'substantial disadvantage'. There are children and adolescents who need more support than their school can provide. In most cases this is dealt with in schools through an individual action plan. The local authority draws up a statement of special educational needs, which in most cases provides extra help of some kind in the school. Details of the procedure are provided in Appendix I.

Early Intervention Programmes

There are several early learning programmes using infant stimulation and parent education, designed to enhance the attainments of disabled and socially disadvantaged children (Carr, 2002). Among those for children aged between birth and 3 years, are the Portage Project Programme (see above). Carr (2002, p. 54) concluded a review of the early learning literature in infancy by stating that:

> programmes of intensive home visiting involving parent education and infant stimulation during children's early tears may prevent cognitive delay and lead to significant gains in intelligence, language development, and scholastic attainment; programmes that were particularly effective spanned the infant's first two years of life and involved at least weekly home visiting.

The Transition to School

■ Anxious Children at School

The definitions of 'play' and 'nursery' schools have become somewhat blurred in recent times in many parts of the UK. So, for the purposes of Chapter 10, it will be broadly children from around five or six years of age upwards, whose developmental progress and problems are considered. The prevalence of anxiety is high at times of transition, such as beginning school, or moving from pre-school to primary school and from primary to secondary school. We examine two specific school-related phobic fears: selective mutism and school phobia.

The question that inevitably arises is: 'When is fear really a problem?' After all, account has to be taken of how essentially 'normal' (i.e. commonplace and universal) fear can be. According to the DSM-IV, a specific phobia is characterized by the marked and persistent fear of circumscribed objects or situations (criterion A, p. 405). Specific fears are present in around 5 per cent of children from community settings and 15 per cent of those referred to outpatient centres or clinics.

Of course, fear is not entirely dysfunctional. Fear is an adaptive reaction to events in many circumstances, having survival and sometimes positive (reward) value. It enhances the individual's effectiveness in 'fight or flight' situations of extreme threat, or tones him or her up for peak performance in activities such as acting (stage fright), examinations, and athletic competitions. Parents also make use of the child's fear of the loss of approval, along with positive reinforcement, as incentives to ensure compliance and the internalization of rules and values.

These considerations underline the importance of context and a developmental criterion for judging the abnormality of fear and anxiety. The parameters that separate behaviours defined as 'phobic' require the question: 'Is the fear proportionate to the objective threat inherent in a particular situation?' And: 'Is the expression of fear appropriate to a child of his/her age and maturity?' The answers will separate phobic fear from the anxieties, avoidance, fears, indecisiveness, and obsessions shown by all children at one time or another, as will their frequency, intensity, their duration and pervasiveness. Clearly, assessment of specific phobias is necessarily multimodal with information drawn from several sources.

Methods of treating school fears are described in Chapter 10.

■ Generalized Anxiety Disorders

Generalized anxiety disorder is characterized by at least several months of persistent and excessive anxiety and worry. The 'age of anxiety' was a rather dramatic metaphor for the psychological and social insecurities of adult life in the twentieth century. In the new millennium, this epithet becomes more and more apposite to the world of childhood and adolescence. Gone, it would seem, for today's children, is that 'golden age' (at least as their parents or grandparents like to describe it) of the safe, carefree, and innocent pleasures associated with growing up. Of course, one has only to read Charles Dickens and Jack London to appreciate how many children from another age had their childhood 'stolen' by grim exploitation and deprivation. But there seems to be a different quality about the insecurity, which I have called 'existential anxiety', restricting the lives of many contemporary children.

What bears down most heavily on them and their concerned parents, is a sense of living in an unsafe world, one in which violence, bullying at school, and outside the school gates, is commonplace. School authorities often seem ineffectual at controlling the intimidation and sale of drugs. What else but worry (for immature, impressionable minds) is likely to be the response to the images of coercive sex and violence, hatred and hostility, they witness in daily TV news items and television drama?

On the streets, adult strangers are not people to turn to as providers of protection when parents are not available, but thought of as potential sources of danger. Abuse of various kinds undoubtedly existed in previous eras, but the consciousness of its existence and prevalence, is drummed into the minds of children – not surprisingly when the names of many thousands of children under 18 years of age appear on the Child Protection Register in England (see Herbert, 2000). The 1996 Commission of Inquiry into the Prevention of Child Abuse found that each year in the UK 500,000 children suffer severe physical assault, up to

100,000 children have a potentially harmful sexual experience, and 400,000 children live in an environment which is 'consistently low in warmth and high in criticism'.

In the course of normal development and the world of mental health clinics the pervasive, often vague, anxieties I referred to as 'existential anxieties' are more focused, individual, and psychologically distressingly real. Such anxieties, when part of normal development may dissipate like so-called 'growing pains', as the child gets older. Those that are more extreme and debilitating they are likely to require clinic-based treatment. This will be a theme of Chapter 11.

■ Children with Educational and Physical Disabilities at School

The differing needs generated by children with educational and/or physical disabilities require different types of educational provision. The UK government has made it clear that it wishes to see more children with special needs entering mainstream schools. Indeed, the majority are now educated in mainstream primary and secondary schools. But who are these children with 'special needs'? Some are youngsters with a physical disability (e.g. deafness) that hinders or prevents them from being able to use the amenities ordinarily provided for their contemporaries. In the widest sense, however, the term 'special educational needs' applies to all those (e.g. children with dyslexia or specific language disorder) whom the school considers would benefit from extra (perhaps specialist) assistance with their studies. A government code of practice offers practical guidance to all local education authorities and state schools in England on how to identify, assess and monitor such pupils (see Appendix III). These themes are discussed in Chapter 12.

CHAPTER 10

Anxious Children at School

The prevalence of anxiety is high at times of transition, such as moving from pre-school to primary school and from primary to secondary school.

■ Selective Mutism (SM)

The child who *elects* to remain silent in the presence of others, or (more accurately) *selects* to whom he or she will talk, is a relatively recent arrival in the clinical literature. Kratochwill (1981) suggested that the earlier diagnostic term 'elective mutism', should be replaced by 'selective mutism' (SM) because these children are reported to have age-appropriate speech development, but appear 'stuck' at a stage of development characterized by excessive shyness (i.e. 2 to 3 years of age). Selective silence appears to be fairly rare difficulty which tends to occur mainly at school. It represents a formidable problem to the classroom teacher (Baldwin, 1985).

Causation

Several studies (e.g. Sluckin, Foreman and Herbert, 1990) have attempted to isolate individual and demographic factors associated with, and possibly predisposing children to, selective mutism. Children with SM have been exposed to greater family discord and a greater number of environmental stressors than controls. Moreover, they frequently come from families with a history of some form of psychopathology. A useful review of the background literature to SM is provided by Standart and Le Couteur, 2003).

▨ Interventions

Reed (1968) was possibly the first to propose that SM might be a learned pattern of behaviour, thus a child's pattern of selective communication might be better understood following a functional analysis of the frequency of talking (speech) in relation to particular situations and/or individuals. Adults (teachers in particular), in response to a selectively mute child's silence, often tend to adopt a pattern of verbal interaction which reinforces simple, non-verbal responses, while peers, in contrast, do not speak, or simply reduce their interaction with the child.

Child and Mental Health Services (CAMHS) have little opportunity to work with children who have SM because of its low incidence. Persistent SM is difficult to treat (Kolvin and Fundudis, 1981). The most promising intervention appears to be a behavioural approach. In 1999 Joseph published a review of treatment options for selective mutism. He concluded that:

> Accepted current therapy combines behaviour modification, family participation, school involvement and possible pharmacology for the treatment of selective mutism. It is likely that even after the mutism is cured the child is apt to suffer symptoms of shyness and social anxiety into adolescence and adulthood. This would suggest that the therapist's role should not end when the child achieves speech in school.

■ School Refusal

Given our concern in this chapter with the transition to school life, this problem is particularly relevant. Among 11- and 12-year-olds, worries associated with school are nearly half as many again as worries about home matters. The most common manifestation of anxiety in children are the refusal to attend school, and fear of being separated from parents and home.

Most children experience periods when they don't wish to go to school. Granted that many children seek to avoid facing a difficult situation at school by feigning illness, this commonplace reluctance is very different to school refusal where the child misses going to school for many days (sometimes weeks or months).

Diagnosis

Reluctance or refusal to attend school often leading to prolonged absence:

- The child usually remains at home during school hours, rather than concealing the problem from parents.
- Displays of emotional upset at the prospect of attending school (excessive fearfulness, temper tantrums, misery) or possibly physical symptoms.
- Reasonable parental efforts to secure the child's attendance at some stage in the history of the problem.

'School withdrawal' is the name given to parental ambivalence or opposition toward the child attending school regularly.

Heyne, Rollings et al. (2002) list the following differences between *school phobia* (more appropriately referred to as *school refusal*) and *truancy*, the other major non-attendance problem:

- Children who 'truant' generally attempt to conceal non-attendance from the family, whereas the parents of children who are 'school-refusers' are well aware of the non-attendance.
- The truant may start out for school in the morning, but fail to arrive there or absent herself during the day; in contrast the school-refuser tends to remain at home.
- Whereas the truant's non-attendance is usually intermittent, the school-refuser may be away from school for weeks or months at a time.
- The truant is often a poor student who dislikes school; the school-refuser is generally a capable student with vocational goals requiring study at school; children who refuse to attend school are usually capable but self-critical students.
- Truancy often involves anti-social behaviour; school-refusers seldom display anti-social behaviour.
- Truants are more often diagnosed as having a conduct disorder rather than the type of emotional disorder commonly associated with school refusal.

Causation

A broad range of precipitating factors associated with the home, the school, and the individual may contribute to the development of school refusal (King, Ollendick and Tonge, 1995; King, Hamilton and Ollendick, 1998), notably:

- the transition from primary school to secondary school;
- illness in a family member;
- other family stresses such as moving home or parental separation; Many children experience emotional distress brought about by the break-up of their homes, often following long and bitter conflict between parents they love.

Fear of some aspect of the school environment such as doing tests, social rejection or isolation, or having to use the school toilets.

- the child's vulnerability as a consequence of biological or environmental factors. For example, the temperament of some children may predispose them to the development of anxiety;
- the parents of school-refusers sometimes experience considerable anxiety or depression, or they experience marital/cohabiting failure, thus contributing to the vulnerability of their offspring at school;
- a very distressed parent may be unable to provide adequate support to the young person at critical times, and thus may fail to help him or her cope with regular attendance;
- the child's perception of his or her ability to cope with school. For example, students who are unsure of their capacity to establish close friendships or to fulfil academic requirements, may wish to avoid school;
- distress resulting from the inexorable pressure on children to achieve academically, an understandable, if undesirable, survival strategy by parents who perceive the diminishing job opportunities available to their offspring.

Treatment

Many cases of school refusal can be worked out successfully over time without psychological or psychiatric counselling, given sympathetic management by the school. If all the 'common-sense' options have failed, a GP or educational psychologist can arrange therapy for the child and family.

There have been many forms of psycho-social treatment applied to SR: psychodynamic psychotherapy, play therapy, and family therapy – all of unproven effectiveness (see Heyne, King and Tonge, 2004). Treatments based on *exposure principles* are the preferred intervention for children exhibiting simple and social phobias (Ollendick, Davis and Muris, 2004). Systematic desensitization is efficacious (Ginsberg and Walkup, 2004). The method consists of three basic steps: (i) progressive relaxation training; (ii) development of a fear-provoking stimuli hierarchy; and (iii) the systematic graduated pairing of situations in the hierarchy (different aspects of school attendance) with relaxation. A large number of controlled and uncontrolled single-case studies, and a number of group studies evaluating systematic desensitization to a variety of phobias, have established the credibility of this procedure.

With exposure methods like *in vivo desensitization* the child is gradually exposed to real-life anxiety-provoking situations instead of to imaginal stimuli. The crucial benefit seems to stem from enabling the child gradually to encounter the situation which triggers the fear. He or she then learns step-by-step that the anticipated threat does *not* materialize. This has to be a carefully planned and timed process. It is often beneficial if the child sees the therapist (or another child on video) carrying out the feared activity. This has of course to be performed in a way that is perceived as supportive of the person – not in a way which makes them feel even more inadequate. This method has been used successfully to treat fears of separation and school attendance and also difficulties with social situations (Heyne, King and Tonge, 2004; Ollendick and King, 2004).

Cognitive behaviour therapy (CBT) is another empirically supported method (Heyne, Rollings et al., 2002; Kendall and Gosch, 1994). There is a detailed treatment manual for CBT with children published by Kendall and Hollon (1994). The primary goals of CBT with anxious children are described on page 159.

A typical programme

The child is encouraged to return to school and attend daily, perhaps for graduated periods of time working in quiet areas like the library. Each morning the child may continue to complain of various physical 'symptoms' that worsen as the time to leave for school approaches (and, incidentally vanish if parents relent and lift the pressure to go to school). However, the 'contract' negotiated with the parents and child requires that he or she is sent to school. It sometimes helps him/her to travel to school with one or more school friends. Confidence usually returns if particular aspects of the child's fear (e.g. bullying or problems at home such as domestic violence) are dealt with.

It is vital to enlist the help of the special needs teacher who can reinforce the efforts made to return to school. The teacher needs to be involved in planning the programme and facilitating it, notably by avoiding in the early stages, fear-provoking activities (e.g. standing in front of the class to read). Where bullying has contributed to the SR as it frequently does, the school's policy on bullying and protective strategies for vulnerable children will have to be discussed. There is a successful 'whole school' approach which achieved a 50 per cent reduction in reported bullying (Olweus et al., 1999).

CHAPTER 11

Generalized Anxiety Disorders

■ 'Normal' Fears and Anxieties

Fear, as we have seen above, is a natural if unpleasant response to events which are threatening to personal security. In fact, it is a vital *adaptive reaction*, which every mother makes use of in training her child to avoid dangers. It can also be adaptive in preparing the person to cope with emergency situations. In such crises, the client experiences a variety of physical sensations such as a pounding heart, shivering and trembling, butterflies in the stomach, dry mouth and perspiring hands. These reactions are due to physiological mechanisms built into the body, and processed by the 'autonomic nervous system'. The physical sensations are by-products of the changes in body chemistry which take place as adrenaline is released into the blood-stream. This outpouring of adrenalin keeps the system toned up for maximum efficiency of the body, until the crisis has passed.

Emergency systems

The human being's appraisals of threat are essentially personal. He or she responds to perceived danger or threat by:

- *fighting* – an aggressive response, to deal by combat with potential threat;
- *fleeing* – a retreat designed to avoid potential threat;
- *freezing* – an alert, but immobile, response, in the hope of escaping the attention of the potential threat.

In modern times it is usually the symbols of danger, rather than real life-endangering threat, to which the body's emergency system reacts. This means that the crisis physical reactions are inhibited and are not resolved in active, vigorous physical activity. If the stress is repetitive and the physical reactions thus 'chronic', we would get a situation in which previously adaptive reactions become dysfunctional and contribute to psychosomatic illness (e.g. hypertension, ulcers, asthma).

If infants and young children experience separation from their mother; later, they tend to be fearful of events that occur in their immediate presence (e.g. animals, imaginary creatures such as monsters, the dark, storms). Fears of bodily injury, physical danger, loss, natural hazards, and anxieties about school performance and social interactions increase as the child gets older in the middle school years and adolescence (e.g. fear of failure, social relationships, physical danger, and death). The reasons for these stage-related changes continue to be debated.

■ Clinical Anxiety (Generalized) Disorders

Diagnosis

Generalized anxiety disorders (GADs) are characterized by at least several months of persistent and excessive anxiety and worry. Worry is the cognitive process during anxiety states that aims to prepare an individual for future threat; in GAD it has reached excessive and uncontrollable proportions.

The main symptoms are:

- distress and agitation when separated from parent and home;
- school refusal;
- pervasive worry and fearfulness;
- restlessness and irritability;
- timidity, shyness, social withdrawal;
- terror of particular objects;
- associated headache, stomach pains;
- restless sleep and nightmares;
- poor concentration, distractibility and learning problems;
- reliving stressful event in repetitive play/dreams.

Clinical features

Four separate systems make up the anxiety response:

- *physiological*: the person's response via the autonomic nervous system – adrenaline is secreted, heart rate increases, sugars flow to the muscles;

- *behavioural*: the person's observable behaviours;
- *affective*: the person's experience and feelings;
- *cognitive*: the person's *self-statement* (what a person thinks/says about and to him- or herself) ('I can't cope with this').

These systems are not neatly synchronized one with another i.e. changes in one system are not immediately reflected by changes in the others.

Epidemiology

GADs are among the most prevalent forms of psychopathology during childhood and adolescence. In childhood 2 to 10 per cent of children under 12 years of age experience a clinical anxiety condition, with these rates increasing to between 15 and 20 per cent in adolescence (see review by Ollendick, King and Yule, 1994; Ollendick and March, 2004).

Causation

Anxiety may be learned or elicited by the following processes:

- *the appraisal of threat* – e.g. separation in young children, distressing life events, conditions of living or work, family relationships especially during childhood, and physical illnesses manifesting themselves with an anxiety component;
- *classical conditioning* – the pairing of a previously neutral stimulus with a situation of pain or fear;
- *modelling* – the person perceives others whom he or she perceives as being like him or herself behaving in an anxious way. This person acts as a model for the acquisition of anxiety.
- *traumatic learning* – an experience of intense fear or pain can lead to acute anxiety being experienced in similar subsequent situations, e.g. following a road accident;
- *generalization of learned anxiety to other settings* – e.g. a person who suffered humiliation in a test at school may experience acute anxiety doing a driving test;
- *vicarious learning* – a person may become fearful through seeing someone else undergoing a fearful event;
- *cognitive processes* – the highly individual way in which people perceive situations is crucial in understanding anxiety. Some people typically see danger in

situations which are simply stimulating or routine to others, e.g. having an argument or travelling by aeroplane.

Treatment

The evidence from well-designed research studies (e.g. Barrett, Dadds and Rapee, 1996; Kendall and Hollon, 1994) suggests that cognitive-behaviour interventions are the treatment of choice for serious GADs. The primary goals of CBT with anxious children are:

- the management of the anxiety;
- reduction of the child's distress;
- increasing the child's mastery and coping skills.

Children are helped to detect early signs and triggers of anxious arousal, and then to utilize these cues as signals for initiating active cognitive and behavioural coping strategies, by means of relaxation and self-instruction. They are coached in self-reinforcement to manage to produce successful coping strategies.

Integrated psychosocial and pharmacological treatment

March and Ollendick (2004, p. 142), in a review of combined psychosocial and pharmacological treatments, comment that 'the past 40 years have seen the emergence of diverse, sophisticated, empirically-supported, cognitive-behavioural, and pharmacological interventions that cover the range of childhood-onset anxiety disorders'. Many clinicians and researchers now believe that the combination of disorder-specific cognitive-behaviour therapy (CBT) and medication administered in an evidence-based, disease-management model is the initial treatment of choice for many if not most children and adolescents with diagnosable anxiety disorders.

Panic disorder

People often do not recognize anxiety for what it is, and may misinterpret the physiological changes they are experiencing, pounding heart, headaches, changes in breathing, as evidence of insanity. This can set up a vicious spiral of *increasing* anxiety, so that people become 'afraid of being afraid' (see Mattis and Ollendick, 2002, for a discussion of theory and practice).

■ Obsessive Compulsive Disorders

Diagnosis

The *Diagnostic and Statistical Manual of the American Psychiatric Association* (DSM-IV) defines obsessions as follows:

- recurrent and persistent thoughts, impulses or images that are experienced, at some time during the disturbance, as intrusive and inappropriate and that cause marked anxiety or distress;
- the thoughts, impulses, or images are not simply excessive worries about real-life problems;
- the person attempts to ignore or suppress such thoughts, impulses, or images, or to neutralize them with some other thought or action;
- the person recognizes that the obsessional thoughts, impulses, or images are a product of his or her own mind (not imposed from without as in thought insertion).

The DSM-IV defines compulsions as:

- repetitive behaviours (e.g. hand washing, ordering, checking) or mental acts (e.g. praying, counting, repeating words silently) that the person feels driven to perform in response to an obsession, or according to rules that must be applied rigidly;
- the behaviours or mental acts are aimed at preventing or reducing distress or preventing some dreaded event or situation; however, these behaviours or mental acts either are not connected in a realistic way with what they are designed to neutralize or prevent or are clearly excessive.

The DSM-IV classification also requires that the obsessions or compulsions cause marked distress, are time-consuming (take more than 1 hour per day), or significantly interfere with the person's normal routine, occupational (or academic) functioning, or usual social activities. At some point during the course of the disorder, the person has recognized that the obsessions or compulsions are excessive or unreasonable (this does not apply to children).

Clinical features

The clinician should meet with the child and ask specific questions about obsessions and compulsions. He or she should also meet with parents or other primary caregivers. The parents and usually the child may also fill out checklists such as the YBOCS (Yale–Brown Obsessive Compulsive Scale). They determine the baseline number and severity of the symptoms. Information from school and other outside sources is useful. OCD can be associated with other disorders which need to be enquired about.

Causation

There have been several theories about the cause of OCD, including psychodynamic, learning and neurobiological theories.

Psychodynamic theories

Sigmund Freud classified obsessive compulsive disorder as a psychoneurosis. The roots of the illness lay in a disturbance in the psychosexual development of the child (Lee and Herbert, 1970).

Biological theories

Most recent research studies point toward a biological basis for OCD. PET scans (showing levels of brain activity in specific areas.) have shown increased activity in the sub-orbital cortex (the underside of the front part of the brain) and abnormality in the basal ganglia. When patients are successfully treated, the brain scan studies resemble those individuals without OCD. Serotonin seems to be involved in mediating the interaction between these two parts of the brain.

Co-morbidity

Some cases of OCD may be associated with Tourette's syndrome. Tourette's syndrome is characterized by multiple tics. (involuntary rapid movement or vocalization) Individuals with Tourette's may also have OCD symptoms, and attention deficit disorder (see Chapter 12).

Children and adolescents with OCD tend to have AD/HD, learning disorders, oppositional behaviour, separation anxiety disorder and other anxiety disorders. Some of the anxiety disorders have similarities to OCD and are called obsessive-compulsive spectrum disorders. These include:

- trichotillomania, (compulsive hair pulling and twirling);
- body dysmorphic disorder (the obsession that part of one's body is unattractive or misshapen);
- habit disorders such as nail biting and scab picking.

Treatment

If not treated, OCD tends to be a long-term disorder. Some individuals experience waxing and waning symptoms over the years. Others experience progressive
worsening of their OCD, leading to depression. When children spend too much
time obsessing or engaging in rituals, they have trouble focusing on schoolwork
or, conversely spend hours of time on homework and be unable to finish projects
because the work is never quite satisfactory.

There are various psychodynamic, play therapy and family therapy approaches
to the treatment of OCD. I will focus on medication and cognitive-behavioural
psychotherapy.

Behaviour therapy

The results of using behaviour therapy for the distressing, and once seemingly
intractable symptoms of OCD, have established its pre-eminence for adults and
children. At the early stages of therapy the child and family are informed about
the biological basis of OCD, so that they find it easier to externalize the problem.
The symptoms are the fault of the disease, not the individual or family. The child
is strongly encouraged to refrain from ritualizing, with support and structure provided by the therapist, and possibly by parents. The method involves the child
or adolescent deliberately and voluntarily confronting the feared object or idea,
either directly or in imagination. As the therapy progresses, the child begins to
expose him/herself to the anxiety-provoking object or situation while trying
to avoid performing the usual compulsive acts. Treatment proceeds on a step-
by-step basis, guided by the patient's ability to tolerate the anxiety and control
the rituals.

This 'exposure and response prevention' has to be done gradually because it is
likely to cause youngsters significant anxiety. The child is given an important role
in determining how quickly s/he is able to progress through these steps.

A more rigorous example (perhaps for a mature adolescent) might be a compulsive hand washing ritual. The patient is encouraged to touch an object believed
to be contaminated, and then urged to avoid washing for several hours until the
anxiety provoked has greatly decreased. The child may benefit from learning relaxation techniques and learning mental self-monitoring to help tolerate the
anxiety engendered by the exposure and response prevention.

When symptoms are eliminated or at least reduced to a tolerable level, the
therapist needs to discuss the future outlook with the child and parents. Symptoms may reappear at a later date and require pre-emptive coping strategies.

Cognitive-behaviour therapy (CBT)

A more cognitively based therapeutic perspective emphasizes changing the patient's beliefs and thought patterns. It is suggested that obsessions persist as long as such misinterpretations continue. The phenomenology of the disorder incorporates cognitive distortions involving risk appraisal and responsibility, which are changed by various cognitive-behavioural strategies (see page 205). An excellent review of the literature is available in Francis and Gragg (1996).

Combined pharmacological treatment (clomipramine) and CBT

Many clinicians prefer to start treatment with behavioural or cognitive-behavioural psychotherapy. If there is no response or only a partial response, medication may then be added. March, Mulle and Herbel (1994) combined a pharmacological treatment (clomipramine) with a cognitive behavioural programme including individual and parent training elements for 15 children and adolescents with OCD. (See also March and Mulle, 1998.) Some 80 per cent showed substantial clinical improvement at the end of the intervention and 56 per cent were asymptomatic at 18 months follow-up. Unfortunately the absence of a control weakens this encouraging finding.

There are difficulties of implementing programmes which use combined pharmacological (SSRIs) and psychological (exposure and CBT) with adolescents. OCD is certainly a disorder which tests the skill and endurance of the therapist as it does (the latter notably) of the patient.

CHAPTER 12

Children with Educational and Physical Disabilities at School

■ Educational Difficulties

Specific Learning Difficulties

The term 'specific learning difficulties' (SLDs) refers to problems involving particular areas of cognitive functioning. In America they constitute the highest number (between 4 and 5 per cent) of school children requiring special educational assistance (American Academy of Child and Adolescent Psychiatry, 1998); the need is also high in the UK. There tend to be specific associations between learning difficulties and behaviour problems, with correlations between (i) reading disabilities and disorders of conduct and attention; and (ii) between mathematical difficulties and internalizing disorders, notably in girls (e.g. Prior, Smart et al., 1999).

Specific Reading Difficulties (SRD)

Severe difficulties with reading, spelling, writing and arithmetic reflect educational rather than medical criteria. SRD is a developmental problem (usually found in boys) which is fairly common. When using a criterion of two standard deviations (or about two years) below expected reading age, it was found in some 10 per cent of inner-London children (Berger, Yule and Rutter, 1975). The implications for these children are serious. A child's inability to read with understanding is a major obstacle to other aspects of school learning. And if not attended to, this can have far-reaching adverse social and economic consequences in later life. Children with SRD:

- tend to be clumsy;
- have concentration difficulties;
- are delayed in their speech development;
- suffer from motor problems;
- tend to have arithmetic and spelling problems
- experience emotional difficulties, and notably
- exhibit anti-social behaviour (in a third of severely impaired readers).

Certain of the symptoms of SRD can be detected during early childhood through the use of screening techniques by educational specialists.

Causes are multi-factorial, and include:

- deprived home situations;
- inadequate teaching;
- lack of home–school cooperation;
- genetic influences.

Remedial treatment

The school psychological service (e.g. educational psychologists) and remedial education services (e.g. special educational needs coordinators; remedial teachers) are the major sources of interventions for children with academic skill deficits. No single educational approach is applicable to all children with reading difficulties (Maughan and Yule, 1994).

The research evidence reviewed by Angela Fawcett (2002) suggests that there is a critical time for intervention. The most effective approach would be to identify children as 'at risk' in the early years of school, and provide them with a short structured intervention. Various studies make it clear that providing support in early school life is much more successful than waiting for children to fall behind, before intervening. This early support is likely to accelerate the literacy skills of a majority of children with SRD, leaving relatively few whose difficulties are intractable. These, it is thought, could then be followed up with a longer intensive intervention targeted on the particular difficulties of an individual child. This approach, by providing carefully designed treatment for the children with the really serious difficulties, should prove not only successful, but also cost-effective.

Dyslexia

Dyslexia is a subset of the reading disabilities above, and it is a contentious concept. Not everyone believes in 'dyslexia' as an independent category of reading disability (see Maughan and Yule, 1994). Nevertheless it is frequently discussed in the educational literature as a separate entity, and as a common developmental problem affecting 3 to 10 per cent of school children (Reason, 2001). The problem is far more common in societies that have phonetic rather than pictorial scripts. Early diagnosis is regarded, as with most if not all developmental disorders, as essential. Once a child is shown to have defects in the processing of visual symbols, appropriate remedial teaching may help the child to avoid the common accompaniments of difficulties in reading and writing: a loss of self-esteem and an image of being a 'failure'.

Although eyes are necessary for vision, seeking causes of dyslexia in abnormalities of the eyes will not identify any. It is the brain that encodes visual stimuli, resulting in visual perception. Indeed, children with or without dyslexia have the same incidence of ocular problems such as refractive errors and muscle imbalance. There are no peripheral eye defects that cause the reversal of letters, words or numbers. Nevertheless, because clues in word recognition are transmitted through the eyes to the brain, it remains a quite common practice to attribute reading difficulties to subtle ocular abnormalities.

Interventions

The remediation of dyslexia begins with a multidisciplinary assessment carried out by, *inter alia*, educational and reading specialists. It does not seem to matter whether children are taught remedially as individuals, in small groups, or as a class. The timing of the intervention is more critical than the type of intervention. The evidence suggests that an early intervention with a range of methods can reduce the severity of children's disabilities, allowing some to keep pace with their peers, and others to improve to a milder category of deficit (see Fawcett et al., 2001).

An eclectic mixed remedial 'package' linking sounds and letters produces the best overall results. As their reading skills develop, guided oral repeated reading is more successful than simply practising silent reading. Studies involving lengthy interventions for 25 hours or more (e.g. the Wise group, which is known for experimental rigour) tend to be low in cost effectiveness, notably for children over seven years of age with recognized disabilities.

Specific Language Impairment (SLI)

In SLI, language development is abnormal, although development is usually normal in other areas. The prevalence rate is about 7 per cent. Problems with language structure are common. There is a high rate of undiagnosed SLI, especially among children referred to clinics for behaviour problems. There is no obvious physical cause. However, short-term memory is poorer in SLI children than in typically developing (TD) children. Family aggregation studies reveal a strong genetic influence in SLI, possibly operating through some type of neuronal mechanism. Environmental factors possibly escalate the risk for SLI, eventually 'pushing' some vulnerable children into a full expression of the disorder.

Treatment

Speech and language therapists work with children who suffer from SLIs. There are sceptical views about the effectiveness of speech therapy and remedial education in producing durable and generalizable results. (e.g. Lyon and Cutting, 1998; Maughan and Yule, 1994), but also more optimistic opinions (Law, Boyle et al., 1998). The results of combined investigations of speech therapy outcomes for early speech and language delays (methodologically uneven studies reviewed by Law et al., ibid.), give median effect sizes of around 1.0. The average treated child might move from the 5th to the 25th percentile on a standard language test. The improvement of expressive language yielded higher effect sizes than those for receptive difficulties (i.e. comprehension).

Physical Disorders

Bronchial Asthma

Diagnosis

Illnesses involving pulmonary functions are the most common chronic diseases of childhood, and bronchial asthma is the most common respiratory ailment It is a lung disorder that can develop at any age. During 'attacks' of asthma the bronchioles (breathing passages) of the lungs are obstructed. The typical pattern is periodic attacks of wheezing, alternating with periods of relatively normal breathing.

Clinical features

Because asthma involves resistance, or obstruction to exhaled air, it is called an 'obstructive lung disease'. The medical term for such lung conditions is *chronic obstructive pulmonary disease* (COPD). COPD is a group of diseases that also includes chronic bronchitis and emphysema.

Asthma attacks can last minutes to days, and may be life-threatening if the airflow becomes severely restricted. The frequency and severity of asthma attacks tend to decrease as an individual gets older; some children 'outgrow' the illness. Symptoms can occur spontaneously, or be triggered by respiratory infections, exercise, cold air, or tobacco smoke. Particular attacks or phases of the illness can be precipitated or prolonged by psychological stresses involving anger, conflict, separation anxiety and fear.

Chronic asthma gives rise to many personal and social costs. It is:

- a major cause of school absence and academic under-achievement;
- one of the most common reasons for admission to hospital emergency departments and in-patient hospitalization.

Epidemiology

- The ailment affects all races.
- It affects all ages, although it is most common in younger people.
- It is the most common chronic disease of children, affecting 1 in 10 children.

Causal mechanisms

Risk factors include a personal; or family history of eczema, allergies, or family history of the disease itself. Personality predispositions (e.g. anxiety, repressed hostility) and dysfunctional parenting (e.g. over-protective, ambivalent mothering) have been posited, but neither confirmed as specific to the illness (Herbert, 1965). Asthmatic episodes are caused by chronic (long-term) inflammation of the airways. This results in the bronchioles of the child being highly sensitive to various precipitants or 'triggers'. When the inflammation is 'triggered' by a variety of external and internal factors, the bronchioles become constricted (bronchospasms), producing narrowing of the airways. This constriction makes it difficult for air to be exhaled from the lungs, and the obstruction to exhaling leads to the typical symptoms of an asthma attack.

Treatment

Unlike other chronic obstructive lung diseases, asthma is reversible, in the sense that although incurable (unless 'growing out of it' constitutes a 'cure'), it can be controlled. There is a better chance of managing asthma if it is diagnosed early and treatment begun promptly. With appropriate medical and (where indicated) psychological treatment, children with asthma tend to suffer less frequent and less severe attacks.

A variety of medications for the treatment of asthma are available and include:

- anti-inflammatory medications (inhaled corticosteroids, e.g. Becotide – used to prevent attacks, not for treatment during an attack);
- bronchodilators (inhaled, e.g. Ventolin);
- steroids (taken orally).

Children with infrequent attacks use inhalers on an 'as-required' basis. Those with significant asthma (symptoms that occur at least weekly) are generally treated with anti-inflammatory medications and additionally, bronchodilators. Severe asthmatic (unremitting, exhausting) attacks may require hospitalization, oxygen, and intravenous drugs. In the absence of treatment, sufferers are likely to suffer frequent and more intense/prolonged attacks which could prove fatal (e.g. status asthmaticus).

Prevention

A peak flow meter (which measures lung volume) can be used at home to check on lung functions on a daily basis. The communication of clear information to parents and child about the nature of the illness and its treatment, in addition to emotional support and advice about child management (where appropriate), can reduce parent–child conflict, parental over-protectiveness, maternal depression, and other problems secondary to the illness. According to a review by Lehrer et al. (1992), psycho-educational approaches (that go beyond the mere imparting of knowledge) also produce:

- increased medicatiom compliance;
- greater perceived self-competence in managing asthmatic symptoms, and
- decreased use of medical services.

(See also: Evans and Mellins, 1991)

If these measures fail, referral for more intensive investigations at a CAMHS (Child and Adolescent Mental Health Service) or Paediatric Assessment Centre, is advisable. Family therapy has been applied to cases of bronchial asthma, with mixed results (see Lask and Matthew, 1979). A behavioural (functional) analysis may provide clues to the contingencies (controlling stimuli) that precede as triggers, or follow as reinforcers, particular attacks of asthma.

Environmental hazards

A potent preventive strategy is to reduce exposure to known allergens by staying away from cigarette smoke, removing animals from bedrooms or entire households, avoiding food products that cause symptoms and pungent odours. Allergy desensitization is rarely successful. Preventive measures will require action on some of these difficult, if not intractable issues:

- Children grow up with less exposure to infection than did previous generations, a fact that which has left their immune systems more sensitive/reactive.
- The air children breathe in as passive smokers (along with petrol and diesel oil odours, etc) is more polluted than the air inhaled by previous generations (see Herbert, 1967).
- Children (addicted to computer games and TV shows) spend more time indoors, where they are exposed to indoor allergens such as house dust (mites) and mould.
- Their lifestyle has led to them taking less vigorous exercise, walking or bicycling to school giving way for many children, to 'safer' car transport, becoming (in the process only too often) victims of obesity, a condition which contributes to asthma attacks.

■ Neurological and Neuro-Developmental Disorders

Motor clumsiness, problems with handedness and fine motor difficulties (e.g., gripping a ballpoint pen) might indicate a neuro-developmental problem such as cerebral palsy. They are often associated with attention deficit/hyperactivity disorder (AD/HD), learning problems and low self-esteem, and require further neurological assessment. Children with cerebral palsy (CP) and other brain disorders have a substantially higher rate of psychiatric problems than do children with chronic disorders or disabilities that are not secondary to brain abnormality – suggesting the existence of direct brain–behaviour links, in addition to any indirect effects of chronic disability and stigmatization. The psychiatric/psychological problems of childhood hemiplegia are persistent as well as common (see Goodman, 1998, 2002). Similarly, the psychological problems that accompany AD/HD (a condition with undoubted brain-related determinants) support my choice of the term neuro-psychological to categorize the disorder dealt with next.

Attention Deficit Hyperactivity Disorder (AD/HD)

Diagnosis

Official guidelines for a diagnosis of AD/HD (also referred to sometimes as ADD, Hyperactivity or Hyperkinesis), suggest that the key features are overactivity and impaired attention – problems that show themselves in more than one situation (for example, home, classroom, clinic, etc.). Waldron and Kern-Jones (2004, p. 321) conclude an extensive review of AD/HD by stating that 'at present it appears that AD/HD should be thought of and treated as a chronic disorder, that requires ongoing treatment over the course of development'.

Symptoms

- *Overactivity.* This implies excessive restlessness, especially in situations requiring relative calm. It may, depending upon the situation, involve the child running and jumping around, getting up from a seat when he or she was supposed to remain seated, excessive talkativeness and noisiness, or fidgeting and wriggling.
- *Impaired attention* is manifested by prematurely breaking off from tasks and leaving activities unfinished. The children change frequently from one activity to another, seemingly losing interest in one task because they become diverted to another.
- *Anti-social behaviour.* The anti-social behaviour (uninhibited, reckless, non-conformist impulsive) is most evident in organized situations that require a high degree of behavioural self-control, in relationships with other people; in situations involving some danger, in the flouting of rules.
- *Interrupting* others' activities.

Clinical features

A child may have poor attention but not be markedly overactive; s/he may be overactive but able to concentrate quite well which is why the literature sometimes uses the letters AD/HD to denote the disorder. Most children have both AD and HD problems, hence AD/HD.

Co-morbidity

James Morrison (1995) provides a guide to complications in making a diagnosis:

- Children with learning disabilities learn slowly and may be overly active and impulsive, but children with AD/HD, once (if) their attention is focused, tend to learn normally.
- AD/HD patients communicate normally, unlike children with *Autistic disorder*.
- Depressed children may be agitated or have a poor attention span, but the duration is not usually life-long.
- Many children with Tourette's syndrome are also hyperactive, but those who have AD/HD only, will not display motor and vocal tics.
- Other behaviour disorders (*oppositional* and *conduct*) may involve activities that annoy adults or peers immensely, but the behaviours appear purposeful and are not accompanied by the feelings of remorse typical of AD/HD behaviour. However, many children with AD/HD also have conduct disorder or oppositional defiant disorder, as well as Tourette's syndrome.
- Children reared in a chaotic social environment may also have difficulty with hyperactivity and inattention.
- In a practitioner's office, many children with AD/HD are able to sit still and focus attention well; the diagnosis is best made on the basis of historical information, and/or multiple observations in varied situations.

At home. What stands out in the 'shell-shocked' minds of many mothers and fathers of a young child with AD/HD is the presence in the house of a 'mobile disaster area'. His or her short attention span, rapidly changing goals and insatiable touching and demanding, is combined with a rather 'muscular' ham-fisted approach to the world. They leave in their wake broken toys, smashed ornaments and upset grocery shelves – if the mother is brave enough to take them to a supermarket.

At school. Teachers tend to be dismayed at their inability to manage such a child's disruptive actions, let alone get him or her to concentrate on lessons (Herbert and Wookey, 2004). Where children with AD/HD differ from other children who are also often naughty and exuberant is in the extent of their unwillingness or inability to inhibit their antisocial and frenetic activities in the face of classroom rules.

Hyperactivity at school

Children who are hyperactive:

- squirm in their seat or fidget;
- leave their seat inappropriately;
- run or climb inappropriately (in adolescents this may be only a subjective feeling of restlessness);
- talk excessively;
- are impulsive;
- answer questions before they have been completed;
- have trouble awaiting their turn;
- interrupt or intrude on others.

Deficits in attention span

Children with ADD:

- fail to pay close attention to details or make careless errors in schoolwork, work, or other activities;
- have trouble keeping attention on tasks or play;
- do not appear to listen when being told something;
- neither follow through on instructions nor complete classroom tasks (*not* necessarily because of oppositional behaviour or failure to understand);
- have trouble organizing activities and tasks;
- dislike or avoid tasks that involve sustained mental effort (e.g. homework, schoolwork);
- lose materials needed for activities (assignments, books, pencils, tools, toys);
- are easily distracted by external stimuli;
- are forgetful.

The referral

Behaviour can be so disruptive and frenetic that they may be referred to a GP, and thence to a psychologist, psychiatrist, or paediatrician, by parents or teachers who feel demoralized by their inability to manage their children and pupils. Many health care professionals, perhaps somewhat hazy about AD/HD and its treatment, have wilted before harassed parents, confronting them with articles from the Internet, magazines or books about *Ritalin* – the 'magical cure' or 'invasive drug' – depending upon the feature author's point of view.

Children with AD/HD require an assessment from a multidisciplinary team, consisting of medical, educational, mental health, paediatric or psychological personnel. Effective multi-agency collaboration is essential in order to identify the child's and family's many problems and needs. Observation, at home or by the classroom teacher, is the initial tool in effectively documenting the child's level of attention and distractibility. Observations should occur in a variety of settings, including the following:

- during solitary, parallel, and group play;
- at home with parents, siblings, and other significant people;
- at the supermarket;
- in other (sometimes novel) environments such as therapy sessions, the psychologists' consulting room.

Developmental features

The onset of AD/HD occurs no later than 7 years of age for more than half of those who receive the diagnosis. Four boys for every one girl are diagnosed as AD/HD. Level of achievement at school is well below normal on tests of maths and reading. The high degree of activity when present in early childhood tends to peak at around 5 or 6 years, and then undergo a slow downward trend by adolescence.

However, while some children outgrow the AD/HD problem altogether; and others certainly improve (although somewhat impaired), estimates suggest that as many as 70 to 80 per cent are likely to continue to display some symptoms in their adolescent years. Only 10 to 20 per cent of children with AD/HD reach adulthood free of any psychiatric diagnosis and able to function without significant symptoms of their previous AD/HD. Antisocial conduct, so closely associated with AD/HD (see Chapter 11), tends to persist if not treated, and, indeed may get worse.

Causation

It has been the hope of many professionals and, not least, parents that the identification of an underlying biological cause would go some way to redress the balance of 'perceived blame' for families, removing the shame of people pointing the finger at parents for their alleged disciplinary inadequacies. A majority of studies of hyperactivity have failed to establish a single, specific medical cause. Inconsistent results seem to be the most predictable aspect of research into the causes of AD/HD.

While little is yet certain, researchers believe that a fault (most likely inherited) in the neurological system causes poor self-control and hyperactivity. A fashionable and convincing view is that deficits (inherited) in the ability to attend may be biochemical in origin. Neurotransmitters appear to play an important role in the AD/HD symptoms. The catacholamine hypothesis suggests that an under-availability of Dopamine and Norepinephrine in the brain is a major determinant, although precise mechanisms which reduce availability have not been delineated.

Advocates for social and familial models of AD/HD believe it is dangerous to 'invent' medical conditions to explain social difficulties and suggest that many children who would previously have been called 'badly behaved', are now being stereotyped as 'medically disordered'. Critics suggest that it is important to investigate environmental conditions (e.g. patterns of activity, home life and upbringing) for the answers to the question about the 'determinants' (they avoid the term 'causation') of AD/HD-type behaviours (not, of course symptoms).

Treatment

Multiple problems, so common in cases of AD/HD, require a multimodal treatment strategy, one that is likely to involve cooperation between several professions (see Sutton et al., 2004).

Primary effects are the improvement of attention span with the reduction of, disruptive, inappropriate and impulsive behaviour. Compliance with authority figures requests and commands is increased. But medication has not been demonstrated to produce positive changes after its cessation. It is not a long-term solution to AD/HD.

Other commonly used approaches in dealing with AD/HD, a problem highly associated (co-morbid) with conduct disorders in childhood, involve:

- creating and maintaining a well-structured ('prosthetic') environment to compensate for the child's poor stimulus control;
- group and/or individual behaviour therapy (notably operant techniques to shape up pr-social behaviour);
- cognitive-behaviour therapy (CBT) to enhance poor information processing and self-control;
- life-skills (e.g. social skills, on-task attention training);
- medication which can be combined with each of the above (e.g. Barkley, 1996).

The most common medication used to treat AD/HD is the stimulant *Ritalin* (generic name *methylphenidate*). Ritalin works by stimulating groups of brain cells that function to maintain attention. Thirty minutes after a child takes medication, it begins to take effect. Ritalin's action peaks two hours after it is taken. Four hours after the child has taken the medication, it is no longer active and has in effect left the body. Although medication (particularly Ritalin) does facilitate the short-term (i.e. day-to-day) management of hyperactive children in about 75 per cent of cases, it is not a panacea; it has little or no impact on the social, academic or psychological adjustment of these youngsters in the long run.

A behavioural approach to treatment (see Herbert and Wookey, 2004) may render the use of drugs unnecessary, or (in combination with medication which provides a 'window of opportunity' for behavioural training) make less likely any prolonged drug dependence or the abdication from personal parental responsibility. A favourable outcome for affected children may be anticipated if parents and teachers (or other carers), from a very early stage, are supportive, set firm limits, and use positive discipline.

Various training programmes have been developed, which focus on increasing parents' skills in managing their child's behaviour, and facilitating social skills development. Endlessly negative criticism and 'put-downs' by parents and teachers to these undoubtedly challenging, indeed, exhausting children, are discouraged. The positive skills which are encouraged and modelled (see Herbert and Wookey, 2004; Webster-Stratton and Dahl, 1995; Webster-Stratton and Herbert, 1993; 1994) include:

- communicating warmly with the child;
- problem solving and negotiating solutions;
- setting clear rules and limits;
- providing appropriate reinforcement;
- using positive disciplinary techniques.

School-based programmes have been devised for the youngsters with AD/HD in their own right (see Webster-Stratton and Dahl, 1995). They focus on specific cognitive skill development in children, enhancing their decision making and cognitive processing by

- raising physical awareness of the premonitory 'danger' signs of anger they experience;
- teaching interpersonal problem-solving skills;
- mobilizing self-talk and other self-control strategies during provocative situations.

A review of the empirical evidence by Nolan and Carr (2000) revealed 20 studies (66 treatment groups or conditions, involving 1096 children, aged 3 to 18 years). ODD and CD problems were the most commonly reported co-morbid conditions. The programme durations ranged from 3 to 16 weeks and occupied 6 to 40 sessions. Randomization of assignment to conditions was used in 70 per cent of the studies. Pre- and post-treatment measures were commonly based on the Conners Parent Rating Scale or the Connors Teacher Rating Scale:

- A BPT programme (see p. 219) and stimulant therapy was more effective than BPT without stimulants in reducing parent- and teacher-rated behaviour problems, and in improving attention in the short term, but not the long term.
- Combined stimulant therapy and a multi-component psychological treatment package were more effective in leading to sustained improvements over a 9 month period in home-based behaviour problems than stimulant therapy alone.
- Additional school-based contingency management was required for treatment programmes to improve classroom behaviour (see Nolan and Carr, 2000, pp. 97–8).

Barkley (1996) has published a guide for parents and practitioners as an aid to managing this most daunting of problems, one which (if not remedied early on) has a particularly grave prognosis (Farrington, 1995).

Preventive work

For children with AD/HD, who are reluctant, unwilling, or unable to learn, school can mark the beginning of resentful attitudes that are expressed in social isolation or a repertoire of rebellious behaviours. A sense of inferiority and failure provide the fuel often, for antisocial attitudes and behaviour. Research has shown that temperamentally difficult hyperactive children receive more critical feedback, negative commands and less praise than less active children (Herbert, 1987a, b).

In a sense, they 'train' (i.e. inhibit) their parents (or teachers) from praising them, because they are so unrewarding to manage. Consequently, children who suffer from AD/HD need desperately to succeed and receive positive feedback about themselves. It is particularly important to praise increased attention span and persistence with tasks: activities such as painting picture books, playing quietly, sitting while reading a book, or being *on-task* in the classroom. Unfortunately, they frequently do not find praise and encouragement positively reinforcing – a daunting problem for parents and behaviour therapists.

Alan Kazdin (1997) has provided a useful discussion of how different types of psychopathology may require different types of treatment delivery. Indeed, it is likely that most children will not derive maximum benefits from traditional time-limited treatment. Kazdin describes six such models of treatment delivery, which vary with respect to dosage, the number of systems targeted, and the degree to which the treatment is continuous or intermittent. He draws parallels between treatment for psychological symptoms and treatments for various medical conditions. Some psychopathologies may require continued care, much like ongoing treatment for diabetes. Treatment is modified over time but is never discontinued. Waldron and Kern-Jones (2004) state that the evidence indicates that the effects of both behaviour therapy and stimulant medication reverse when the treatments are withdrawn.

Epilepsy

Diagnosis

Epilepsy is a chronic neurological disease characterised by recurrent spontaneous seizures. The seizures ('fits') occur because of sudden abnormal bursts of electrical brain activity that disrupt the functioning of the brain. During a seizure, neurones in the cerebrum generate abnormally increased electrical activity, preventing the brain from processing normal signals.

Clinical features

Epilepsy shows the following features:

1   *Grand mal seizures.* The patient loses consciousness after a sharp scream, falls to the ground with generalized muscular spasticity, dilation of the pupils, intermittent convulsions of all four extremities, facial cyanosis, incontinence of urine and stool and biting of tip of the tongue. The seizure may last for a few minutes, after which the child falls into a deep sleep and has no recollection of the attack upon awakening.
2   *Absence seizures (petit mal seizures).* These seizures are non-convulsive. Discrete eye movements (myoclonic jerks) may appear, lasting between 5 and 30 seconds, and may be quite difficult to observe in the child, as the body posture and muscle tone remain the same. The eyes appear somewhat glazed and the child is literally 'absent in mind', unaware of his or her surroundings staring into space, and appearing 'frozen'. Nor can their unawareness be

disrupted by prompting. Such interruptions in consciousness occur dozens of times a day in some children. They are not aware that these episodes take place. There is either a very short, or no post-seizure period.

Causation

No underlying cause is found in most cases of epilepsy. In some children the seizures are the result of an underlying brain disorder, such as:

- a former brain anoxia during delivery;
- a brain tumour or stroke;
- brain injury or lesions following a trauma, such as, respectively, a severe blow to the head or brain surgery;
- an infection of the brain, e.g. encephalitis or meningitis.

Other cases of the illness may be attributed to an imbalance of neurotransmitters in the brain. This is usually the case in children with epilepsy.

Epileptic seizures may arise from different brain regions and can cause abnormal motor activity, sensory changes, mood changes and unconsciousness. For example:

- motor phenomena (e.g. tonic-clonic seizures or jerks) are associated with the frontal lobe;
- sensory phenomena, with the parietal lobe;
- changes in mood and smell and gastrointestinal symptoms, with the temporal lobe;
- changes in consciousness, with the limbic system;
- if the seizure spreads to other regions, various brain functions may be involved resulting in a generalized seizure.

A family history of seizures, use of antidepressant drugs and alcohol misuse are risk factors associated with epilepsy in young people and older adults. Low blood sugar and changes in electrolytes (especially sodium) can cause seizures.

Co-morbidity

Epilepsy occurs quite commonly in autism, and provides one of the early indications that the pervasive disorder is a neurobiological condition. Early studies suggest that up to a third of children with autism will develop epilepsy either in early childhood or in adolescence.

Developmental features

The cognitive attributes of epilepsy are very variable and multifactorially determined. Cognitive dysfunction varies, depending on:

- timing (during an epileptic event, post seizure, or between attacks);
- location of the focus of the seizure;
- onset of seizures;
- type and severity of seizures;
- medications.

Children with epilepsy appear to be at significantly greater risk for learning difficulties. Besag (1988), following an extensive review of the research literature on epilepsy and cognitive impairment, suggested that most children with epilepsy are of normal intelligence and the intellectual ability does not deteriorate; but a small subgroup does deteriorate intellectually. Although there is conflicting evidence, it appears that what contributes to the intellectual deterioration may be:

- early age of onset;
- frequent seizures;
- prolonged seizures;
- association with pre-existing brain damage;
- mixed seizure types occurring together;
- status epilepticus.

Epidemiology

The incidence of epilepsy in developing countries is nearly double that found in developed countries. It is one of the most common neurological disorders, affecting males and females of all ages. Most children with epilepsy experience their first seizure between the ages of 2 and 14. People with a family history of seizure disorders are also at risk of suffering from epilepsy.

Prevention

Prevention is not an option for most epileptic disorders. However, knowledge of the precipitants of episodes of epilepsy may affect, in a limited way, whether or not seizures can be pre-empted. Children and adolescents can contribute to the control of their seizures by avoiding (where possible) the common triggers of an epileptic seizure. Common triggers include:

- stress;
- lack of sleep;
- fever (in infants and small children);
- menstruation;
- exposure to flickering light;
- alcohol.

Treatment

Generally speaking, there is no cure for epilepsy. Most children are prescribed an antiepileptic drug to help prevent the onset of further seizures. An estimated 70 per cent experience symptom relief while on medication; around 30 per cent may experience a reduction in seizures. Fortunately, with the appropriate treatment, many epileptic children will not experience a seizure for many years, and can bring to an end, eventually, their medication. Indeed, after 2 to 5 years of successful therapy, medication can cease in many children, without relapse.

Medication

Anti-epileptic drugs work by restoring the normal electrical activity in the brain. However, there is no received wisdom to inform clinicians which epileptic children should or should not be treated with an anti-epileptic drug.

- A single seizure is not generally treated unless the patient is at high risk of experiencing further seizures, e.g. children with brain tumours.
- Some neonatal seizures are not treated with anti-epileptic drugs, e.g. febrile convulsions.
- Children who have experienced two or three seizures within a short time period are likely to be prescribed medication.

There are approaches that help to inhibit excessive neuronal firing and prevent a seizure from spreading throughout the brain. This is achieved by enhancing the inhibitory activity of neurotransmitter gamma aminobutyric acid (GABA), or reducing the activity of excitatory neurotransmitters such as glutamate. Some drugs act on neuronal membranes and help to stabilise them, while others block sodium channels to stop the seizure from spreading across the brain. The mechanisms of action of these drugs are complex and not all fully understood.

Those with severe forms of epilepsy that do not respond to medication may receive surgery to treat their illness. This can be performed if the area of the brain affected by seizures can be identified, and removed without significant side-effects.

Several types of surgery are used, including (for example) temporal lobe surgery which removes part of the *temporal lobe*, especially the hippocampus and amygdala.

Ohtahara Syndrome

Epilepsy is not a unitary disease; the plural 'epilepsies' would better serve as a generic term to accommodate the different syndromes that involve neurologically based seizures as major presenting symptoms. An example of a condition that progresses for some infants ('regresses' would be a more apt description) into two other syndromes, is the Ohtahara syndrome (OS) – a rare and particularly tragic syndrome.

Diagnostic history

Ten cases of early infantile epileptic encephalopathy with suppression-bursts on EEG were reported by Ohtahara in 1978. The disorder was finally recognized as a separate disease entity in 1989 by the International League Against Epilepsy which classified it under 'symptomatic generalized epilepsies and syndromes with non-specific etiology'.

Diagnosis

The OS – a form of epilepsy – has its onset after what appears to be a period of normal development in infancy, and wreaks havoc with the child's development. The types of seizure in Ohtahara syndrome are variable. The most frequently observed is a tonic seizure, which may be either generalized and symmetrical or lateralized. The tonic seizures are usually brief, but often occur in series. Other seizure types include clonic seizures and erratic myoclonic jerks. Later in the course, there may be generalized tonic-clonic seizures. Partial seizures are frequent in cases with focal lesions.

Symptoms

Soon after the onset of seizures, infants become inactive and hypotonic. Their psychomotor development is arrested and they usually develop severe neurological abnormalities such as spastic diplegia, hemiplegia, tetraplegia, ataxia, or dystonia.

Between 2 and 6 months of age, the cases may evolve into West syndrome. The clinical manifestations are spasms and a hypsarrhythmic pattern on EEG.

A very small number have developed Lennox–Gastaut syndrome, with its characteristic slow spike-waves on EEG and minor motor seizures.

Clinical features

- onset in early infancy;
- main seizure pattern: brief tonic seizures;
- suppression-bursts in EEG, during both waking and sleeping states;
- severe psychomotor retardation;
- intractable seizures;
- poor prognosis;
- polyaetiology;
- progression to *West syndrome.*

Developmental features

The seizures develop within the first 20 days of life in the majority of reported cases, and may occur as early as the first hour after delivery. The onset is acute in a previously normal infant. Du Plessis and colleagues extend the earliest age of onset into the prenatal period with intrauterine seizures (du Plessis, Kaufman and Kupsky, 1993). The disorder takes a progressively deteriorating course with increasing frequency of seizures and with severe retardation of psychomotor development. The infants are usually left profoundly handicapped. Boys are affected more often than girls in the reported cases.

Causation

Cerebral malformations are cited as a common aetiology for Ohtahara syndrome. Despite the presence of different neuropathological pictures, the syndrome is now believed to be secondary to a cerebral malformative disorder. Because of the close relationship of Ohtahara syndrome, West syndrome, and Lennox–Gastaut syndrome, it is suggested that they all represent age-specific reactions of the brain to heterogeneous, non-specific external factors (Ohtahara, 1984).

Incidence

The incidence and prevalence of Ohtahara syndrome are unknown, and there is no information about prevention.

■ Pervasive Developmental Disorder (PDD)

Autism and Asperger's Syndrome

The combination of social communication impairments and idiosyncratic skills (impressive ones in some children) can convey an impression of eccentricity in children with PDDs. And appearances of being 'unusual' or 'different' are not always acceptable to a peer group or, if they are awkward in the classroom, to their teachers. Children with autistic or Asperger traits may be mercilessly bullied, becoming anxious and afraid. Those who are more fortunate in their schools, may be accepted as benign 'aliens', and respected if they possess unusual abilities.

It has to be said that some of their behaviour patterns can irritate teachers and alienate classmates alike. For example, they may try to dominate play and disrupt rule-based games with outbursts of temper. After mastering (with difficulty) classroom routines and rules they may resist small changes vociferously, or 'report' minor transgressions of fellow pupils. Such rigidity and literalness frustrate the teacher who wishes to be flexible, and antagonize the child who has been 'grassed on'. Among other reasons why children with AS unwittingly disrupt the class are: (i) inability to focus; (ii) extensive confusion; (iii) inability to interpret social rules and subtle cues; (iv) absence of a desire to 'please' or 'be liked'; (v) difficulty in conveying or explaining their feelings; (vi) a sensory overloading due too much physical stimulation, such as sights and sounds.

Disabled children, who receive no help in decoding the complexities and ambiguities of school norms, are quite likely to become increasingly aware, as they enter adolescence of the social conformity of teenagers, and of being different from their peers. In consequence, they are quite likely to become anxious, hyper-sensitive to criticism, and withdrawn from the 'hurly burly' of teenage social life.

The Autistic Spectrum

Clearly, disabled children with communication disorders need empathic understanding and down-to-earth (i.e. practical) help, as do their parents (Wolf, Noh et al.) and their teachers. Such all-round help begins with the ability to recognize the disability. The following features should alert teachers to the presence of an autistic spectrum disorder in one of their pupils:

Social impairments

The autistic child shows the following features:

- easily overwhelmed by social stimulation;
- fails to join in with the play of other children;
- is inappropriate in joint play (e.g. shows aggressive or disruptive behaviour);
- is unwilling to cooperate in classroom activities;
- is too intense or withdrawn in relationships with adults;
- reacts in an extreme manner in the face of what is perceived as an intrusion into his or her personal space;
- shows extreme resistance to being rushed or 'chivvied'.

Impairments of communication

The autistic child shows the following features:

- has a limited use of language for communication or a tendency to talk freely only about very specific topics;
- is mute and odd or uses inappropriate prosody;
- demonstrates other abnormalities (e.g. echolalia) of language;
- refers to self as 'you', 'she', or 'he' (i.e. after the age of 3 years);
- uses an atypical vocabulary for his or her age or social group.

Asperger's Syndrome (AS)

The following features should alert teachers to the possibility of Asperger's syndrome in one of their pupils:

Social impairments

Children with Asperger's syndrome show the following features:

- often become quite interested in other people as they grow older, but they are socially inept and inappropriate;
- show abnormalities of social imagination;
- tend to be egocentric;
- fail to learn from their experience in a manner that provides social meaning and useful guidelines for living;

- accumulate knowledge that is fragmented, lacking in 'common sense';
- lack ability to understand and use the rules governing social behaviour;
- do not have the intuitive knowledge of how to adapt to the needs and per-sonalities of others;
- have relationships with the opposite sex that provide exemplars of their more general social ineptitude;
- tend to convey a picture of naïveté and childishness. Some adults respond to these traits with empathic understanding of what they perceive as the child's vulnerability. But they can also lose sympathy when repeated inanities begin to pall, and are simply exasperating.
- parents tend to complain: 'The trouble is my child looks so normal to others, but in fact, isn't!'

Impairments of communication

The child shows the following communication impairments:

- language development may have been slow to begin with and also very odd in the way it is used for communication;
- ability to speak fluently by the age of 5 is a notable feature of the syndrome;
- content of speech tends to be pedantic, often consisting of lengthy disquisi-tions on favourite subjects;
- use of speech which seems more for self-gratification than for communication;
- failure to understand subtle verbal jokes;
- misinterpretation when ignoring non-verbal signs;
- inability to use or understand facial expression, tone, gestures and other body language for expressing emotions;
- use of a vocal intonation that tends to be monotonous and droning, or exaggerated;
- abnormal eye contact – either gaze avoidance or prolonged intense gaze;
- tendency to interpret speech literally.

Skills and interests

- Children with AS tend to be of average or above average intelligence.
- In general, on psychological tests requiring good rote memory they perform well, but have deficits on those dealing with abstract concepts, or timed sequencing.

- Visuo-spatial abilities are variable, and the test scores tend to be markedly lower than those for expressive speech.
- Sport is not a tension-releasing outlet for children with AS.
- Most are poor at games involving motor skills, because gross movements are clumsy and ill-co-ordinated.
- Posture and gait appear odd.
- Artistic interests may be inhibited because executive problems sometimes affect the ability to write or to draw.
- They may excel at board games like chess, which require good rote memory.
- Hobbies generally consist of one or two narrowly focused areas, such as astronomy, train timetables, stamps, or prehistoric animals, to the exclusion of all else.
- They obsessively collect and organize every known fact about their chosen interest, and talk incessantly about it at length quite unconscious of the fact that they may be boring their audience.

Interventions

Academic and intellectual status

Children with Asperger's syndrome (AS) suffer from a particular form of the autistic spectrum (some theorists prefer the term high functioning or mild autism), so in considering school-based interventions, I will deal with them for the most part together. Children diagnosed with autism and AS should benefit from the use by teachers of various strategies suggested by Tony Attwood (1993) in his book *Asperger's Syndrome: A Guide for Parents and Professionals* – an invaluable text designed to facilitate the academic attainment of children with AS, and reduce their challenging behaviour in the classroom. The actions and attitudes teachers might try are adapted and summarized below:

- encouragement of the child to ask for help with explanations of the appropriate methods for carrying out classroom tasks;
- provision, as far as possible, of a predicable environment and consistent routines;
- provision of a setting that has opportunities for individual attention and the use of small work groups. (a classroom assistant is helpful);
- allowing opportunities for social interaction and facilitation of social relationships in fairly structured and supervised activities;
- preparation for alterations in routines or timetabling;

- issuing of brief, precise, and specific instructions;
- giving the child enough time to process information;
- reducing tasks into manageable segments;
- training the child to schedule and plan his or her work;
- positioning the child in the least distracting place possible in the classroom; with particular attention to the placement of pupils who provoke the child some distance away;
- not expecting the student to have the ability unaided, to generalize instructions;
- not presuming that the child will wish to please;
- indicating to the child how others feel when appropriate opportunities occur (such as when fellow pupils are hurt or distressed).

Supportive strategies (child-focused)

(Also adapted and summarized from Attwood, 1993.) Attwood suggests that the teacher try to organize:

- a formal 'peer support network' (e.g. 'buddy' system) for the security and guidance of the child;
- social situations constructed to allow him or her the opportunity to take the leadership in an activity, explaining, demonstrating, or teaching others how to improve in the particular activity;
- clearly defined and monitored rules of social conduct so that the child does not constantly interrupt from over-zealousness, literalness, or irrelevance;
- a strategy for times when the child can't cope with over-stimulation or confusion; perhaps a 'time out' or 'calming down' area when required. It is particularly important, given the nature of autism and AS, to ensure that the 'time out' procedure is not more attractive than the classroom activity;
- a simple written timetable to help the child organize him/herself.

Adaptive skills designed to boost the child's self-sufficiency have to be taught explicitly without assuming that general explanations will prove sufficient, nor that generalization from one specific situation to similar ones will take place automatically.

Professional help with pervasive developmental disorders

1   A *counsellor* might focus on an individual's psychological well being, monitor progress, serve as a resource to other staff members, and liaise with disabled pupils and their families.

2   A *speech therapist* with expertise in pragmatics and social skills is invaluable for individual and small group work. The child may need to be taught to monitor his or her own speech style in terms of volume, rhythm, modulation, naturalness, adjustment to the nature of the speaker, context and social situation. In terms of formal properties of language, the child may benefit from a discussion of idiomatic language, and practice identifying its use in both text and conversation. It is important to help the child to increase the flexibility with which he or she both uses language with other people, and to develop the ability to make inferences, to predict, and explain motivation.

3   A *clinical* or *educational psychologist* might focus on behavioural change (see below) and social skill training (Goldstein, 1995; Ladd 1984). Individuals with AS often exhibit a variety of challenging behaviours. It is important that these disruptive actions are not reified by being attributed to some intrinsic disability trait *per se, rather than difficulties of a socially interactive nature.* The maladaptive behaviours are often a consequence of the child's *social tunnel vision* – a restricted and overly concrete understanding of social life which, in turn, results in an overwhelming bewilderment when faced with intrusive interpersonal interactions. This dilemma requires management by means of *therapeutic* and/or *educational strategies*, rather than by unpredictable punishments that imply (simplistically) that a disease entity is 'at work', or that the challenging behaviour is malicious in intent.

Behavioural interventions

Possible behavioural interventions might involve:

- specific problem-solving strategies dealing with recurring troublesome situations plus social awareness training for the recognition of relevant aspects of given situations;
- discussion of discrepancies between the child's perceptions regarding particular situations;
- practising how to interpret visual information simultaneously with auditory information, i.e. how to interpret other people's non-verbal behaviour accurately while also interpreting what is being said in conjunction with these non-verbal cues;
- role-play of social problem-solving and self-evaluation;
- learning (and re-learning) how to differentiate situations which are manageable from those that are not;
- strengthening self-esteem by maximizing situations in which success can be achieved, by identifying and, if necessary, adapting them.

The curriculum content requires an emphasis on skills that correspond to relative strengths in the individual, as well as skills that may be critical for the child's future vocational life (e.g., writing skills, computer skills, science).

■ Sensory Impairments

Government policy in the UK is to facilitate the education of children with special needs in mainstream schools. Children who are blind or deaf are likely to require additional educational provision – be it input from specialist professionals, special equipment, or modifications of the curriculum. Early diagnosis of sensory impairments is vital, as prompt interventions make possible developmental benefits, while undue delays can affect adversely the acquisition of skills.

The identification of deaf children with moderate multiple disabilities tends to come at a later age than that for deafness-only students. This often results in years of education for them as students with a hearing loss alone. Many experience underachievement as a result of the failure to recognize their additional disabilities. The shortage of teachers with the specialist skills to work with them exacerbates their deprivation. Deaf and blind children with multiple disabilities may come to be alienated from schooling for these and other reasons, and begin to present disruptive behaviour problems (see Herbert and Wookey, 2004, on the management of disruptive behaviour). These issues are discussed separately for deaf, blind, and blind-deaf children.

Hearing Impairments

Diagnosis

Deafness is not a homogeneous condition. It can vary in frequency (measured in hertz, Hz) or intensity (units of sound measured in decibels, dB). The frequency range for the normal ear is from around 20 to 20,000 Hz. The frequencies that are important for speech development fall between 250 and 4000 Hz. A child with a hearing impairment involving a loss of intensity up to 55 dB would hear sounds, but have difficulty interpreting them without a hearing aid. These children are described as partially hearing.

Communication

Clearly, deaf individuals are seriously disadvantaged when it comes to the linguistic skills so valued by society, especially in educational settings. The development of sign language and speech in children with hearing difficulties is described in detail by Vicky Lewis in her classic (2003) book *Development and Disability*. She makes the point that sign languages are *naturally occurring languages* in their own right, and describes the undoubted advantages to children who learn the skill of signing early in life. Sign bilingualism for deaf children is widely considered to have advantages over mono-lingualism.

Assessment of hearing loss

Sound is of critical importance for the development of speech in children who can hear. Not surprisingly, the restriction, distortion or absence of sound, often results in a severe impairment of communication which is the greatest barrier to social and educational inclusion. Just as important, however, is the family's and school's *awareness* of the implications of deafness, the child's capacities and the vital role of communication.

Early assessment of hearing is important for planning interventions designed to help the child adjust to a 'hearing' world. In addition, there is a need for a differential diagnosis providing an accurate learning profile for the individual student, one which includes a clear determination of the disabilities influencing that profile. Assessment can be complicated for children with partial hearing loss. Intermittent hearing loss, associated with recurrent ear infections, is thought to interfere with speech and language development.

The assessment would consist of teacher observations and appropriate standardized assessment measures as well as informal assessment procedures. The professionals involved are likely to include educational and clinical psychologists, classroom teachers, occupational and physical therapists, speech and language therapists/pathologists, audiologists, and any necessary medical personnel. The team should provide a detailed formulation of the assessment results, with recommendations and suggestions for an educational programme.

The earlier hearing difficulties are detected and treated, the more successful are the developmental and educational outcomes. So it is important to be aware of behaviours suggestive of possible hearing loss. The infant, for example: (i) does not respond to sounds by becoming still and quiet, as is the normal response to sound in very young hearing infants; (ii) turns to follow visual stimuli but not to locate sounds; (iii) does not babble, or ceases to babble after a period of normal babbling.

Education of deaf children

According to the *UN Report on Disability and Human Rights*, most countries legally define basic education as every citizen's *right*. Studies among people with disabilities, however, suggest that education amounts usually to a *privilege*. In general, individuals with hearing difficulties have less access to education than those with other kind of disabilities. Some 80 per cent of deaf people in the developing world have no access to education, according to the World Federation of the Deaf. The more fortunate opportunities for deaf children in the developed world do not eliminate the limitations and particular challenges they face in an academic world designed for children with normal hearing. For example, with regard to the following:

- *academic achievement*: most evidence indicates that deaf children are not as successful academically as would be anticipated when compared with hearing children of similar intellectual ability;
- *academic subjects* such as reading and writing: many deaf children have difficulties;
- *communication with teachers*: Lewis (2003) reports the finding that more than 50 per cent of a large sample of 16-year-olds with a profound hearing loss in mainstream schools, communicated through speech (according to their teachers) with difficulty. In another sample cited by Lewis, teachers rated 80 per cent of a sample of profoundly deaf 10–17 year-olds as not understandable at all.
- *multiple impairments*: additional disabilities may include learning disabilities, AD/HD, visual impairment, cerebral palsy, or other physical disabilities. Children with a hearing loss combined with other disabilities generally need services beyond those provided for a child with the single disability of deafness. The combined effect of hearing loss and an accompanying disability presents a unique and complex problem to professionals and parents. Unfortunately, the professional literature yields surprisingly little specific information on educational programmes for such children. The fact that there are many differences among children with multiple disabilities adds to the difficulties of providing appropriate programmes.

Choosing a school for a deaf child is a daunting decision for parents, and may involve (i) a mainstream school where the instruction is delivered orally, requiring an assistant to interpret if he or she uses sign language; (ii) a specialist unit for hearing impaired children which is based at a mainstream school, sometimes functioning as a 'half-way house' to integration into the mainstream; (iii) a special school catering for hard of hearing children or for children with a range of disabilities including deafness. Many researchers and teachers of deaf children are of the opinion that all students with hearing impairments (including those with additional learning problems) should receive individually designed instruction programmes (see Powers and Elliott, 1993).

▨ Visual Impairments

Diagnosis

Most so-called 'blind' children can see something, although their vision may be severely restricted, or limited to a minute area of their visual field. This preponderance of partial-sightedness has led to a preference for the term visual impairment (VI). The incidence of VIs in children and adolescents under the age of 18 is 12.2 per 1,000. Severe VIs (legal or total blindness) occur at a rate of 0.06 per 1,000.

There is a wide range of visual impairments from blurred vision and short-sightedness to total blindness. What visually impaired partially sighted children can see will depend on whether their vision is peripheral (which means they cannot see straight ahead or read the printed page), or central only (allowing them to read print but restricting ease of getting around). Two children with the same limited visual acuity may see things very differently if one, say, learns to use his residual vision efficiently, a sign perhaps of a higher intellectual level.

Causes

Eye disorders which might give rise to visual impairments are:

- congenital disorders;
- cataracts;
- glaucoma;
- muscular problems that result in visual disturbances;
- corneal disorders;
- diabetic retinopathy;
- retinal degeneration;
- albinism;
- infection.

VI can be the consequence of a functional loss of vision, rather than an eye disorder *per se*.

Early screening for VI

Vision screening in the child's first year is important, given the need for early intervention, in detecting VI problems. The infant shows the following features:

- is behind with developmental milestones, for visual tracking and following;
- is behind with motor milestones;
- moves too little or seems uninterested in moving about;
- does not follow objects which make no noise;
- is difficult to make or maintain eye contact with;
- tilts head to the side frequently after good head control is established;
- has unusual eyes (various features such as jerky eye movements, dull appearance, unusual eye colouring, rapid eye movements back and forth when at rest);
- is poorly coordinated when older.

Developmental features

Children who are blind begin to talk at around the same age as sighted children and their early vocabulary increases at about the same rate. These are crucial developments as speech is a counter to the restrictions of experience that follow from a lack of vision. Speech needs encouragement, especially as the parents of blind children can find it difficult, because of (*inter alia*) their lack of eye contact and somewhat expressionless faces to communicate with their babies.

Training and education

As soon as blindness is diagnosed, a peripatetic teacher who visits regularly should be assigned to the family. Beginning playgroup or nursery school can be a very distressing experience for young visually impaired children. Various strategies are required to help children with VIs so as to familiarize themselves with their new social and physical environment – a very different and daunting world to adjust to (see Lewis, 2003. p. 313).

Educational aids

Pupils and older students with VIs may need help with special equipment including the large print materials, Braille books and books on tape which should be available. There may be a need for creative changes to the conventional curriculum, with an emphasis on communication, listening skills, orientation, mobility, and social and daily life-skills. Technology in the form of computers and low-vision optical and video aids enables many partially sighted and blind children to participate in regular class activities. Pupils and older students may need help in using their residual vision more efficiently, and in working with special aids and materials.

It is important to remind ourselves, as Lewis (2003, p. 313) does, that blind children without any other disability can achieve just as much as sighted children. They may, however, have other (their own) idiosyncratic ways of achieving the goals set for sighted children.

Multiple impairments

Instruction for students with the single disability of a visual impairment, relies heavily on information received through auditory and tactile channels. For example, a child with a VI might learn to associate a sound (music or ringing) with the amorphous objects on different tables at the end of the classroom in order to differentiate between a record player and a telephone. Visually impaired pupils who have multiple impairments (e.g. additional hearing difficulties) do not always possess that advantage. They are likely to require an interdisciplinary approach and may need an emphasis on self-care and daily living skills – a subject returned to below.

Deaf-blindness

Diagnosis

Deaf-blindness does not necessarily refer to a total inability to see or hear. In fact it is a condition in which the combination of hearing and visual losses in children cause such severe communication and other developmental and educational needs that they cannot be accommodated in special education programmes solely for children with deafness or blindness, or multiple impairments. Some individuals are deaf-blind from birth. Others may be born deaf or hard-of-hearing and become blind or visually impaired later in life; or the reverse may be the case. Still others may be adventitiously deaf-blind, that is, they are born with both sight and hearing but lose some or all of these senses as a result of accident or illness.

Throughout their lives, generally speaking, the eyes and ears of these children either distort or altogether omit incoming information. Their only experience of any experience is fragmented, and consequently they have difficulty learning through observation or individual exploration. The ability to orient and travel independently is deeply affected by deaf-blindness. Various environmental cues must be found (sight or sound aids are not available as they would be for blind-only or deaf- only children) to teach them to find their way around. Without the attraction of auditory and visual stimuli, children with deaf-blindness may be less likely to explore and interact with the world around them.

However, the range of sensory impairments included in the term 'deaf-blindness' is wide. If children who are deaf-blind have some vision, as is quite common, they may be able to move about in their environments, recognize familiar people, read sign language at close distances, and perhaps read large print. Some may have sufficient hearing to recognize familiar sounds, understand some speech, or develop speech themselves.

Assessment

Assessing the skills of deaf-blind children is difficult because of the lack of normative data for assessment instruments for this population. Another difficulty is engaging them in a psychometric exercise given their 'inwardness' (see Mar, 1998).

Causation

There are several causal possibilities, including:

- multiple congenital anomalies such as fetal alcohol syndrome; hydrocephaly, maternal drug abuse, microcephaly;
- congenital prenatal dysfunction such as AIDS, herpes, rubella, syphilis and toxoplasmosis;
- post-natal causes such as asphyxia, encephalitis, head injury/trauma, meningitis, and strokes;
- prematurity.

Education and training

It is important to remember that these children can learn. Cognitively, socially, and in language skills, children with deaf-blindness have an experiential and conceptual background that differs significantly from all other disabled children. They therefore need unique educational programmes to ensure that they have the opportunity to reach their full potential. Children with deaf-blindness learn best when information is presented in a consistent and repetitive fashion. Information and input from the family is vital to a well coordinated programme. Principal communication systems for persons who are deaf-blind include:

- touch cues;
- gestures;
- object symbols;
- picture symbols;
- sign language;
- finger-spelling;
- Braille writing and reading;
- large print writing and reading.

The professionals who work with a child with deaf-blindness include: teachers of the visually impaired, teachers of the hearing impaired, orientation and mobility instructor, general classroom teacher (regular education and special education) and instructional aide, behaviour therapist, diagnostician, and often occupational and physiotherapists as well as speech/language therapists and audiologists.

The children, and all of the people working with them, require training in how to use all the adaptive devices and other instruments that are essential aids to coping with life. Deaf-blind children require:

- *the opportunity to access information* which has been unavailable to them because of their sensory losses (e.g. extended time with carefully planned 'hands on' activities to acquire information that other children pick up incidentally);
- *communication training*: this involves a variety of practical options – one of the highest priorities in the educational programming;
- *communication system*: this typically includes signals, tactile sign language, object symbols, tactile symbol systems, and Braille. Generally, children with deaf-blindness use a variety of adaptive equipment, for example, a personal hearing aid and an FM auditory trainer, glasses, a monocular, and a cane. They may rely on a communication book for much of their communication. They may need to use a vibrating alarm to wake up in the morning. Each child's communication system needs to be individually designed and used with a high degree of consistency across the day.

The constant stress and frustration of sensory deprivation these children experience often result in behaviour problems. Many children with deaf-blindness suffer additional disabilities, which further complicate their lives. Many dislike being touched, they may have disrupted sleeping patterns, feeding difficulties, and generally poor health.

Transition beyond school

When an individual who is deaf-blind nears the end of his or her school-based education, transition and rehabilitation help will be required to assist the individual find suitable work and living situations. Because of the diversity of needs, such services for a person who is deaf-blind can rarely be provided by a single agency.

V

Late Childhood and Early Adolescence

■ The Transition to Adolescence

The establishment of a clear sense of identity is one of the major tasks of adolescence (Erickson, 1968). There are three aspects of identity that particularly concern teenagers: (i) the way they see their present abilities, status and roles; (ii) having an acceptable body-image – a favourable representation of what it is like, and how it looks to others; and (iii) fulfilling their aspirations for themselves, becoming what they would like to become.

What is meant by adolescence? As a time period, it begins with the physiological changes of puberty and 'ends' at an indefinite time, when the young person is supposedly both mature and independent – as 'defined' by a variety of social and economic indicators. These include the end of education, the attainment of economic independence, personal status, duties, and privileges, also rights to bear arms and to marry. Clearly, adolescence is not a homogeneous stage of development.

Because individual rates of development are variable, the differences between teenagers at 13 and 17 years of age or, indeed, between two adolescents of the same age, may be dramatic – the dissimilarities between an individual who is still child-like, and one who is, in many respects an adult. The developmental tasks and preoccupations of teenagers, and their cognitive maturity, also vary to such an extent that it becomes necessary to divide adolescence into its early, middle, and late stages. The first two are the subject of Chapter 12.

■ Self-Awareness (Self-Image)

Adolescent self-awareness is strongly influenced by cultural norms, especially those of peers at school. The perception of one's appearance (what they should be, and look like) to others – the 'subjective public identity' – is important for the individual's self-esteem. The importance of body image to our culture, and adolescents in particular, is obvious given the widespread attention paid to the body's appearance. Vast expenditures of money, time, and effort are invested in fashionable clothes, skin preparations, cosmetics, and dieting. For many girls and young women, intense dieting and exercising, and sometimes purging, are the extreme measures required by fashion. Girls are particularly influenced by peer group pressures and media propaganda on the desirability of a thin 'prepubescent' body-image, and are thus prone to adopt 'Spartan' eating and exercise regimes which, when rigorous to extremes, indicate a weight phobia (anorexia nervosa).

■ Risky Sexual Activity

The hormonal changes of puberty bring in their wake many psychological changes for teenagers who will have to manage a dramatic heightening of sexual awareness and increased sexual arousal, both of which contribute to their evolving identity. Sexual identity and risky sexual behaviour are among the subjects addressed in Chapter 13, including the issue of sexual difficulties (if any) in intellectually disabled teenagers.

■ Depression and Suicide

This is another topic discussed in Chapter 13. Depressive reactions in children are frequently treated as concomitants of school refusal, truancy, failure to thrive, substance abuse and delinquency. But depression has only fairly recently achieved the status of a problem of childhood in its own right, joining the concern already in existence about the adolescent form of the illness. Suicide is a related issue. Incidence rates rise sharply during adolescence, to the point that it ranks among the half-dozen most common causes of death among older adolescents.

■ Conduct Problems and Delinquent Activity

As a relatively small (but growing) core of children approach adolescence and grow stronger, more assertive and rebellious, what were 'merely' difficult situations for parents can become menacing, and in some cases, dangerous – especially where they have been granted too little control and supervision when young (the conduct disorders). This is the topic of Chapter 14.

Delinquency is perhaps the most notorious of adolescent activities, reaching a peak at 15 years for boys and 14 years for girls. Although conduct problems can create misery for everyone concerned with the younger child, the disturbance can often be restricted, although often at great cost, to the home or classroom. As children grow older, the persistent defiance of authority, and their refusal or inability to show self-restraint, become more serious in their implications. They extend more and more beyond the confines of the child's life at home and school, into the domain of the criminal system and courts. Delinquency is often associated with depression in the adolescent years.

All of these issues are explored in the following chapters, together with the serious personal and social problems they give rise to, and the possible remedies that can be applied.

CHAPTER 13

The Transition to Adolescence

■ Self- and Body-Image Problems

▨ Anorexia

Diagnosis

The word 'anorexia' means loss of appetite, which is not what this extremely serious condition is really about. The disorder (affecting up to 1 per cent of healthy young 15- to 18-year-old females, and a lesser number of males and pre-pubescent children), is essentially about weight rather than eating. Young persons who are anorexic deliberately restrict their food intake. Their persistent dieting and food restriction can take them to the limits of starvation, and even death.

Clinical characteristics

At the core of the disorder is a body weight that is abnormally low for the age, height and sex of the young person, the result of self-inflicted near-starvation. Sufferers fear being overweight and insist on perceptions of their body-shape that are distorted. Because they believe (despite contrary evidence and countless reassurances) that they are fat, they attempt to lose weight by eating as little as they can 'get way with', and/or by purging any minuscule amounts (or 'fattening' contents) of meals they have been persuaded to eat. Deceiving parents and controlling food intake become a way of life. What makes life particularly difficult for parents and professionals is that sufferers with anorexia tend not to be honest about their avoidance strategies and innermost feelings, and usually resist treatment.

Despite a striking resemblance among anorexic patients, there is evidence that anorexia nervosa is a heterogeneous syndrome. There appear to be three patterns of food consumption and elimination:

1 *Restricters* keep to a regime in which there is a consistently extreme limitation on the amount of food ingested. They exclusively starve themselves and indulge in excessive exercise.
2 *Purgers* starve and purge but do not binge.
3 *Bingers* are notable for a severe dieting regime which is interspersed with episodes of bingeing followed by vomiting or other means of purgation. In *bulimia nervosa* – a bingeing subgroup – the pre-morbid weight level is generally higher than is the case in anorexia nervosa.

Physical attributes might involve:

- emaciation;
- anaemia;
- Autonomic Nervous System regulation (e.g. hypotension, hypothermia, bradycardia);
- complications from the eating disorder which can affect almost every organ;
- primary or secondary amenorrhoea.

Psychological attributes: The anorexic individual is described variously as:

- withdrawn
- isolated
- introverted
- stubborn
- selfish
- manipulative
- perfectionist
- hyperactive and controlling.

Causation

The causes of anorexia are multifactorial and poorly understood. Adolescent dieting provides the entrée into an eating disorder if such dieting is exacerbated by negative identity development (low self-esteem and poor body concepts) and emotional problems. The risks are intensified if, in addition, there is a family history of depression (common in the mothers), eating disorders, and alcohol or substance abuse. Clearly, treatment requires multi-level therapeutic work. Once established, anorexia nervosa requires specialist referral for individual psychological and family therapy.

Behavioural approaches

In the case of a relatively simple behavioural model of treatment, a functional analysis would be considered vital in order to understand the development and particular circumstances of the eating disturbance for the individual. Following a formulation of likely causes and contingencies, the concern is to tackle specific aspects of the problem with behavioural techniques. One such aspect – food refusal – is considered a manifestation of avoidance behaviour. In anorexia, it is suggested, a learned association develops between negative thoughts and images about weight gain and eating. Gradually this learning process becomes strengthened and leads to an association between thoughts or images of food and feelings of revulsion. This aversive affect then occurs in association with the actual eating of food. A conditioned aversion to food intake becomes established, and the idea that eating will lead to weight gain, becomes fixed. The reinforcing influence maintaining this sequence is the anxiety reduction associated with food restriction, the affirmation of self-control, and also (more broadly) control over one's life.

The operant paradigm

Hospitalization for controlled feeding and pharmacotherapy, are aspects of a multi-level intervention. The operant paradigm includes (*inter alia*) restricting the anorexic patient to his or her hospital room and making activities and privileges contingent on weight gain. Both lenient and strict applications of such programmes appear to be effective (Touyz, 1995). However, according to the review by Mitchell and Carr (2000), behavioural interventions focusing solely on this goal are not sufficient to cope with the multi-level subtlety and complexity of anorexia, and are not always effective over the longer term. Short-term gains may be made more durable by interventions that address issues such as interpersonal problem-solving and concepts/dynamics of self-esteem (e.g. family therapy; conversational therapy and cognitive-restructuring).

The cognitive-behavioural paradigm

Cognitive-behavioural therapy (CBT) is a preferred major component in any multilevel therapeutic work. Garner and Bemis (1985) have described a cognitive-behavioural treatment model focused on modifying faulty thinking patterns about body weight, food, and eating and its effects. They teach the patient to examine the validity of his or her beliefs on a here-and-now basis; looking at such distortion of thinking as selective abstraction, over-generalization, magnification, dichotomous thinking, personalization and superstitious beliefs. A variety of cognitive-behavioural techniques are used to remedy cognitive distortions and also to enhance self-esteem.

Systematic desensitization combined with cognitive restructuring has been used to reduce the anorexic individual's extreme fear of obesity (Ollendick, 1979).

At a more mundane but no less important level, both parents and child benefit from advice on healthy eating and information about normal development. The measures above, together with frequent monitoring of the youngster's eating behaviour, can be effective in secondary prevention of anorexia nervosa. Early diagnosis and intervention are vital if the development of a chronic psychiatric disorder is to be avoided, one which has a mortality rate from starvation and suicide of around 5 per cent.

Obesity

The potential adverse consequences of obesity (body weight exceeding ideal weight for height by 20 per cent) justify early intervention. About 80 per cent of obese adolescents will become obese adults. Obesity was discussed in Chapter 7.

Body Dysmorphic Disorder

Body dysmorphic disorder (BDD) is an excessive preoccupation with an imagined defect, or real but usually slight, 'imperfection' in normal physical appearance. It was first described in 1886 by an Italian psychiatrist. The term he used *dismorphobia* comes from the Greek word 'dysmorphia', meaning ugliness of the face. ICD-10 adopted the term as a classified disorder in 1992 (WHO, 1992); DSM-111-R took it up earlier, in 1987 (APA, 1987).

The disorder usually has its onset in adolescence and tends to be chronic. At present the causes of BDD are largely speculative, based on theories ranging from psychological and socio-cultural influences, to physical (e.g. neurotransmitter) dysfunctions. Theoreticians classify BDD as part of the obsessive-compulsive disorder (OCD) spectrum, for the following reasons:

- there are many phenomenological similarities;
- BDD responds preferentially, like OCD, to pharmacological treatment with SSRIs and clomipranine;

- there appears to be an increased incidence of OCD among family members with BDD.

■ Risky Sexual Activity

The National Survey of Sexuality and Lifestyles (Wellings, Field et al., 1995) indicates that during adolescence the majority of adolescents (one in five under the age of 16 years) engage in some sexual activity, usually within the context of brief romantic relationships. This may include kissing, sexual fondling, mutual masturbation, oral sex, and intercourse. The average age of first sexual intercourse has declined over the past two or three decades by at least three years.

Harmonious sexual relationships are relatively infrequent, feelings of insecurity fairly common. Gerrard (2000) concludes an extensive survey by stating that in Britain there seems to be a strange disconnection between sex and pleasure. In most first sexual experiences, either the girl (two or three in every four), or both the girl and boy regret the encounter. Young people appear to be having sex earlier, becoming pregnant more often, but not necessarily enjoying it, some even regarding it with a sense of dread. Clinical evidence suggests that adolescents are as secretive and wary about sex as ever. Most of them believe that they have sexual problems of one kind or another and often comment on the intense anxiety they suffer.

Sexuality in Disabled Adolescents

Young disabled adults undoubtedly have the same right as typically developing males and females to culturally appropriate sexual expression, hopefully emotionally and physically gratifying. However, if the development of a confident sexual identity is a difficult task for typically developing adolescents, the problems are magnified for youngsters with physical or intellectual disabilities. The emergence of sexual interests and activities in individuals with Down's syndrome (DS) (or other disabilities) are likely to provoke alarm, anxiety, and frequently, disapproval by parents and carers. In the past, the living arrangements in institutions were segregated in terms of gender. So there were either few or no social outlets to meet the opposite sex. The presumption seemed to be that people with disabilities were asexual. Even in society today, supposedly more progressive in its attitudes, prejudice is commonplace.

Not all of this negativity can be dismissed as patronizing hypocrisy or ignorant bigotry. There may be genuine concern that cognitive and language disabilities can place adolescents with DS (for example) at risk of exploitation, unwanted pregnancy, and sexually transmitted disease. There is good cause for concern given the experience of the sexual risks taken by typically developing adolescents. Between a third and a half of sexually active teenagers in Britain do not use contraceptives during first sexual intercourse (Gerrard, 2000). One in five sexually active American teenagers contracts a sexually transmitted disease (STD) such as syphilis, gonorrhea, chlamidia, genital herpes or AIDS.

Individuals with DS may be at increased risk for sexually transmitted disease (STD); there is a substantial transmission risk of gonorrhoea. While no reports estimate the incidence of HIV infection in DS, HIV has been reported in the intellectually disabled population. Clearly, other sexually transmitted diseases are potential concerns in the sexually active individual (Stone, 1994). Risk factors associated with HIV infection in DS are the same as those of the general population and include heterosexual activity, homosexual activity, injected drug abuse, and contaminated blood transfusions (Rani, Jyothem et al., 1990).

Unfortunately, little research has been published on the subject of psychosexual development in DS or other disability syndromes. Masturbation is a developmentally normal part of sexual self-discovery, one that provides self-gratification for both typically developing and atypically developing children (Monat-Haller, 1992; Pueschel, 1986). In some severely intellectually disabled individuals, it may also appear as a compulsive form of self-injurious activity.

Dating is a normal part of adolescent social development. There are no studies of dating patterns or related social behaviours in DS. Nevertheless, the social skills needed for dating can be taught as part of a life-skills-based curriculum (Fegan, Rauch and McCarthy, 1993). Such preparation is best provided before the actual dating experience.

Contraception and Pregnancy

Contraception is often a concern of parents of individuals with DS. Health care providers and professionals need to discuss contraception and provide clear information tailored to the developmental level of the individual (Grant, 1995). Although it is the case that males have long been assumed to be sterile, and evidence in the DS population points to impaired fertility in both sexes, nevertheless a number of reviews document women with DS carrying pregnancy to term, and delivering infants with and without DS (Bovicelli, Orsini et al., 1982; Rani. Jyothem et al., 1990). Infants born to mothers with the syndrome are at increased risk of premature delivery and low birth weight. The presence of maternal cardiac, thyroid, or hepatic disease, as well as seizure disorder, complicates a pregnancy.

The high incidence of congenital heart disease in any offspring with DS contributes to pregnancy risk, including stillbirth and neonatal death. Offspring with the syndrome have a greater than average number of congenital anomalies.

Sex Education

Numerous investigations of physical and sexual abuse report that the intellectually disabled individual is particularly vulnerable to sexual exploitation and abuse (Herbert, 2000; Schwab, 1992). Personal safety and self-esteem become important issues for adolescents and young adults. To prevent such adverse sexual experiences, sex education is a high priority. Because of significant variations within the disabled population in cognitive levels, learning styles, living arrangements, and health problems, the children require an individualized approach to sex education. Personal safety education, accompanied by open discussion, begins ideally early in childhood (see Haka-Ikse and Mian, 1993).

Young children and those individuals who have severe cognitive or language impairment, may learn best from a 'good touch/bad touch' model (Haka-Ikse and Mian, 1993; Monat-Haller, 1992). Older children and individuals with mild language and cognitive deficits may be able to learn the 'Circles Concept', a paradigm of physical and emotional distance, in which coloured circles represent levels of personal relationship and physical intimacy. Individuals learn appropriate touching behaviours for each circle of intimacy, and are cautioned that 'sometimes a friend may want to be closer to you than you want. You must explain to your friend and say "STOP"' (see Walker-Hirsch and Champagne, 1992).

Carr (2002b) has produced a manual for reducing risky sexual behaviour in adolescence.

■ Depression

It is now recognized that clinical depression occurs in children, becoming progressively more common following puberty. It may present in a unipolar form (depression alone) or as a bipolar, manic-depressive disorder. The former is the focus of the present discussion.

Diagnosis

The disturbances due to depressive disorders range in intensity from mild to very severe and disabling, and involve the following:

- affect (emotions of sadness and misery);
- behaviour (slowness and inertia);
- cognitions (thoughts of hopelessness, despair and sometimes suicide);
- motivation (apathy, disinterest, lassitude, little in life appearing worthwhile);
- biological functions (reductions in sleeping, eating, sexual and other activities).

In adolescence there is a higher incidence of symptoms of irritability and feelings of worthlessness and guilt; but less social withdrawal, changes in weight or appetite, thoughts of death or suicide, somatic complaints, and feelings of hopelessness.

Epidemiology

Epidemiological studies covering children and young people from the ages of 4 to 20 years suggest prevalence rates of some 2 per cent among children and 2 to 5 per cent in adolescents (e.g. Lewinsohn and Clarke, 1999). The rate of depression seems to peak in the mid-teen years between the ages of 14 and 17. A family history of mood disorder and a favourable response to antidepressant medication indicate an increased risk of further depressive (including bipolar) disorder in adult life.

Developmental features

A depressive disorder seriously affects social, emotional and educational development. It is often indicated by an increasing neglect of self. It may be masked by a constant search (notably in adolescence) for distraction in uncharacteristic activities such as heavy smoking and drinking, dangerous risk-taking and sometimes delinquent activities. Depression is the most important predictor of suicidal behaviour in young people aged from 15 to 24 years (see below).

Causation

Depression can be understood as a final pathway of multiple interacting influences: genetic, biological, psychosocial and socio-economic. Their particular contribution to the symptomatic manifestation of the illness varies in significance, as do the influences (e.g. personal resilience and environmental supports) that protect the individual from succumbing to the illness. The issues of resilience and vulnerability are discussed in Chapter 16.

Researchers have highlighted several psycho-social factors that increase the vulnerability to depression, and require attention in preventive and treatment programmes. Some examples are:

- chronic exposure to a rejecting family in which harsh punitive discipline is the norm, or socially impoverished conditions, which give rise to feelings of hopelessness, powerlessness and negative self-evaluations;
- loss of self-esteem due to failure at school, inability to get a job or loss of employment; lack of friendships;
- the impact of traumatic accidents;
- changes in important relationships, particularly bereavement and divorce;
- abuse arising from prejudice, bigotry, racism and discrimination;
- cumulative psychosocial stresses of various kinds which make it more likely that a child will succumb to physical illness, leading in turn to depression;
- faulty cognitive processing of life experiences such as distortions and errors of interpretation.

Treatment

The options for treatment include:

- *Physical treatment.* Current evidence consistently suggests the superiority of tricyclic antidepressants over other drugs for both children and adolescents (Ambrosini, 2000). Nevertheless, in the words of Fonagy, Target et al. (2002, p. 96), their effectiveness is somewhat doubtful and of 'potential dangerousness'. As with all drug treatment, concern about side-effects requires great caution on the part of practitioners. This is a particular worry when tricyclic antidepressants are prescribed.
- *Psychosocial therapy.* Fonagy, Target et al. (2002) make the point that much attention in the clinical literature, is now belatedly paid to individual therapy and to associated family problems of children and adolescents suffering from depression (also Kazdin, 1990; 2000). Seligman, Goza and Ollendick (2004) admit, following a review of these treatment studies, that until the late 1980s, the answer to the question 'What works?' was 'We don't know'. Now, it is possible for them to describe several successful (i.e. 'well-established' or 'probably efficacious') programmes. The longer-term prognosis for depression appears to be most favourable when the depression is secondary to life stresses, and responds to psychosocial treatments, notably cognitive behaviour therapy.
- *Cognitive-Behavioural Therapy (CBT).* The evidence suggests that cognitive-behavioural therapy (CBT) is the effective remedy of choice (see reviews by Chorpita et al, 2002, Kazdin, 1990; 2000; Lewinsohn and Clarke, 1999; Lewinson, Clarke, et al., 1996; Target and Fonagy, 1996). It is the component most favoured in multi-component work.

A study by Lewinsohn, Clarke et al. (1990) illustrates a successful CBT approach. The researchers assigned 59 depressed school-going adolescents aged 14 to 18 to (i) a 14-session CBT group treatment for the adolescent only, (ii) 14 session CBTt groups for the depressed adolescent and separate 7 sessions for his or her parents, and (iii) a waiting list control group. The cognitive-behavioural intervention addressed itself to experiential learning, skills training (e.g. relaxation and mood monitoring), communication enhancement, and negotiation/conflict resolution. Parents were helped to encourage and acknowledge their offsprings' adaptive changes. Fewer adolescents in the active treatment conditions, compared with the waiting list controls, continued to meet diagnostic criteria post-treatment. Treatment gains were maintained at a 2-year follow-up.

The Risk of Suicide

Any discussion of clinical depression that failed to mention suicide would be incomplete, given the significant rise in its incidence during adolescence, and its clear relationship (among other causal influences) to the disorder.

Definitions

Suicide involves the person bringing about his or her own death, and doing it knowingly. Parasuicide is *attempted suicide* involving any non-fatal act of self-injury or taking of substance in excess of the generally recognized or prescribed therapeutic dose. By convention, alcohol intoxication alone is excluded.

In about 60 per cent of cases, there have been months of emotional or behavioural problems before the attempt, and no access to help. These youngsters usually require specialist psychological help for mental health problems such as depression and anxiety. In about 20 per cent of cases, individuals have experienced long-term problems (e.g. with family or school, a delinquent peer group, the police) of a serious nature. These young people are most at risk of further attempts. Some seek an escape or solace through the misuse of drugs or alcohol.

Incidence

Attempted suicide peaks in the age range 15 to 19 years, more than 13 suicides per 100 000 youngsters. It is somewhat rare in children under the age of 14. There has been a tenfold increase in adolescent boys and a fivefold rise for girls in such incidents, causing about 150 000 hospital attendances in the UK every year. The number of young people who actually die after attempting suicide is very small in the UK; never the less, suicide ranks among the half-dozen most common causes of death among older adolescents. Poisoning with *paracetamol* which causes serious liver damage, is the commonest type of overdose in Britain and leads to many fatalities each year.

There are several significant factors that are related to current parasuicidal episodes:

- depression, which may be accompanied by suicidal thoughts;
- persistent insomnia and social withdrawal;
- feelings of hopelessness and worthlessness;
- use of violent methods of self-harm, or serious overdose.

Kreitman (1983) indicates the following risk factors of suicide occurring after a parasuicide:

- risk increases with age;
- males are more at risk than females;
- social isolation: especially after loss of an important relationship;
- unemployment;
- substance abuse: especially following the recent loss of a job;
- psychopathic/sociopathic personality;
- history of multiple previous suicide attempts.

Interventions

It is common for Accident and Emergency departments in hospitals to see young people who have tried to commit suicide because of the despair and desperation they feel. The decision to end their life is made on the spur of the moment, without thought. They do not know where to turn for help, and feel that the only escape is 'to end it all'. It has been found that in most cases young individuals soon regret the attempt. All such incidents require serious assessment and an appropriate intervention – ranging from counselling to therapy. An empathic and knowledgeable adult is needed to explore how they have been feeling, and to provide some constructive problem solving and other appropriate forms of assistance. Usually, help involves individual or family work for a small number of sessions.

Two sources of valuable information for parents about depression in young people are:

- Graham, P. and Hughes, C. 1995: *So Young, So Sad, So Listen.* London: Gaskell.
- Burningham, S. 1994: *Young People under Stress: A Parent's Guide.* London: Virago.

The Samaritans provide a 24-hour service offering confidential emotional support to anyone who is in crisis (see Appendix IV).

CHAPTER 14

Conduct Disorders and Delinquency

As children with 'conduct problems' (see Chapter 4) reach puberty and grow stronger, more assertive and rebellious, what were 'merely' difficult situations for parents can become menacing, and in some cases, dangerous – especially when their offspring have received too little control and supervision when young.

■ Conduct Disorders

Diagnosis

The conduct disorders (CDs) overlap somewhat with the oppositional defiant disorders (ODDs). According to DSM-1V, CD criteria entail the violation of others' basic rights, of age-appropriate norms and rules of society. At least three of the following 15 behaviours (categorized under four headings) must have been present over the preceding year to meet the criteria, with one present in the last six months:

1 *Aggressiveness to people and animals* (e.g. bullying, fighting, cruelty to people and animals, using a weapon, forced sexual activity, stealing with confrontation of the victim).
2 *Property destruction* (e.g. fire setting, other destruction of property).
3 *Deception or theft* (e.g. breaking and entering, lying for personal gain, stealing without confronting the victim).
4 *Serious rule violations* (staying out at night, truanting before the age of 13, or running away from home).

Clinical features

Youngsters with incipient or serious conduct disorders demonstrate (among other problems) an inability or unwillingness to adhere to the rules and codes of conduct prescribed by society at its various levels. Such failures may be related to:

- temporary lapse of poorly established learned controls;
- failure to learn these controls in the first place; or
- behaviour standards a child has absorbed, that do not coincide with the values of the society that enacts and enforces the rules.

Developmental features

A number of investigations (as we saw earlier) have demonstrated the continuity between disruptive problems in the preschool years and externalizing problems in adolescence (Sutton, Utting and Farrington, 2004). Developmental theorists suggest that there are two developmental pathways related to conduct disorders: the 'early starter' versus 'late starter' model. The hypothesized early onset pathway begins with the emergence of oppositional defiant disorders (ODD) in early pre-school years and progresses to aggressive and non-aggressive (e.g. lying and stealing) symptoms of conduct disorder (CD) in middle childhood and then on to the most serious symptoms by adolescence (ibid.). In contrast, the 'late starter' pathway first begins with symptoms of CD during adolescence, after a normal history of social and behavioural development during the pre-school and early school years. The prognosis for 'late starter' adolescents is more favourable than it is for adolescents who have a chronic history of conduct disorders stemming from their pre-school years.

Behavioural profile

- *Aggression.* The child's aggression can take various forms and be directed towards various targets; the overall impression conveyed by parents is one of the child being a tyrant in the family. They often describe feeling deeply insecure when around their children as a consequence of this abuse. Aggression also occurs against siblings/other children/animals. It is the unpredictability of the negative behaviours and their escalating nature that cause parents always to be vigilant.

Repeated episodes of verbal and physical aggression towards other children lead to their children being disliked, rejected and ridiculed by other children.

Moreover, other parents do not want their children to associate with the aggressive child. Frequently parents report that their child has no friends.

- *Non-compliance.* Parents report that their children's refusal to obey parental requests controls not only the parents but the entire family by virtue of the power they command through their non-compliance and defiance.
- *Hyperactivity.* Many parents talk about their children's high temperamental intensity, describing them as highly active, easily 'wound up', overexcited, loud and wild and out-of-control. Their children's activity level is so high as to make their safety and their survival a major care and protection issue.
- *Failure to learn from experience.* Parents express concern about their child's inability to learn from experience. They see their child suffer the negative consequences of a particular action, yet repeat the same self-defeating behaviours on other occasions.

Impact on the Family

Children with CDs are not only non-reinforcing to their parents' efforts but actually physically and emotionally punishing. As described by the parents, a child's conduct problems create a 'ripple effect', impacting on the family in ever-widening circles; first the parents, then the marital relationship, then other siblings, then the extended family, and then the family's relationships with the community are affected.

Qualitative analyses by Carolyn Webster-Stratton (in Webster-Stratton and Herbert, 1994) of interviews with parents indicate that the process of parenting a child with conduct disorders involved four phases: 'treading water' (hoping they'll outgrow the problem); recognition (admitting the seriousness of the problem); searching for reasons (attributions) and eventual learned helplessness. The learned helplessness hypothesis proposes that people who undergo experiences in which they have no control over what happens to them often develop certain motivational, cognitive, and emotional deficits. The motivational deficit which occurs is characterized by retarded initiation of voluntary responses. The cognitive deficit is a belief or expectation that outcomes are uncontrollable. The emotional deficit is characterized by depressed emotion, and eventually a resigned mode of giving up.

The need to help families with conduct disordered children is particularly urgent, for these 'aggressive' children are at increased risk of being abused by their parents as well as for school dropout, alcoholism, drug abuse, juvenile delinquency, adult crime, anti-social personality, marital disruption, interpersonal problems, and poor physical health. Thus, in the absence of treatment, the long-term outlook for conduct-problem children is grave (Sutton et al., 2004).

Causation

There is a particular dilemma for many of the parents of conduct disordered children. The youngsters, in many cases, seem to be arrested at a demanding (egocentric) stage of development – whatever their age. The period between approximately 1 and 3 years of age is often a 'sensitive period' with regard to the development (and therefore prevention) of many conduct disorders. Social learning theorists suggest that the children with these serious anti-social problems are deviant because (*inter alia*) their early social learning/conditioning has been ineffective. The disorder takes root because of the inability of parents (for a variety of reasons, structural, emotional or social) to confront their child's coercive behaviour in a manner that will launch him/her into the vital later stages of moral development, and those processes of socialisation which have to do with empathy and impulse control.

Following this theory, which posits the primacy of parents in the development of conduct and delinquent disorders, early interventions have been aimed directly at training parents (Sutton, Utting and Farrington, 2004). Reviews of a variety of behavioural parent training programmes based on one-to-one therapy or group work, have generally supported their effectiveness.

Treatment/Intervention

Rationale

Intervention approaches based on the consultation model are aimed directly at the parents of the aggressive/anti-social child rather than at (or in addition to) the child him/herself; the aim is to change the child's behaviour by changing the parents' behaviour. One of the major strategies that has been followed in attempting to reduce conduct disorders among children involves training the parents to alter the reinforcement contingencies that support the anti-social behaviour of their children. The rationale for this approach is supplied by the research indicating that parents of conduct-disordered children have an underlying deficit in certain fundamental parenting skills. For example, it has been found that the parents of problem children differ from other parents in being:

- more punitive;
- issuing more commands;
- providing more attention following deviant behaviour;
- being less likely to perceive deviant behaviour as deviant;
- being more involved in extended coercive hostile interchanges;
- giving more vague commands;
- failing to stop their children's deviant behaviour.

Gerald Patterson (1982) has shown that whoever in the family is involved, a hostile response to an aggressive act serves to perpetuate the aggression. If a punitive response is part of a hostile interchange, far from stopping the aggression, it may actually make things worse. The consequence of this accelerating effect of hostile reactions is a family pattern of *coercive negative interchanges* that spreads to involve other family members. Such parent–child interactions are not conducive to internalized moral and social development. Norm-abiding behaviour ultimately depends not merely on avoidance of externally imposed consequences, but, more importantly, on the avoidance of aversive stimulation (anxiety/guilt) which has its source within the individual (i.e. his or her conscience).

Lax discipline (especially with regard to the offspring's acts of aggression) combined with hostile attitudes in the parents, produces very aggressive and poorly controlled behaviour in the offspring (Herbert, 1987a). There is a positive relationship between the extensive use of physical punishment in the home by parents and high levels of aggression in their offspring outside the home. Violence begets violence; what the child appears to learn is that might is right. Delinquents have more commonly been the victims of adult assaults – often of a vicious, persistent and even calculated nature – than non-delinquents (Herbert, 1987b). The consequences tend to be lasting unless pre-empted by radical changes in children's life experiences – the goal of the programmes described below, and in Chapter 16.

Individual Parent/Family Training Programmes

There is a large body of literature describing the 'content' of parent training programmes. For example, behavioural principles such as Time-Out, Beta Commands, Praise, Differential Attention, Response Cost, are outlined in detail, in manuals containing structured courses designed for use with individuals (e.g. Herbert and Wookey, 2004). Otherwise behavioural strategies are taught on an *ad hoc* basis, depending on an individual assessment. Among those most commonly used are the following:

- *Giving commands.* Parents role-play and learn how to give clear and reasonable commands and requests.
- *Differential attention.* The differential use of attention and ignoring is widely advocated as the first step in behavioural interventions with families. It is particularly pertinent if the child is not receiving enough positive reinforcement (attention) and/or is receiving it at inappropriate times. If the child is not receiving positive attention, he or she will work to receive negative attention.
- *'Quality time'.* Happy adult–child relationships result from mutually reinforcing interactions (e.g. planned play sessions). House rules must be fair.
- *Problem solving.* The feeling of being in control is vital to self-empowerment and the successful working through of difficult situations – be it in day-to-day or crisis circumstances. The problem is 're-labelled' for the clients ('cognitive structuring'), defining what they once thought of as impenetrable as 'manageable' – given thought and calm application of a series of interpersonal problem-solving strategies. The emphasis is very much (but not exclusively) on how the person thinks; the goal in therapy or training is to generate a way of thinking, a way of utilizing beliefs and values in decision-making when problems arise.

Group Programmes

These programmes emphasize methods designed to reduce confrontations and antagonistic interactions among family members, to increase the effectiveness of positive interactions and moderate the intensity of parental punishment. In these groups, parents learn (it is argued) not only a new model of behaviour but also how to understand the consequences of their behaviour and the role it plays in the maintenance of their child's 'problem' behaviour. In effect, they learn a new language – verbal and non-verbal – for communicating with their children.

The Oregon Social Learning Center (OSLC)

The seminal influence on parent training theory and practice, is the work of Patterson, Reid and their colleagues at the Oregon Social Learning Center (OSLC), where they have treated over 200 families with extremely aggressive, anti-social children over a period of some two decades. Patterson (1982) summarizes encouraging evidence that changing family management styles (by means of manuals and personal therapeutic input) can produce significant changes in such anti-social behaviours as aggression, non-compliance, destructiveness, disruption and hyperactivity.

Five family management practices form the core components of the OSLC programme:

- Parents are taught how to pinpoint the problematic activities of concern and how to track them at home (for example, compliance versus non-compliance).
- They are taught reinforcement techniques (for example, praise, point systems) and disciplinary methods.
- When parents see their children behaving inappropriately, they learn to apply a mild consequence such as time-out.
- They are taught to 'monitor' (that is, to supervise) their children even when they are away from home. This involves parents knowing where their children are at all times, what they are doing, and when they will be returning home.
- Finally, they are taught problem-solving and negotiation strategies and become increasingly responsible for designing their own programmes.

Twenty hours of direct contact with individual families is the typical pattern in the OSLC treatment package. The therapist must be skilled in coping with the resistance to change that characterizes the majority of the families referred for treatment. Ordinarily, this level of clinical skill requires several years of supervised clinical experience.

Problem-Solving Skills Training (PSST) and Parent Management Training (PMT)

Kazdin and colleagues have combined the cognitive-behavioural-based PSST and behaviourally rooted PMT, to treat pre-adolescent youngsters. Procedures are applied in a flexibly designed individualized programme. Kazdin and Wassell (2000) found improvements in:

- child functioning;
- family functioning (i.e. quality of relationships);
- systemic family functioning;
- parenting functioning;
- personal functioning (reductions in depression; overall symptoms, stress; perceived social support).

The Incredible Years Programmes

Carolyn Webster-Stratton (see Webster-Stratton, 1991) has developed a successful series of parent training programme for the homes and schools of young conduct-disordered children. The programmes are notable for their imaginative use of videotape modelling methods and puppets:

- The *Basic* programme. The first two segments focus on teaching parents to play with their children, building interactive and reinforcement skills. The third and fourth segments teach parents a specific set of non-violent discipline techniques including commands, time out and ignoring, as well as logical and natural consequences, and the importance of monitoring their child. The fourth segment also shows parents how to teach their children problem-solving skills.
- The *Advanced* programme concentrates on adult interpersonal skills, such as effective communication skills, anger management, problem-solving between adults, and ways to give and get support.
- The *Supporting Your Child's Education* programme addresses parenting approaches that promote children's academic skills, including fostering reading skills, setting up predictable homework routines, and building collaborative relationships with teachers.

The use of videotape modelling training methods for parents of young conduct-problem children has been shown to be not only more effective in improving parent–child interactions (in comparison to group discussion approaches and one-to-one therapy with an individual therapist), but also highly cost-effective as prevention. Furthermore, videotape modelling has the potential advantage of being accessible to illiterate parents and to those who simply have difficulties with reading assignments and verbal approaches in general. Videotape modelling has potential for mass dissemination and low individual training cost.

The Child Wise Behaviour Management Programme

An example of a British effort is the Herbert and Wookey programme (described in Chapter 12) which was developed for, and validated on, typical mental health and social service clientele.

Conclusion

All the above programmes have received high ratings from parents on acceptability and consumer satisfaction. Significant changes in parents' and children's actions, and in parental perceptions of child adjustment, have indicated encouraging short-term successes. Observations in the home setting have suggested that parents are successful in reducing children's level of aggression by 20 to 60 per cent. All of the programmes report generalization of behaviour improvements from the clinic setting to the home over follow-up periods ranging from six months to four years.

Webster-Stratton and Herbert (1994) have reviewed the evidence relating to Behavioural Parent Training (BPT). Most of the evaluations of BPT have taken place in America. However, a growing number of reports is now appearing in the UK (see Scott, 2002). Judy Hutchings and her team work with children and families in Wales. They have reported highly encouraging outcomes of a standard and structured, practice-based behavioural programme for children with severe behavioural problems (see Hutchings, Gardner and Lane, 2004). The intensive programme utilized video feedback to parents of their own interactions with children and repeated practice of new management skills (parents doing things rather than being given advice). A four-year follow-up investigation has indicated that the gains made by the intensive treatment group have been maintained. These findings demonstrate that video feedback and coaching help parents but are costly and require highly skilled personnel, thus making the intervention available to very few children and families.

This led to the development of a practice-based training programme for health visitors (nurses with statutory duties for health care of young children), which has been researched and demonstrated evidence of positive outcomes for health visitors, parents and children. This is now an accredited Master's level module within the University of Wales.

■ Delinquency

Diagnosis

It is clear from self-reports of delinquent-type behaviour that large numbers of young people engage in delinquent acts (e.g. petty thefts, vandalism) for several years before they receive a police caution or are found guilty. These activities tend to be transitory for a majority of young delinquents. By their twenties most of the former offenders have gradually become broadly law-abiding members of the community. However, there is a relatively small hard core of adolescents who continue habitually to break the law (Herbert, 1987a).

Delinquency reaches a peak at 15 or 16 years for boys and 14 years for girls. Although conduct problems can create misery for everyone concerned with the younger child with this disorder, as they mature physically, the problems that involve a persistent defiance of authority, together with a refusal or inability to show self-restraint, become more serious in their implications. They extend more and more beyond the confines of the child's life at home and school and may pass the threshold dividing anti-social activity from criminal offences.

Causation

A background of extreme social disadvantage and deprivation is consistently found to be a risk factor for ODD and conduct problems, delinquent behaviour, and adult mental health problems (Kazdin and Wassell, 1999). Compared with children not reared in more affluent surroundings, those from socially disadvantaged backgrounds also tend to have delayed development of cognitive abilities (e.g. language development, academic attainment, and IQ scores) (Guralnick, 1998).

Children born to teenage mothers (who tend to come from large families, have low educational achievement, low income, and low occupational status) are more likely to grow up in lone-parent families, become offenders, and become teenage parents themselves (Herbert, 2004). Early learning programmes have been initiated as one way of tackling these formidable problems.

Delinquency is the field of anti-social behaviour where we observe the most significant interaction between the forces of nature and nurture. For example, the susceptibility to anti-social activity is very marked when adverse parenting is associated with genetic risk. Adverse environments, on the other hand, tend to have only a weak effect in increasing anti-social behaviour, when there is no genetic risk as indexed by its presence or absence in the birth parents. Bohman (1996) found that, in the absence of either genetic or environmental risk, the rate of adult criminality was 3 per cent. With environmental but no genetic risk, the rate rose to 6 per cent. With genetic but no environmental risk, it rose further to 12 per cent. However, when both genetic and environmental liability were present, the rate reached 40 per cent (see Rutter et al., 1999a, b).

Treatment

Given the social impact of the delinquent disorders, and the fact that for many young people, the transition to adolescence is marked by impulsiveness, independence-seeking and a dramatic expansion and complexity of their social lives, important therapeutic agendas are likely to be about self-control, the resolution of conflict and confrontation within the family, in the school and residential settings, and the acquisition of social skills.

Multimodal programmes

Behavioural methods are most useful when embedded within multimodal interventions (e.g. Henggeler, Schoenwald et al., 1998). The treatment package might involve:

- communication training
- feedback
- positive interruptions
- problem-solving
- decision-making skills
- providing rationales
- happy talk
- positive requests
- non-blaming communication
- negotiation skill-training
- didactic dialogue and
- family games.

There are different training and rehabilitation programmes, such as:

1   *The Reasoning and Rehabilitation Programme*, developed by Ross and Fabiano (1985), incorporating as it does several methods, is an example of useful multimodal work. It is reviewed among other methods in Lilienfeld et al., 2003.

2   *Aggression Replacement Training (ART)* (Glick and Goldstein, 1987) includes three main approaches to changing behaviour: structured social skills learning (social skills and social problem-solving), anger control training, and moral education. Lochman (1992) reported a three-year follow-up of aggressive young adults (males) participating in a school-based anger control programme. The results were positive: the treated group had lower rates of substance abuse and higher levels of self-esteem and social problem-solving skills than untreated controls. There was no evidence, however, that the programme had a significant long-term effect on delinquent behaviour.

While there are encouraging demonstrations from these studies that, on a variety of outcome measures (notably behavioural indices, cognitive functioning, family relationships, and different academic and social skills), short-term changes can be brought about, there is less room for optimism on the issues of temporal generalization and (in the case of delinquents) generalization to actual offending behaviour.

The literature suggests there is a moderately encouraging if short-term effect for the non-offending conduct problems of adolescence. Much of this evidence accrues from individual therapy studies. Whether the conduct problems reviewed are functionally related to offending such that changing targeted behaviours will modify delinquent activities is debatable.

Cognitive-behavioural (CBT) approaches

The CBT approaches to interventions for delinquent adolescents consist usually of techniques which have their roots in cognitive therapy (e.g. Socratic questioning, persuasion, challenging, debate, hypothesizing, cognitive restructuring, verbal self-instruction and internal dialogues). Others are drawn from behaviour therapy (e.g. operant procedures, desensitization, exposure training, social skills training, role-play, behaviour rehearsal, modelling, relaxation exercises, redefinition, self-monitoring) (see Kendall and Hollon, 1994).

Treatment programmes are designed to meet particular difficulties, but generally involve:

- relaxation training;
- modelling and reinforcement of confident behaviours;
- formulating more positive thoughts (cognitions) and self-attributions to alter maladaptive beliefs;
- self-appraisal;
- the experience of rewarding structured tasks and activities;
- using operant conditioning to develop pro-social behaviour and improve social skills.

The evidence for the effectiveness of cognitive-behavioural treatment approaches is sufficiently substantial to make them the preferred treatment option (Cooke and Philip, 2001).

VI

How and Where to Find Help

■ The Care-Plan Formulation

The formulation of problems associated with a child's development is generally a means to an end, a multi-agency plan of action or an individual treatment intervention. It might also be an end in itself: an expert assessment for the social, health or educational services, or an independent report for the courts. The individual or multi-agency team exercise of piecing together a formulation, bridges the processes of assessment, analysis of causes, and allocation of resources, which inform the choice of an intervention. The particular rationale for that intervention will be based on a variety of contributory causal factors – genetic, medical, psychological and social – which are described in Chapter 15.

Many *psychological difficulties* of development in childhood and adolescence differ in degree, rather than kind, from normal behaviour, with implications to be examined in the chapter.

■ Service Provision

Two styles have been described in the literature on intervention:

1 In the 'waiting' mode, professionals remain physically within a service system (e.g. hospital, clinic) and wait for patients/clients to come to them; it tends to be associated with remedial therapies. The waiting mode stresses late tertiary preventive activity. This mode can, regrettably, be a metaphor for inertia in the face of urgent requests by stricken parents of children with mysterious

disabilities, for more information, more understanding, and more medical or non-medical initiatives. As the mother of a child suffering from the long-term consequences of very low birth weight and brain damage, said: 'If you just wait, nothing will happen!' Her unremitting search for help did not result in the hoped-for cure, but she mobilized innovative technical assistance that enhanced her child's life style.

2   In the 'seeking' mode, professionals usually operate physically outside the traditional service system and seek to intervene in problems before they become long-term. The seeking mode involves more active, primary prevention.

In Chapter 16, we address the How? question. How do we help disabled children and their families or, better still, help them to help themselves, in the most effective way? This raises the issues of practice models and the provision of resources.

CHAPTER 15

The Care-Plan Formulation

■ Introduction

In this chapter we change our earlier diagnostic perspective on specific developmental problems in order to take a broader view of the way in which disabilities and disorders in general, are assessed and formulated for planned individual and group interventions. The formulation of problems associated with a child's development is generally a multi-agency plan of action or an individual treatment intervention. It might also be an expert assessment for the social, health or educational services, or for the courts. The formulation bridges the processes of assessment, analysis of causes, and allocation of resources. As such it is central to most therapeutic or rehabilitative interventions.

Taylor and Rutter (2002) comment that: (i) diagnosis is seldom the 'automatic generator' of a plan of management; and (ii) that a formulation encompasses more information than a restrictive diagnosis. The reality is that many signs of atypical development ('abnormality') are, by and large, on a continuum with, or manifestations of physical, behavioural, cognitive and emotional attributes common to all children. Their quality of being dysfunctional lies in their inappropriate intensity, pervasiveness, frequency and persistence. Many psychological difficulties of development in childhood and adolescence differ in degree, rather than kind, from normal behaviour.

The exceptions to this generalization are, of course, many qualitatively exceptional genetic conditions (more than 2,000 single-gene defects are known), medical diseases and physical impairments (Buys, 1990). This fact raises ethical problems for the practitioner. Whereas the medical model provides a reasonably unambiguous ethical rationale for treatment by means of *a priori* standards of 'health' and 'pathology', psychological (particularly behavioural) definitions tend to construe abnormality as not usually different qualitatively, from normal behaviour. If this is the case, therapists are involved in making judgements that some alternative behaviour would be preferable – a social, subjective and, therefore, potentially discriminatory decision.

This leads inexorably to the following questions, the answers to which have the status of ethical imperatives for the therapist as agent of change: 'To whom is the behaviour undesirable?', 'Is it really in need of changing, and if so, to what must it reasonably change?', 'Is it the environment that needs to change?' These questions have resonances with the concerns surrounding the classification of the disabilities (see page 248).

■ The Formulation Procedure

The skills involved in formulating explanatory hypotheses, choosing and evaluating a test of the formulation, and translating it into a plan of action, are rooted (depending on the presenting problems) in medical, psychological, social or educational theories and practices. The knowledge base is frequently empirical; experimental and evaluative research constituting the sources of information about aetiology and likely treatment outcomes.

There are also intuitive and creative aspects to work with children and their families. The balance between convergent scientific thinking and a divergent approach (a creative element) to child practice, varies within professions, between individual professionals, and most particularly, between therapeutic interventions. For example, family-oriented behavioural work can be said to be a blend of applied science and 'art', and as such has many of the qualities of craftsmanship. Practice has a foundation of empirically tested theory. However, because of the particular demands of work with children, its boundaries cannot be restricted to the letter rather than spirit of scientific method. There needs to be a place for intuition, insight, imagination, and empathic communication. There needs to be:

- an intuitive feeling for the 'world' of developmentally delayed children and their parents, particularly the need to normalize their day-to-day activities and enhance their sense of self-worth;
- insight into other special needs of emotionally distressed and disabled children, and the resources they require in order to improve the quality of their lives;

- the imagination to find play and teaching materials that will captivate and extend children's learning, while stimulating the interest and participation of the adults who teach and care for them;
- the empathic communicative skills for teaching children and adult care-givers: explaining abstract principles, unravelling complex problems, and negotiating solutions with them.

There is, additionally, the vital art of increasing children's and parents' self-confidence (self-efficacy) by means of a therapeutic alliance that is consistent and non-patronising. Other no less important skills may involve the *socio-political* and *economic* knowledge required to influence people and policy. It might be community organizational expertise that:

- mobilizes funds for an increase in the number of classroom assistants for 'statemented' children;
- creates pressure for improved access facilities for children permanently in wheelchairs;
- advocates laws reversing the social exclusion of disabled children (e.g. demands for inclusive sports and social clubs, and 'user-friendly' playgrounds).

■ Assessment

The way a formulation is conceptualized and the consequent selection of data describing the patient's (client's) problem vary according to its nature, purpose, and the theoretical assumptions of the professional. Different disciplines have designed assessment or diagnostic protocols, for example the social work core assessment leading to a multi-agency plan of action for a 'child in need', or the educational statement of need for 'special' educational provision. There is no one right way of arriving at a remedial, preventive or treatment programme. Two examples of assessment procedures follow: (i) a statutory social work protocol; and (ii) an assessment leading to a general casework formulation.

Assessment of Children in Need by Social Workers

Social workers who have statutory responsibilities for child protection, use the Framework for Assessment of Children in Need and their Families (see Appendix I) as a guide to the steps required following a referral, and the time allowed for each stage of the informal enquiry, and the formal investigation.

The initial assessment is a brief assessment of a child referred to social services, which begins after the single 'working day' allowed for clarifying the referral and deciding whether to proceed or not. It leads on to the recruitment of a variety of expert opinions for the detailed 'core assessment of need' that follows, if justified.

Its purpose is to ascertain:

- why the assessment is required, and whether the child is in need (Section 17 of the Children Act 1989);
- whether there is suspicion of harm (Section 47 of the Children Act, 1989);
- whether there is reasonable cause to suspect that this child is suffering or likely to suffer significant harm;
- the nature of services required;
- who should provide services;
- within what timescales;
- whether a core assessment is necessary.

Timescale: within 7 days for this.

Key sections of the Children Act, 1989, are described in Herbert (1993).

The main assessment is called the *core assessment*. This is an in-depth assessment which addresses the central or most important attributes of a child and the capacity of his or her parents (or caregivers) to respond appropriately to these needs. Its purpose is:

- to gain an understanding of the child's developmental needs and the capacity of his or her parents or care-givers to respond appropriately;
- to provide an analysis of the findings (formulation); to inform planning, case objectives, and the nature of service provision.

Time scale: within 35 working days.

Dimensional criteria

Among the criteria used in the formulation, are those related to the child's developmental needs (Herbert, 2003). These include health; education; emotional and behavioural development; identity; family and social relationships; social presentation and self-care skills. Dimensions of 'parenting capacity' involve: basic care; ensuring safety; emotional warmth; stimulation; guidance and boundaries; stability. The 'family and environmental factors' include: family history and functioning; wider family; housing; employment; income; family's social integration; and community resources (Sutton, 2000).

▓ A Casework Assessment

This assessment framework is well suited to problem solving like the experimental method it resembles. The process of formulating is, figuratively speaking, like the action of a funnel containing a series of filters that represent choice and decision points. They have the function of distilling a many-sided problem into a relatively brief, formal statement about one's conclusions and recommendations. The resulting formulation may serve as the ground plan for a hoped-for alleviation of the presenting difficulties, or as an expert report of some kind (see below). Whatever its purpose, it is likely to be an amalgam of analysis, explanation and intentions that emerges at the end of the figurative funnel.

The stages of working up a case involve four kinds of activity, represented by the mnemonic ASPIRE (Sutton and Herbert, 1992): The stages are as follows:

Stage 1   Assessment (AS) (in medicine referred to as diagnosis)

> Focusing on the 'What?' question,
> i.e. what is/are the problem(s)
> Focusing on the 'Which?' question,
> i.e. which of the problems are to be addressed,
> and in what order
> Focusing on the 'Why?' question,
> i.e. why have the problems arisen?

Stage 2   Planning (P)

> Focusing on the 'How?' question,
> i.e. how are we (practitioner and patient/clients) going to
> address the problems?

Stage 3   Implementation of the intervention (I)

> i.e. the detailed planning of the programme, and consideration
> of possible difficulties that may arise.

Stage 4   Rigorous Evaluation (RE)

> i.e. the choice of measures (or other means) of evaluating the progress and
> outcome of the intervention.

The preventive and treatment approaches adopted by practitioners, and indeed agencies, may be based on a variety of theoretical models drawn from different 'schools' of thought within the disciplines, among others, medicine, psychiatry, education, sociology and psychology. These theoretical models, acting as 'filters' in the figurative assessment funnel, play a significant role in determining what information is pertinent to the investigation of the client's problems, and which assessment methods will generate the data necessary for an intervention. As the funnel narrows, so does the focus of the three questions: What?, Why? and How? that give direction to the assessment.

The 'What' Question

Rigorous assessment – finding out precisely *what* constitutes the problem whether in a narrow personal/family or broader social focus – is critical to effective intervention. The formulation that bridges these activities depends upon the professional's practice-wisdom and skill in eliciting the data on which it is to be constructed. The different stages of the ASPIRE process leading towards the formulation involve a sometimes daunting array of practical choices, decisions, actions and caveats for the practitioner. Not infrequently, incoming data – sometimes as far forward in client contact-time as the intervention – demands a re-formulation and possibly a 'rethink' of the intervention.

A developmental perspective

There are several questions to ask about children's development in formulating whether their difficulties merit serious concern:

• Is the child's adaptive behaviour appropriate to his/her age, physical status, intelligence and social situation?
• Is the present course of development typical, atypical (e.g. delayed) or a mixture of both?
• Does he or she wet the bed regularly?
• Does he or she soil themselves?
• Does he or she sleep and eat well?
• Are height and weight within normal limits?
• Is the environment making reasonable demands of the child?
• Is the environment satisfying the crucial needs of the child, i.e., the needs that are vital at his/her particular stage of development?
• Does the child's continuing presence at home (or attendance at school) interfere with a forward momentum in his or her development?

- Do they represent a developmental 'cul-de-sac', taking him or her in the direction of a self-defeating life-style (e.g. delinquent activities)?

Particular ages are associated with specific developmental achievements, such as learning to walk, use language and become toilet trained. The concept of sets of behavioural characteristics and learning tasks that occur together at certain *stages* of the life span can be helpful in finding answers to the 'diagnostic' developmental questions above. The issue of competence is central to these age- and stage-related tasks; indeed, both parents and children worry about the 'timetable' they imply. Failures or delays may lead to loss of dignity, self-esteem and the confidence needed to tackle further developmental tasks. As we shall see when we deal below with the 'how' question dealing with interventions, this makes the physical and social training and the education of children with disabilities, a matter of critical importance. The likelihood that children and teenagers will successfully overcome developmental and other life tasks, whatever the 'hurdles', is immeasurably increased when parental influence and professional help are committed, authoritative and wise.

Clinical assessment

Clinical assessment provides answers to the 'what' question that go beyond the sort of testing procedures that use precise psychometric instruments to inform decisions at school and in the clinic by measuring children's attributes and attainments. As defined by Rune Simeonsson and Susan Rosenthal, the term 'clinical assessment' has a broader meaning which encompasses the use of varied procedures to evaluate and record developmental and psychological characteristics (see Appendix III).

The 'Why' Question

The assessment of why problems have come about – the causal influences – should, in an ideal world, inform the choice of an interventive approach.

Physical causes

Many major developmental disorders, mental health conditions, psychological and psychosomatic problems such as Down's syndrome, depression, anorexia and bronchial asthma, have contributory genetic, organic and biochemical causes. Multi-factorial causation, in the form of complex interactions of predisposing and precipitating influences, is found in most mental health and psychological disorders. Even with effective medical (notably drug) treatment, follow-up psychosocial interventions are frequently a necessity in both the short and long term.

Psychosocial causes

The term 'social ecology' is used to describe the system of psychosocial influences impinging on the child and adolescent and their environment. As Urie Bronfenbrenner (1989) conceptualizes them, they are:

- The *microsystem*, which comprises all relationships and transactions in a particular setting, e.g. the social and physical family environment.
- The *mesosystem*, which includes the interrelationships between the major settings such as home and school where children do their growing up.
- The *macrosystem*, which contains the general beliefs, values and traditions of the culture or subculture that control the interactions between the various layers of the social system, and the tenets that reflect the meaning and value of life.

It is necessary to underpin the diagnosis and treatment of children with developmentally related problems, with a broad-based knowledge-base drawn as appropriate, from an interdisciplinary team of professionals: developmental psychologists, geneticists, ethologists, developmental neurologists, cognitive-behavioural theorists, and social learning theorists.

The 'How' Question

The final question leads to the strategic formulation of a plan of treatment or rehabilitation, the tactical specification of methods/techniques for bringing them about, and (crucially) the services and personnel to undertake the tasks. If help is to be provided for children with particular disabilities and needs, it is necessary to know how many children there are with those impairments, and what services they are likely to require. This is the epidemiological issue that pervades all the considerations of service provision.

Goals and Perspectives

Whatever the purpose of an assessment, or the remedial and preventive tasks to be undertaken, individuals and agencies hold assumptions that determine the operational choices and decisions that are made at the opening to the figurative funnel described above. These are in operation before work has even begun, and concern the broadly based perspectives and theoretical models adopted for the case. It has to be admitted that in the absence of clear working protocols, they are not always explicit, carefully thought through, or agreed by collaborating professionals – especially when they come from different disciplines, or are driven by ideology rather than science (see Lilienfeld, Lynn and Lohr, 2003).

There are three major perspectives that public health and mental health goals have in common:

1   *The prevention of specific problems.* The aim is to target populations that include individuals who are at high risk for a variety of physical and psychological problems. This requires the identification of factors that cause specific disorders.

2   *A medical-biological perspective.* For a medical practitioner the emphasis is on pathology: a physical disability may be categorized as an abnormality (e.g. blindness, heart disease), a dysfunction (e.g. paraplegia), or as a specific diagnosis (e.g. bronchial asthma, arthritis). Medical classificatory systems and taxonomies are based on the assumption that specific syndromes (disease patterns) or handicapping conditions (disabilities) with identifiable and specific causes (aetiologies) can usually be diagnosed. Ideally, diagnostic categories should generate reliable descriptive criteria and imply clear causal theories. Implications for treatment or some other intervention should also flow from the chosen diagnosis. These desiderata are something of a rarity in child psychiatric taxonomies.

3   *An ecological perspective.* The assumption here is that similar psychosocial influences can give rise to a variety of psychological disorders. It may not be possible to predict with precision, specific disorders; however it should be feasible to mount general intervention programmes in a variety of sensitive areas where there are common stressors. Professional services are likely to be sought where it is possible to anticipate child and adolescent psychological problems. For example, sexually abused children are particularly at risk (Babiker and Herbert, 1998); among the many adolescents in need of intensive (possibly long-term) support and counselling are single teenage mothers – a particularly vulnerable group according to the research evidence (e.g. Egeland, Yates et al., 2002).

Vulnerability

Children are likely to be identified as 'vulnerable' if:

- they suffer from disabilities;
- they have insecure attachments;
- they are isolated;
- they have experienced trauma early in life;
- they are in institutional care;
- they have a criminal parent;
- they are from ethnic minorities; or
- they have experienced, or continue to experience neglectful care and hostile rejection.

Life-events involving divorce, loss and separation constitute periods of high risk. It is estimated that around a quarter of the children born to married couples will experience the separation of their parents before their sixteenth birthday.

'Cumulative protection' strategies have been developed to target multiple problems. These are discussed in the next chapter.

CHAPTER 16

Service Provision
How and Where to Find Help

■ Epidemiology

Effective service provision requires reliable information about need: what and where help is needed. This is where the data from epidemiological surveys is so critical. Epidemiology functions at the level of population needs rather than individual needs. It is defined as the study of the distribution and determinants of health, disease, and disorder in human populations (see Hatton, 1998a, b). Hatton discusses, *inter alia,* Asian people with intellectual disabilities as an example of epidemiology in practice. A survey found that there were substantial numbers of Asian adults with intellectual impairments who were not known to the specialist services, and thus less likely to use residential and respite services compared with their non-Asian counterparts. This information on prevalence (the number of cases, old and new, existing in a population at a given point in time or over a specified period) allowed local agencies to increase Asian awareness of what resources were available in the community, and to fill gaps in the provision of services.

Hatton makes the point that knowledge of the incidence of a disorder (the number of new cases in a population in a stated period of time) can answer important questions for service planners. As an example, he mentions the increase in the birth and survival rates of the very low birth-weight babies thought of as at particular risk for intellectual disability. However, this improved survival rate does not appear to be accompanied in these infants by an increase in intellectual impairment, presumably because of parallel improvements in health care.

■ Primary Care Services

There are three main sources for the delivery of primary care to children with developmental, mental health, and other problems:

- GPs (family practitioners);
- child health clinics (frequently associated with pre-school as well as school medical services);
- hospital casualty departments.

In the UK, a GP practice provides health care (assessment, treatment and preventative services) for some 2000 patients drawn from the local general population, in surgeries situated throughout the country. Many practices have nurses and health visitors attached to them, and increasingly there will also be psychologists, physiotherapists, chiropodists and counsellors in attendance, or available.

GPs are the main source of referrals to hospital medical services, many going on to be referred to paediatricians. Although paediatricians identify, in a high proportion of their inpatients, emotional problems that require mental health consultation, relatively few are sent to child psychiatrists. Reasons for the liaison difficulties between paediatric and child psychiatry departments have been explored by Rauch and Jellinek (2002).

Few follow-up services are carried out nowadays by primary providers. Currently, service provision, managed care and cost containment are among the 'preoccupations' of the social services and health or education departments which deal with the emotional, physical, psychological, and academic needs of children (and families) of all ages. The resulting reduction in the duration of care and number of contact sessions for most types of service, together with increasingly stringent demands for results, encourages professionals to discover the most effective ways of working, and requires them to form working alliances with social, voluntary, and other support systems. For example:

- Community-based personnel are increasingly engaged in arranging for children in need to be looked after in foster or adoptive homes, and in implementing training programmes for health visitors, teachers and parents. These are designed to mitigate disruptive behaviour and prevent delinquency (e.g. Herbert and Wookey. 2004; Patterson, 1982; Webster-Stratton and Dahl, 1995; Webster-Stratton and Herbert, 1993; 1994).

- Follow-up work by various support services for patients after intensive care has produced not only long-term benefits, but also 'unearthed' new or more serious problems. Mentoring, for example, is an important source of after-care, emotional support and monitoring following a programme of therapy or rehabilitation (see below).
- Other individuals requiring support might include those at risk of domestic violence and child abuse, frail disabled clients, teenage mothers, school non-attenders, drug addicts and homeless adolescents.
- Interventions for the developmental problems of children and adolescents tend to take place in multidisciplinary teams and (with encouragement from the government) by means of multi-agency co-operation. Most children currently attending mental health agencies have multi-service needs. The conduct disorders, to take one example, are likely to involve the educational, health and social services and possibly (given their poor prognosis), the criminal justice systems. This collaboration is necessary given the complex interaction of physical, social, economic and psychological causes of disability.

■ Tertiary Care Services

Paediatric Neuro-Developmental Services (NDS)

The regional NDSs offer specialist assessment and diagnosis of children with neuro-developmental disorders of the kind (particularly) that are not evident at birth. An example (Katingo Giannoulis and colleagues, 2004, p. 65) is the Newcomen Centre where the following assessment procedures are applied to all referred families:

- a single, half-day, outpatient attendance at the centre;
- multidisciplinary assessment;
- detailed parental interview (child's developmental history and present condition);
- standardized questionnaires (e.g. Autism Diagnostic Interview);
- play, cognitive and communication assessments;
- informal observations of the child;
- staff conference; formulation and diagnosis;
- feedback of findings to family;
- written report provided for the family.

The authors of this paper collected information from 37 main-caregivers of referred children, on their expectations and experiences of attending the clinic. The most commonly cited expectations were:

- to have what was wrong with their child assessed;
- to be given a diagnosis;
- to be given detailed information on the diagnosis/condition;
- to be given advice on educational issues;
- to receive guidance on behaviour management issues.

With regard to whether their needs were met:

- 81 per cent said 'totally' or 'largely', with regard to diagnosis;
- 46 per cent said so, in relation to educational advice;
- 38 per cent with regard to behaviour management guidance.

With regard to satisfaction with the service received:

- 46 per cent were 'very satisfied';
- 22 per cent were 'satisfied';
- 24 per cent were 'fairly satisfied';
- 8 per cent were 'not satisfied'.

The researchers discuss these findings in relation to the value of regional vs. local; paediatric assessment services, and improved ways of working together.

■ Community Support Services

Communities That Care (CTC)

CTC, a community prevention programme in the United States and the United Kingdom, applies a 'Social Development Model' that reinforces social bonds, opportunities, cognitive skills and other influences capable of protecting youngsters against risk in otherwise adverse circumstances. Local audits are conducted in order to identify and target priority risk factors in their particular neighbourhoods (Hawkins and Catalano, 1992; Communities that Care, 1997).

Home Visiting Programmes

There are several American programmes that have produced measurable reductions, over time, in children's offending behaviour (or dysfunctional parenting), by supporting families with very young children:

- from age one: the Houston Parent–Child Developmental Center (Johnson and Walker, 1957);
- over the first two years of life: the Yale Welfare Project (Seitz, Rosenbaum and Apfel, 1985);
- from 0 to 5 years: the Syracuse study (Lally, Mangione et al., 1983);
- infants: the Nurse–Family Partnership (Olds, Hill et al., 1998).

Examples of British schemes are:

- Home-Start;
- the Parent Adviser Service;
- Community Mothers Programme;
- Childwise Programme (Home-Visit Variation).

Home-Start

Home-Start is a voluntary home visiting service which offers practical support and friendship to any family with young children which is experiencing difficulties – most commonly young mothers who are exhausted and isolated. They may be single parents, mothers with new babies and toddlers – each family involves different circumstances. Some families will already be receiving assistance from other helping agencies. Families needing help are usually referred by workers in various helping agencies. Other referrals come from schools, pre-schools, churches, doctors, community centres. Families themselves can ask Home-Start to help.

Home-Start co-ordinators make an initial visit to the family to assess needs and discuss the Home-Start philosophy. If it can assist, staff will introduce a visitor to the family. It is up to the visitor and family to determine when the visits will happen and how long they will continue.

Home-Start visitors assist by giving low key support and friendship on a short or long term basis. Families are visited once a week or fortnightly. Sometimes visits consist of playing and talking with the children, on other visits it may be important to help the parent cook a meal – or go with the family on a picnic. Volunteer(s) offer both friendship and practical support, such as transport, help with the children, outings and help with the shopping.

The staff members maintain close links with both family and visitor to ensure arrangements are working out. All visitors are parents or grandparents themselves – and come from a variety of backgrounds and age groups. They are selected for their caring attitudes and ability to relate to others. They need to pass volunteer screening and attend a 10-week (one day per week) preparation course.

Support is offered to all Home-Start volunteers by means of:

- training;
- supervision;
- regular phone calls;
- meetings with other volunteers;
- newsletters;
- functions.

Parent adviser service

This service was established in disadvantaged areas of London. The home visiting programme is focused on families with pre-school children (Davis et al., 2003). The parental difficulties involve relationship and emotional problems (low self-esteem, stress, depression and anxiety); the children have behaviour problems. An evaluation of the service to 55 disadvantaged families by Davis and Spurr (1998) found significant improvements in all those areas of concern.

Community mothers programme

In this programme (Johnson, Howell and Molloy, 1993) trained volunteer mothers give monthly home-based support to vulnerable mothers with children aged 0 to 2 years. Among further positive findings for parents and children, a 7-year follow-up evaluation conducted by Johnson, Molloy et al. (2000) indicated enhanced parenting skills and maternal self-esteem

Sure start

This is a government programme which has the aim of giving every child a good start in life by integrating: (i) early education; (ii) child-care; and (iii) health and family support. The assumptions upon which this extremely costly nation-wide programme were based derive from evidence collected during a governmental review of child-care and early education (2002). It was demonstrated that:

- Children, parents and communities benefit when child-care, early education and health and family support are offered together.
- There are significant benefits in offering these services to disadvantaged young children, parents and communities. They can help enhance children's achievements at school, enable parents to choose work as a route out of poverty, improve health and reduce crime.

The child-wise programme: home-visiting version

This programme (Herbert and Wookey, 2004) provides a practical resource for birth parents, foster parents and teachers who are struggling with offspring (age 2 to 10 years) and older pupils who are disruptive at home and in the classroom respectively. It has been empirically established that restoring a balance of authority and control within the family/classroom is most effectively achieved by *triadic* behaviour management training (BMT) for parents/teachers.

The cognitive-behavioural (applied social learning) approach directly addresses the major conditions (e.g. failures of care-giving and distortions of socialization) that are known to contribute significantly to the development of childhood behaviour problems. If problematic behaviours of childhood are acquired largely as a function of faulty learning processes, then there is a case for arguing that certain problems can most effectively be modified where they occur, by changing the 'social lessons' the child receives. Children can unlearn self-defeating behaviours; they can learn new, more advantageous ways of going about things; and in all of this, parents and teachers are generally the best persons to help them achieve the necessary changes.

Parents use common-sense methods to rear their children, shaping and changing their behaviour in ways not too distant from the learning theory techniques of behaviour therapists. The authors of this manual claim that the basic tactics and broad principles of behaviour therapy (if not the theoretical small print, or ability to formulate strategically) are readily understood, and relatively straightforward to communicate to parents individually and in groups. The home visiting version has proved to be highly successful in disadvantaged homes.

■ Individual Support Services

▨ Mobilizing Human Resources

A professional can assist clients by putting them in touch with people, clubs, specialized self-help groups, and other resources. Surveys have shown that an important way in which people cope with their problems is to turn to family and friends rather than to professionals for help; they in turn act as a buffer against some of the harmful effects of stress. As social networks, ties, and contacts promote psychological well-being, it is important to identify their presence or absence for the client. Sources of support might include the following:

- social worker
- general practitioner
- school counsellor
- educational or clinical psychologist
- teacher
- psychiatrist
- child and family guidance (psychiatric clinic)
- probation officer
- youth/community worker
- priest/vicar/minister
- marriage guidance counsellor
- psychotherapist
- police
- volunteers and professionals operating helplines.

Intimate or close relationships of the type provided by primary groups (those people with whom one has face-to-face interaction and for whom, one feels a sense of commitment) are the most significant sources of support. The supportiveness of relationships is reflected by the availability of the following:

- emotional support (the expression of liking, respect, etc.);
- aid (material assistance, services, guidance, advice);
- social companionship;
- affirmation (the expression of agreement);
- social regulation (appropriate role-related support such as mothering, fathering, partnership – husband/wife/companion, etc.).

Different kinds of support are required for different life crises. The particular persons and circumstances involved in a potentially disruptive life event determine what is likely to be the most effective input. The support of peers and encouragement at work are positively related to an individual's continuing or recovering their sense of well-being.

Crisis Counselling

Counselling has, as its main aim, the production of constructive behavioural change. Such change emerges from a relationship of trust, one which emerges from confidential conversations between the professionally trained counsellor and the client (Egan, 1986). In the case of emergencies – acute crises – the task is to respond rapidly to lessen the immediate disruptive impact of stressful events, and thus alleviate (hopefully) longer-term effects of an adverse nature. There are many potential crises in family life:

- child diagnosed as mentally/physically disabled;
- separation/divorce;
- loss of a member of the family (bereavement);
- a successful or attempted suicide (parasuicide) in the family;
- physical illness or injury;
- mental illness (e.g., schizophrenia, depression) in a member of the family;
- the discovery of sexual abuse of a child/adolescent in the family;
- police involvement (a child's delinquent act) or a court appearance;
- drug abuse discovered;
- anorexia nervosa diagnosed;
- youngster runs away from home;
- truancy;
- family violence.

Non-Directive Therapeutic Counselling

Carl Rogers (1960) has played a major part in developing the client-centred, non-directive approach to counselling and therapy. Non-directive counselling and therapy are based upon the assumption that the individual has not only the ability to solve his or her own problems satisfactorily, but also a growth impulse that makes adult behaviour more satisfying than childish behaviour. In the Rogerian approach the goal of the intervention is to work in a facilitative, non-intrusive manner to increase the person's positive self-regard and self-direction.

Mentoring

Mentoring involves a relationship that requires eventual separation of worker and 'client'; one in which the mentored individual is encouraged to move on, to exercise individual choice, ability, and direction. Mentors provide a useful extension of the help given by professionals (see Herbert and Harper-Dorton, 2002). Putting adolescents in touch with adult mentors and with each other is a useful way of supporting them during their formative and (at times) turbulent years. Although they are relatively new to social work, counselling, and psychology, the business and education worlds are very familiar with mentoring. A major role for supervising trainers is to mentor trainees in their early experience of diagnosis and treatment; they also serve as role models guiding the trainee in patient/practitioner relationships.

Practice Approaches

Medical Practice

There is no denying the immense contribution of medical science to the understanding and remediation of disability, in its many forms. It has come in the fields of diagnostics, surgery, genetics, neonatology, orthopaedics, neurology, to mention a few. They certainly figured importantly in the chapters so far.

It is in the area of diagnostic taxonomy that much of the controversy arises. The issue of categorization is highly politicized in the area of disability. Activists challenge the jurisdiction of medicine, which is concerned primarily with illness, over the concept of disability, 'something' (reification is difficult to avoid) that may affect entirely healthy persons. Critics are concerned that the 'medicalizing' of developmental problems reduces complex life problems to reductionist medical categories. For one thing, impairments are highly variable both across populations and within an individual child or adolescent. For another, official definitions of disability may not coincide with a specific person's self-image. Persons, for example, who have difficulty walking because of an old rugby knee injury, or who suffer from activity-restricting angina, might well be mortified to be described as 'disabled'.

Most worrying is the absence of a clear relationship between many of the global diagnostic classifications applied to children who have psychological difficulties, and any clear aetiology or therapeutic/remedial programme. The clinical ideal in medicine is for a single diagnosis to be made. Child and adolescent psychiatric co-morbidity rates imply that this ideal is rarely attained in clinical settings.

Psychological Practice

The therapies subsumed under this subtitle can be differentiated along several dimensions:

- the goals (or purpose) of therapy: e.g., *supportive, prescriptive, exploratory,* or *collaborative;*
- the means by which goals are sought. This encompasses the theoretical rationale, e.g., *behavioural, cognitive, client-centred* or *psychodynamic.* (In child therapy these approaches may be mediated by talking to, playing with, rewarding the child or rehearsing skills with him or her.)
- the modality of therapy, e.g., *individual, group, couple* or *family;*
- the means of bringing about change: *training, therapy* or *self-help manuals;*
- the level of training and/or expertise of the therapist; the 'integrity' of therapeutic programmes is undermined by the *laissez-faire* attitude of some agencies with regard to these vital requirements.

The adoption of a collaborative approach to clients has advantages. Effective therapists tend to develop more positive therapeutic alliances with their patients than do ineffective therapists (Webster-Stratton and Herbert, 1994). Moreover, this tendency is independent of factors to do with attributes of the patient. The practitioner in collaborative mode engages parents in the intervention by (*inter alia*):

- actively soliciting their ideas and feelings;
- negotiating, which means involving them in joint decisions about treatment goals;
- educating, which means providing explanations, empowering parents by giving reasons, sharing information, and increasing their knowledge;
- understanding their cultural context;
- discussing and debating ideas, sharing their experiences, and solving problems together;
- eliciting support: If necessary, and if the client permits, other members of the family, or outside helpers are brought in as aides and mentors.

A good example of crucial 'outside' help is the Lovaas approach to training autistic children (see Lovaas, 1996, and Chapter 8).

Self-help

The function of helping relationships can become that of solving problems to the exclusion of defining client strengths. Focusing on client strengths is a shift from the traditional approaches of deficits and disease that have characterized much of social work practice (Cowger, 1997). Identifying strengths and supporting client capacities for growth and change are essential to the empowerment process. Empowerment in clinical practice is an internal process which is fuelled by identification of strengths, encouraged through support from others, and fostered by growing self-esteem through experiencing success in coping with daily living.

An example of the empowering process at work by Webster-Stratton and Herbert (1994) is described above in their application of the collaborative approach. The perceptions of parents with seriously disruptive children have important implications for treatment because their learned helplessness and low self-efficacy beliefs can be reversed by experiences of success. The promotion of effective parenting skills undoubtedly starts such a reversal process giving parents some expectation that they will eventually be able to control outcomes – notably their children's behaviour.

Webster-Stratton and Herbert (1994) suggest that the collaborative process which gives parents responsibility for developing solutions (alongside the therapist), is more likely to increase parents' a sense of confidence, self-sufficiency and perceived self-efficacy than are therapy models which do not hold parents responsible for seeking solutions. Recognizing the strong capacities of people to access and utilize personal and community support systems and to grow in personal and social ways validates their strength and *resilience*.

Resilience

'What makes for a vulnerable child?' was at one time the question most frequently asked, and investigated in the earlier trauma literature. A change in emphasis was inevitable in the light of evidence from longitudinal studies that an estimated half to two-thirds of children growing up in extremely adverse environments emerge intact, or nearly so (Herbert, 2003). Resilience does not mean 'unscathed' or 'invulnerable'. Stressors that most affect children tend to occur at transitional periods of life, notably when they are transferring to a new school, adapting to a reconstituted family (one in seven families with dependent children is a step-family), or moving from childhood (via a possibly awkward puberty) to adulthood. Other high-risk circumstances ranging from emotional deprivation, poverty and war conditions to 'parenting' by alcoholic, criminal, mentally ill or abusive adults, make resilience a compelling subject for research.

Resilience has been described as the ability to thrive, mature, and increase in competence in the face of adversity. In a parallel with the curvilinear relationship hypothesized between anxiety and efficiency, Luthar (1991) suggests a similar relationship between stress and adjustment so that stressors can actually enhance competence if stress levels are not too high. Competence is an aspect of resilience which depends upon the context within which it is required. The environmental influences that give rise to resilience in one context may not arouse resilient behaviour in others. For example, a child's physical resilience in the face of illness or injury may be irrelevant when his/her home has broken up following a divorce – a time when emotional resilience is required.

Many of the characteristics of the collaborative or partnership model described earlier, feature in the 38 different UK group-based parenting programmes (published or unpublished) reviewed by Smith (1996). Two broad groups were identified: (i) those with a behavioural focus with a main aim of changing children's behaviour; and (ii) those that mainly address interpersonal relationships within the family. Their objectives overlap despite their particular emphases, as both approaches help parents improve their parenting skills and their family relationships. Six main theoretical approaches were identified:

- transactional analysis stresses the transactions between people and the processes important to personality development;
- behavioural methods (applied social learning theory as described by, among others, Gerald Patterson, 1982);
- humanistic methods (as developed in 'Parent Effectiveness Training' (PET) and the work of Carl Rogers, 1961);
- psychodynamic methods that stress play and dream analysis (e.g. Anna Freud, 1958) and parent–child empathy (e.g., exploring the links between intra-psychic perceptions and family experiences);
- family systems theories that emphasize the importance of understanding individual children's behaviour in relation to that of other family members (e.g. Herbert, 1998);
- Adlerian theory (the ideas of Alfred Adler, 1927; 1930, developed by Dreikurs and Stolz, 1964, and Dinkmeyer and McKay, 1976, for their Systematic Training for Effective Parenting (STEP) programme).

■ Treatment and Prevention

The question 'what works?' is an imperative ethical and (these days) political question when planning intervention and prevention programmes, In the past two decades, the search for the *active* ingredients of treatments, have been aided by the randomized controlled trial (RCT) experimental design (see Fonagy, Target et al., 2002). To evaluate the specific effectiveness of a medical therapy, patients are randomly assigned to the experimental treatment and to an inert placebo treatment condition. In the case of a trial of a particular type of psychotherapy, clients would be assigned to a placebo treatment that includes some of the non-specific influences, and sometimes (when the effect of time alone may be suspected) to a waiting-list control group.

░ Psychosocial Interventions

Ollendick and King (2004, p. 21) confirm, after a widely ranging review of psychosocial interventions, the disappointment that has followed the initial inflated optimism about their effectiveness. They conclude that:

> somewhat unexpectedly our present overview of empirically supported psychosocial treatment for children reveals that our armamentarium is relatively 'light' and that more work remains to be done. We really do not have very many psychosocial treatments that possess well-established data in research settings let alone clinical settings.

There are many evaluative investigations but they tend to suffer from various design flaws – omissions and commissions – which undermine confidence in the validity and/or generalizability of the results. Among the various omissions are those that concern referral relevance (i.e. the clinical value of data based on work with: participants who are self-referred or respondents to advertisements); the failure to randomize allocation to groups; the absence of appropriate controls or comparison groups; the loss of 'power' and causal specificity due to small sample numbers; inadequate criterion measures of outcome; neglecting to make statements about co-morbid disorders in the patient-samples and about the programme's integrity (i.e. the quality of the experience/training of the therapists and the *real-life clinical reality* of the therapy venue and the intensity of the therapy input).

Most outcome research involves demonstrations of efficacy rather than demonstrations of effectiveness or clinical utility. Efficacy studies are directed at establishing whether a particular intervention works (e.g. reduces symptoms, increases adaptive functioning) and they are usually conducted under tightly controlled conditions. Effectiveness, or clinical utility studies are directed at establishing how well a particular intervention works in the environments and under the conditions in what treatment is typically offered (see Lonigan et al., 1998). A treatment with demonstrated efficacy in clinical trials may fail to be effective in the hurly burly of clinical practice as a result of difficulty in implementing the intervention in clinical settings, ease of dissemination, acceptability of the intervention to clients, or the increased heterogeneity of clinical populations and problems in clinical settings (e.g. co-morbidity) compared to research settings.

The issue of treatment effectiveness is discussed in detail by Fonagy, Target et al. (2002) and Kazdin (2000). Kazdin (1997a) has provided a useful discussion of how different types of psychopathology may require different types of treatment delivery. Indeed, it is likely that most children will not derive maximum benefits from traditional time-limited treatment. Kazdin (1997b) describes six such models of treatment delivery, which vary with respect to dosage, the number of systems targeted, and the degree to which the treatment is continuous or intermittent. He draws parallels between treatment for psychological symptoms and treatments for various medical conditions. Some psychopathologies may require continued care, much like ongoing treatment for diabetes. Treatment is modified over time but is never discontinued. Other psychopathologies may be nest treated within a 'dental' model. With this approach, ongoing psychological treatment is discontinued, but the child is monitored at regular intervals (particularly during important developmental transition points). Such treatment delivery models differ from the more standard notion of booster sessions. Booster sessions are typically used to reinforce treatment already provided; the types of care Kazdin (1997) is advocating are entirely different from 'treatment-as-usual'.

Epilogue

We have observed children with developmental problems at five early stages of their life journeys: beginning with the intrauterine periods, next, infancy, followed by pre-school and middle childhood, and ending with adolescence. I am conscious at the end of this sequel to my book on typical and atypical development in children and adolescents, of a similar paradox when it comes to discussing the prevention and treatment of the disorders described there. There is so much information on the remediation and prevention of childhood and adolescent disabilities, and their impact on parents and families, and yet so relatively little.

I will comment briefly on successes and failures in three areas: (i) psychosocial prevention and treatment; (ii) physical prevention and treatment; and (iii) social change.

■ Psychosocial Prevention and Treatment

Anxiety Conditions

With regard to the literature devoted to anxiety, so much a part of the world of children, there have been many successful treatment programmes, but not sufficient progress to allow for any triumphalism. As Nemeroff, Gipson and Jensen (2004, p. 498), conclude, following a rigorous 10-year review:

> unfortunately, as much as our review reflects state-of-the-art knowledge in the field, the most disappointing lesson seems to be an awareness of how little we truly know about treating childhood anxiety problems. Evidence for the efficacy of current anxiety treatments is limited by alarmingly little research with experimental designs,

small sample sizes that limit the ability to discern true outcome differences, and inconsistent results across different outcome assessment measures.

They add that 'unfortunately, as little information as we have about the efficacy of childhood treatments, we have even less information about the effectiveness of these treatments in real-world settings'.

The Consultation Model ('Triadic Approach')

One of the modest success stories in the area of preventive work – especially with regard to the risk of aggressive anti-social behaviour – has been the consultation (triadic) approach, rooted in applied social theory. The 'triadic model' begins from an assumption that parents, surrogate parents, teachers and other caregivers have a profound effect on children's development and mental health. Because they exert such a significant, foundational influence during the impressionable years of childhood, they are usually in a strong position to facilitate skill and pro-social learning, and moderate the genesis of unskilled behaviour or behavioural disorder.

There is a case for arguing (as we have done in earlier chapters) that certain problems can most effectively be modified, or skills taught, where they occur or fail to be achieved. Children can unlearn self-defeating behaviours; they can learn new, more advantageous ways of going about things; and that in all of this therapists, parents and teachers are generally the best people to help them achieve the necessary changes.

In the past two decades, the encouraging search for the success rates and active ingredients of this approach (e.g. parent and health visitor training; home visiting; early learning programmes), has been aided by the randomized controlled trial (RCT) experimental design (Fonagy, Target et al., 2002; Sutton, Utting and Farrington, 2004).

The highly systematized theories and methods of applied learning theory involved psychologists in the task of 'sharing' (e.g. teaching) their skills. The basic principles of behavioural work are clear and relatively easily communicated to professionals and para-professionals, also parents and other care-givers (Herbert and Harper-Dorton, 2002; Herbert and Wookey, 2004). This sharing of expertise reflects an important strand in the present climate of collaborative work with carers, and between agencies.

■ Physical Prevention and Treatment

There have undoubtedly been positive developments in our physical knowledge of disability, advances in screening and treatment technology; also increases in the number of skilled professional and agency teams (official and voluntary) who provide expert help and support to families. Successes in medical science research have made some potentially disabling diseases remediable, by environmental intervention. Nevertheless, the vast majority of genetic diseases continue to be poorly or not at all understood. Some are fatal, many physically or intellectually disabling for life.

Much of the hope for the present and future of chronic developmental problems lies in genome discoveries, and the preventive genetic engineering or remedial gene therapies to which they might lead. Optimism has to be tempered by the fact that many developmental problems arise from multiple genetic faults which are less accessible to manipulation than single gene disorders.

It is difficult to refer to genetic screening or modification for the prevention of disabilities, without appearing to denigrate the individuals who have the disabilities. Developmental problems may restrict their lives in different ways, and they may constitute a hardship, but they do not necessarily hinder the enjoyment or sense of fulfilment of countless productive people.

■ Social Awareness

What does prove a major hindrance to people with disabilities is the paucity of improvements – a failure of social policy and community sensitivity – in the provision of equal opportunities and facilities for children and adults in their day-to-day lives. One of the significant theoretical developments in the field of disability has been the insistence by many theoreticians and practitioners on a 'social model' of disability which challenges the discrimination and social exclusion (e.g. segregated schools, residential homes and day-centres) suffered by so many disabled people. Its beginnings in 1976 emerged from a conference of the Union of the Physically Impaired Against Segregation (UPIAS). A later development in Britain was the founding of the Disabled Peoples' Movement. Members aim to enforce in legislation, their rights and responsibilities as citizens, and also highlight failures in the provision of services for disabled people.

■ Conclusion

The subject of the prevention and treatment of developmental problems is so vast, that a book like this can only cover a relatively restricted range of disorders, and then only scratch the surface with some of them. What it can do, I hope, is to describe many of the major disorders in terms of their diagnoses, causes and available treatments, and the effectiveness of their application. My wish has also been to offer some insights into the world of children with developmental disorders, and to guide the interested reader to further reading on themes I haven't the space to explore.

Any professional help offered must take account of the unique qualities of each child who has a particular disability; but also those aspects of their development and needs that are universal – held in common with other non-disabled children. Margaret Mead in her 1949 book *Male and Female* used these words: 'We need every human gift and cannot afford to neglect any gift because of artificial barriers of sex or race or class or national origin.' Not to be forgotten are the gifts (their humanity and potential) brought to the community by the children of this book, no matter how disabled or socially disadvantaged.

The Statement of Special Need

The UK government has made it clear that it wishes to see more special needs children entering mainstream schools. As a result, special schools for children with moderate difficulties have been closed in many areas. The local authority draws up a 'statement' of special educational needs, which is meant (arguments over funds and resources are perennial) to provide extra help, such as classroom assistants or special equipment, in the school. Just over 3 per cent of children in England and Wales have a statement. Provision varies between authorities. Parents have a right to appeal to a Special Educational Needs Tribunal if they disagree with the statement. In 2000, 60 per cent of pupils with statements were in *maintained mainstream schools*, 35 per cent in *special schools* and 5 per cent in *independent schools*. There are children with serious developmental delays or disorders, sensory difficulties (visual and hearing deficits), physical impairments, chronic illness, and epilepsy, who may lack (perhaps temporarily) the cognitive, linguistic or social skills, necessary to cope with mainstream schooling (see below).

There are about 2,000 special schools (both day and boarding) for pupils with special educational needs. Some of these are run by voluntary organizations and some are in hospitals. Some independent schools provide education wholly or mainly for children with special educational needs, and are required to meet similar standards to those for maintained special schools. It is intended that pupils should have access to as much of the National Curriculum as possible. The pupil–teacher ratio in special schools is 6.5 : 1 compared to 18.6 : 1 in mainstream state schools, and 9.9 : 1 in independent schools. In mainstream schools a Special Educational Needs Co-ordinator (SENCO) is appointed to be responsible for these pupils. Also, with a concern for their welfare, is the educational social worker.

■ The Code of Practice on Special Needs

The Code of Practice on Special Needs (revised in April 2002) is published by the Department for Education and Employment (DfEE). It is based on the legal requirements for special educational needs which are laid down by the 1996 Education Act. It gives practical guidance to all schools, LEAs, Social Services Departments and Health Authorities, on how to fulfil their responsibilities under the 1996 Act. All schools are required to publish their policies based on the Code of Practice guidelines, on pupils with special needs.

A statement of *special educational needs* (SEN) is a legal document detailing the special educational needs that a child is considered to have. It outlines the specific help which will be made available to meet these needs. This is called special educational provision. In many cases, there may be no need for a statutory assessment or a statement of special educational needs. An important theme in the Code of Practice is that of *partnership*. It is essential that everyone – parents/carers, schools, LEAs, the Health Service, Social Services, voluntary organizations and other agencies – works together. This is a worthy ideal, but a formidable task.

A statement of special educational needs is set out in six parts:

Part 1: The Introduction

This gives basic details about the child, such as name, address and date of birth.

Part 2: Special Education Needs

This gives details of the child's special educational needs which have been determined from the advice given during the assessment.

Part 3: Special Education Provision

This describes:

- the special help the LEA thinks the child should have to meet the needs set out in Part 2;
- the long-term objectives to be achieved by that special help;
- the arrangement to be made for setting short-term targets and regularly reviewing the child's progress towards those targets.

▨ Part 4: Placement

This informs parents about the school where their child will go to get the special help set out in Part 3, or the alternative arrangements for education.

▨ Part 5: Non-Educational Needs

These are needs agreed between the Health Services, Social Services or other organizations and the LEA.

▨ Part 6: Non-Educational Provision

This describes how the child will get the help described in Part 5. This part could also include details about home-to-school transport.

Parents can appeal to the tribunal if the LEA:

- refuses to make a formal assessment of their child's special educational needs, or refuses to issue a statement of their child's special educational needs after making a formal assessment;
- has changed a previous statement it has made.

Parents can appeal against:

- the description in the statement of their child's special educational needs;
- the description in the statement of the special educational help that the LEA thinks their child should get;
- the school named in the statement for their child to attend;
- the LEA's not naming a school in the statement.

Parents can also appeal if the LEA:

- refuses to change the school named in the statement;
- refuses to re-assess their child's special educational needs if they have not made a new assessment for at least six months;
- decides not to maintain the statement.

Parents *cannot* appeal to the tribunal against:

- the way the LEA carried out the assessment, or the length of time it took;
- the way the LEA is arranging to provide the help, for example, the level of funding it is providing, set out in the child's statement;
- the way the school is meeting their child's needs;
- the description in Parts 5 and 6 (for example, transport costs) of the statement of their child's non-educational needs or how the LEA plans to meet those needs;
- the LEA not amending the statement after the annual review.

■ Special Education

There are exceptional (atypical) pupils with developmental delays or disorders, sensory difficulties (visual and hearing deficits), physical impairments, chronic illness, and epilepsy who lack the necessary cognitive, linguistic or social skills, to cope with ordinary schooling. Among them are:

- children with pervasive genetic disorders such as some of those described in Chapter 1, autistic spectrum disorders, and severe learning disabilities;
- children who have specific learning difficulties in reading, spelling, writing, mathematics and motor skills – which may require temporary help in order to move into or back to mainstream education;
- children presenting severe emotional and/or disruptive problems;
- children with a combination of these difficulties.

The differing needs, both within and across these groups, generate different types of educational provision.

■ The Gifted Child

The term 'atypical' or 'exceptional' applies to the high end of the normal curve of intellect as well as the lowest extreme. Less than 3 per cent of children have IQs above 130 and an infinitesimally small number score above 145 on tests specially designed to identify intellectually bright children. Using a unitary quantitative criterion puts us in the anomalous position of asserting that an extremely intelligent and exceptionally gifted child (think of the prodigy Mozart) is 'abnormal'. The prejudice or fallacy that what is rare is pathological has led to the widespread belief that geniuses and child prodigies are generally weedy, non-athletic, scholarly creatures who are distinctly odd.

Terman and Oden in their 1947 book *The Gifted Child Grows Up*, produced a summary portrait of the typical gifted child that gives the lie to the mythology that such statistical abnormalities as child geniuses are also mentally and physically 'abnormal'. It is worth looking at the evidence. Although there are exceptions to the rule, the typical gifted child is the product of high achieving parentage – exceptional not only in cultural and educational background, but also apparently in heredity. As a result of the combined influence of heredity and environment, such a child is advanced *physically* compared to the average child in the general population. Educationally, in class placement, he or she is about 14 per cent ahead of their age; but in mastery of the subject taught, he or she are about 44 per cent ahead. The net result is that, during the primary school period, a majority of gifted children are kept at school tasks two or three full classes below the level of achievement they have already reached.

Here may lie the source of problems – boredom and lack of incentive – for many of these youngsters. The advanced and distinctive progress of the gifted child generates demands on his or her emotional and social development, which often lead to social isolation and emotional hypersensitivity. The interests of gifted children are many-sided and spontaneous. They learn to read easily, and read many more and also better books than the average child. At the same time, they engage in a wide range of childhood activities and acquire far more knowledge of play and games than the average child of the same age. Both sexes show a degree of interest in the world, and a general maturity, two or three years beyond the norm for their age. They are rated above average on tests of character, and a variety of intellectual, personality, physical and social characteristics. Gifted children, like their adult genius counterparts, far from falling into a single pattern, represent an almost infinite variety of patterns.

These youngsters may not be 'disabled' in the technical meaning of the term, but without thoughtful attention to their educational and emotional needs behaviour problems are likely to emerge (see Cline and Schwartz, 1999; Kerr, 1991).

Needs of Developmentally Disabled Children and their Families

■ Informing Parents

Around 28,000 children in the UK are born or diagnosed with a disability. One of the first priorities in helping families is finding the 'right' way to tell them what many have been dreading: the news that their child has a disorder or disability. There is probably no right way for all, or any parents. Not all parents receive this information at the same stage of their child's life. Some are told at, or soon after birth; others are informed at a later consultation when their supposedly 'normal' child begins to display the adversely life-changing effects of an inherited disorder, or an accident. For others, the realization that something is 'not quite right' comes gradually, as their child fails to reach particular milestones of development, and is later diagnosed as having a *developmental delay*.

The charity SCOPE has published a research-based report *Right From The Start* which examined parents' first experiences of hearing of their child's condition. What became clear was the fact that professional practice in conveying significant news is very mixed. Two quotations from the study indicate how crucial sensitive communication is at this time for vulnerable parents.

among the most frightening and confusing pieces of information that a parent will ever receive.
Informing parents of a life-threatening or severely disabling condition in their child is one of the most challenging duties faced by staff working in the child health services.

No matter how minimal or severe the disability, or how traumatic the impact of the revelation, feelings tend to run a recognizable course: shock, anger, sadness, denial, and grief. When asked, most mothers express the view that it is best for them to be told as soon as the doctor suspects a physical or an intellectual disability in the infant. They wish to be given truthful and clear information.

However, some mothers adopt what seems like a defensive stance and deny the diagnosis. They often continue to hope that the doctor will be proved wrong. Such denial is not uncommon immediately following diagnosis and may go on for some days or weeks, or even longer, before it finally abates. The doctor has to decide how soon he or she is in a position to tell the parents of their infant's disability. A further problem faced by the paediatrician or GP is not only when and what to tell them, but also how much and what definitely not to tell her. This last point is controversial. Nevertheless, it is often a question of not giving the parents information that (at that particular time) could be overwhelming or misinterpreted. It is a matter of fine judgement; sparing parents any unnecessary worry and grief. Young mothers, in particular, and childless women who have been waiting desperately for a pregnancy, are sometimes so overwhelmed by the initial news that they cannot absorb much more than the minimum of information.

■ Helping Strategies

There are several useful strategies that can ease the shock a little once the news about a disabled or disordered child has been received, or at an early stage. It is suggested to parents that they talk to other parents with disabled children. The parents of disabled children generally develop expertise in the specialist care of their child and management of their disorder, particularly when it is a rare condition. Many health professionals acknowledge that such parents frequently know significantly more than they do about the condition and its management Other suggestions to parents are: (i) to take time to come to terms with their feelings; (ii) to develop constructive outlets for them; (iii) to give support to their disabled child's sometimes 'overlooked' siblings (e.g. finding time to spend alone with each of the other children); (iv) to seek advice and information from experienced professionals: therapists from different disciplines, doctors, social workers, special education co-ordinators, school and mental health counsellors; (v) to seek help and support from trusted family members, friends, professionals, and voluntary agencies.

Parents should not feel ashamed of needing and asking for assistance, but would benefit by arranging for their child's access to an appropriate Early Intervention Programme (see pp. 66, 85, 108, 110, 145).

■ Family Needs

A vital consideration for professionals at a more personal level than usual, are the responsibilities and needs of families who care for children with developmental disabilities. Bryony Beresford at the Social Policy Research Unit, University of York, conducted a national survey in 1992, to explore issues of this kind, by asking parents about their needs and circumstances arising from rearing a severely disabled child. A sample of over 1100 parents drawn from the database of the Family Fund (arguably the most representative database of families with severely disabled children in the United Kingdom), completed a questionnaire about their needs and circumstances. While this survey is somewhat dated, it has to be said that comparisons with data collected in the 1970s indicated little improvement in the circumstances in which families were then caring for their severely disabled child.

■ Synopsis and Summary of the Findings

- Severely disabled children of all ages are highly dependent on their parents to meet their basic care and treatment needs.
- Older children are likely to have social, communication and behavioural problems.
- The most common unmet needs of the child related to learning skills, meeting physical needs, and having someone to discuss their disability with them.
- A third of the parents had unmet needs related to skills which would encourage their child's development, as well as those which would resolve or ease sleep and behaviour problems.
- Certain groups (families from minority ethnic groups, lone parent families and those caring for the most severely impaired children) were particularly vulnerable to high levels of unmet need and poor living circumstances.
- Only half of the parents described their relationship with professionals as positive and supportive.
- Household incomes of these families were lower, on average, than families with non-disabled children and substantially lower than the incomes of the

general population; a particular burden as a disabled child places extra demands on the household budget.

- 90 per cent of single parents, and over a third of two-parent families, had no income other than benefits.
- Employment for mothers in the study, who made up 96 per cent of the respondents, was much lower than mothers with non-disabled children as identified in the General Household Survey of 1992.
- The most common unmet needs of the parents were financial resources, help in planning the child's future, help with care, and knowledge of available services.

For further information about this project, Bryony Beresford can be contacted at the Social Policy Research Unit, University of York, Heslington, York YO1 5DD. A national survey of parents caring for a severely disabled child, is published by the Polity Press in association with *Community Care* magazine, as part of the Community Care into Practice series.

Assessment

■ Clinical Diagnosis

Effective treatments depend upon reliable diagnoses. The term 'diagnosis' has been the source of some intellectual difficulties for developmental theorists, psychologists and psychiatrists in their desire to work within a scientific and (notably, for psychiatrists) a medical framework. Diagnostic skills, and concepts like aetiology, have served physical medicine well. Research over many decades, firmly rooted in scientific philosophy and methodology, has built on these skills and generated an impressive array of rational treatments, which have done much to reduce human suffering.

Ideally, a diagnosis would give rise to the following:

- reliable descriptive criteria: the 'what' (is the problem) question?
- clear causal theories: the 'why' (has the problem come about) question?
- appropriate (validated) interventions: the 'how' (do I help my patient/s) question.

Fulfilling all these desiderata is somewhat rare in child development work and psychiatry. Early detection of disorders is crucial for both children and their families. Undoubtedly, the younger the age at which children with physical, intellectual, emotional or social difficulties are identified, the more likely it is that appropriate interventions can be planned to enable them to develop their independence and the potential to participate in everyday life. It often proves difficult at an early stage to distinguish between typical (normal) and atypical (abnormal) development. The relationships between them are far from simple or dichotomous.

Taylor and Rutter (2002) comment that: (i) diagnosis is seldom the 'automatic generator' of a plan of management; and that (ii) a formulation encompasses more information than a restrictive diagnosis. The reality is that many signs of atypical development ('abnormality') are, by and large, on a continuum with, or manifestations of physical, behavioural, cognitive and emotional attributes common to all children. Their quality of being dysfunctional lies in their inappropriate intensity, pervasiveness, frequency and persistence.

■ Clinical Assessment

As defined by Rune Simeonsson and Susan Rosenthal (2000), the term 'clinical assessment' has a broad meaning which encompasses the use of varied procedures and multiple activities to evaluate and record developmental and psychological characteristics; for example:

- screening
- testing
- observing
- interviewing
- formulating
- planning
- monitoring progress
- evaluating outcomes.

The rationale of this approach is based on recognition that the idiosyncratic and complex nature of problems of children with disabilities and chronic conditions requires methods that are flexible and comprehensive to an extent not possible with standardized tests (Simeonsson and Rosenthal, 2001, p. 3).

Different disciplines have designed assessment or diagnostic protocols, for example, the social work *core assessment* leading to a multi-agency plan of action for a 'child in need', or the educational *statement of need* for 'special' educational provision. There is no one right way of arriving at a remedial, preventive or treatment programme. Two examples of assessment procedures: (i) a statutory social work protocol and (ii) an assessment leading to a general casework formulation, were provided in Chapter 15. They illustrate the way in which a formulation is conceptualized, and how the consequent selection of data describing the patient's (client's) problem varies according to its nature, purpose, and the theoretical assumptions of the professional.

■ Assessment Methods

The following texts have descriptions of test and other assessment methods:
BPS-Blackwell, Oxford: *PACTS SERIES 1* (edited by M. Herbert):

* *Post-Traumatic Stress Disorder in Children.*
* *Assessing Children in Need and their Parents.*
* *Coping with Children's Feeding Problems and Bedtime Battles.*
* *Toilet Training: Bedwetting and Soiling.*
* *Social Skills Training for Children.*

BPS-Blackwell, Oxford: *PACTS SERIES 2* (edited by M. Herbert):

Carr, A. *Depression and Attempted Suicide in Adolescence.*
Carr, A. *Avoiding Risky Sex in Adolescence.*
Griffiths, M. *Gambling and Gaming Addictions in Adolescence.*
Guerin, S. and Hennessy, E. *Aggression and Bullying.*
Heyne, D. and Rollings, S. (with King, N. and Tonge, B.) *School Refusal.*
Hollin, C.R., Browne, D. and Palmer, E.I. *Delinquency and Young Offenders.*
Mattis, S.G. and Ollendick, T.H. *Panic Disorder and Anxiety in Adolescence.*

Other titles include:

Carr, A. (ed.) 2002: *Prevention: What Works with Children and Adolescents?* London: Brunner-Routledge.
Murray, L. and Carothers, A.D. 1990: The validation of the Edinburgh postnatal depression scale on a community sample. *British Journal of Psychiatry*, 157, 288–90.
Simeonsson, R.L. and Rosenthal, S.L. (eds) 2001: *Psychological and Developmental Assessment: Children with Disabilities and Chronic Conditions.* New York: Guilford Press.

■ Useful References

Low birth-weight babies

Resnick, M. and Packer, A. 1990: *Infant Development Activities for Parents.* New York: St Martins Press.
Wasik, B., Bryant, D. and Lyons, D. 1990: *Home Visiting.* Newbury Park, CA: Sage.

Communicating with children

Jones, D.P.H. 2003: *Communicating with Vulnerable Children: A Guide for Practitioners* (Department of Health). London: Gaskell.

Risk and protective factors (resilience)

Grizenko, N. and Fisher, C. 1992: Reviews of studies of risk and protective factors for psychopathology in children. *Canadian Journal of Psychiatry*, 37, 711–21.

Early childhood intervention

Yoshikawa, H. and Zigler, E. 2000: Mental health in Head Start: New directions for the twenty-first century. *Early Education and Development*, 11, 247–64.

Postnatal depression

Cox, J.L., Holden, J.M., Sagovsky, R. 1987: Detection of postnatal depression: development of the 10-item Edinburgh Postnatal Depression Scale. *British Journal of Psychiatry*, 150, 782–6.

Down's syndrome

Kumin, L.A. 1986: Survey of speech and language pathology services for Down syndrome: State of the art. *Applied Research in Mental Retardation*, 7, 491–9.

Kumin, L. 1994: *Communication Skills for Children with Down Syndrome: A Guide for Parents*. Bethesda, MD: Woodbine House.

Pueschel, S.M., Anneren, G., Durlach, R. et al. 1995: Guidelines for optimal medical care of persons with Down syndrome, International League of Societies for Persons with Mental Handicap (ILSMH). *Acta Paediatrica*, 84, 823–7.

Van Dyke, D.C., Mattheis, P., Eberly, S.S. and Williams, J. (eds) 1995: *Medical and Surgical Care for Children with Down Syndrome: A Guide for Parents*. Bethesda, MD: Woodbine House.

Autism and Asperger's syndrome

Attwood, T. 1998: *Asperger's Syndrome: A Guide for Parents and Professionals*. London: Jessica Kingsley.

Frith, U. 2003: *Autism: Explaining the Autism*. Oxford: Blackwell.

National Autistic Society, http://www.nas.org.uk/ (Provides information about autism and Asperger's syndrome and about support services available to people with autism, families, and professionals.)

Primary care

Garralda, M.E. 1994: Primary care psychiatry. In M. Rutter, E. Taylor and L. Hersov (eds) *Child and Adolescent Psychiatry: Modern Approaches.* Oxford: Blackwell Scientific Publications.

Parent guides

Douglas, J. and Richman, N. 1984: *My Child Won't Sleep.* Harmondsworth: Penguin.
Duker, M. and Slade, R. 1988: *Anorexia Nervosa: How to Help.* Milton Keynes: Open University Press.
Wood, D. 1988: *How Children Think and Learn.* Oxford: Blackwell.

Deaf children

Marsscark, M. 1993: *Psychological Development of Deaf Children.* Oxford: Oxford University Press.

Assessment

Bayley, N. 1993: *Bayley Scales of Infant Development* (2nd edn). New York: Psychological Corporation.
Cassidy, J. and Shazer, P.R. (eds) 1999: *Handbook of Attachment: Theory, Research, and Clinical Applications: Attachment.* London: Brunner-Routledge.
Elander, J. and Rutter, M. 1996: Use and development of the Rutter parents' and teachers' scales. *International Journal of Methods in Psychiatric Research,* 6, 63–78.
Gibbs, E.D. and Teti, D.M. 1990: *Interdisciplinary Assessment of Infants: A Guide for Early Intervention Professionals.* Baltimore: Paul H. Brookes.
Gregory, R.J. 2000: *Psychological Testing: History, Principles, and Applications* (3rd edn). Boston: Allyn & Bacon.
Griffiths, R. 1954: *The Abilities of Babies: A Study in Mental Measurement.* London: London University Press.
Ritter, S.H. 1995: *Assessment of Preschool Children.* New York: Eric Digest.
Sluckin, W., Herbert, M. and Sluckin, A. 1983: *Maternal Bonding.* Oxford: Basil Blackwell.

Dyslexia

Snowling, M.J. 2000: *Dyslexia.* Oxford: Blackwell.

Language

Messer, D. 2000: Language acquisition. *The Psychologist,* 123, 138–43.

Johson, M. and Wintgens, A. 2001: *The Selective Mutism Resource Manual.* Bicester: Speechmark.

Government publications

Department of Health, 1991: *Welfare of Children and Young People in Hospitals.* London: HMSO.
Department of Health, 1995: *A Handbook on Child and Adolescent Mental Health.* London: HMSO.
Health Advisory Service, 1995: *Child and Adolescent Mental Health Services.* London: HMSO.

Services

Kraemer, D. 1993: *The Case for a Multi-Disciplinary Child and Adolescent Mental Health Community Service, The Liaison Model: A Guide for Managers, Purchasers and GPs.* London: Child and Family Psychiatric Service, Whittington Hospital.
Kurtz, Z., Thornes, R. and Wolkind, S. 1984: *Services for the Mental Health of Children and Young People in England: A National Review.* London: South Thames Regional Health Authority.
Rutter, M. 1991: Services for children with emotional disorders: Needs accomplishments and future developments. *Young Minds Newsletter*, 9, 1–5.

Self-help

Rosen, G.M., Glasgew, R.E., and Moore, T.E. 2003: Self-help therapy. The science and business of giving psychology away. In Lilienfeld, S.O. et al. (ed.) *Science and Pseudoscience in Clinical Psychology.* New York: The Guilford Press.

Resource Material

■ Community Phone Helplines

The National Society for the Prevention of Cruelty to Children (*NSPCC*) is the UK's leading charity specializing in child protection and the prevention of cruelty to children. It has been protecting children and campaigning on their behalf since 1884. The work includes (*inter alia*):

- A *Child Protection Helpline* (free, and with 24-hour coverage) that provides information, advice and counselling to anyone concerned about a child's safety. Also available is an Asian helpline in five Asian languages, a bilingual Welsh helpline, and a text-phone service for people who are deaf or hard of hearing.
- *Child protection training* and *advice* for organizations involved in the care, protection and education of children.
- *Information resources* on child protection and related topics for professionals, the press and the general public.
- The *NSPCC Kid's Website* makes itself known (on the Internet) to children, in this way: 'The NSPCC believes that every child has the right to be safe, valued and happy. Our mission is to end cruelty to children. . . . And if you've got a problem and need to talk, find out how the NSPCC Helpline can help.'

Childline is a confidential, free 24-hour helpline for children and young people in the UK. Children and young people can call the helpline on *0800 1111* about any problem, at any time – be it day or night.

The Samaritans provide 24-hour confidential emotional support for people in distress or despair. Individuals contact them by phoning *08457 90 90 90*, emailing *jo@samaritans.org* ,writing or by visiting a local branch. They have helpful information on *bullying*, and a helpline which tells children: 'If you're being bullied and feel you can't cope any longer and want to speak to someone about it then contact Samaritans. You can phone them [see above] or you can find your nearest branch in your phone book.'

Bullying Offline was founded in 1999 by Liz Carnell and her son John, as a direct result of their experience of dealing with bullying at his school. They decided to share their experience with other parents and pupils by using the Internet as a cost-effective medium. Bullying Online became a UK-registered charity in May 2000. It has leaflets which describe 12 of the most common problems endured by parents and pupils. Individual leaflets are free and can be obtained by sending a stamped addressed envelope to *Bullying Online*, 9 Knox Way, Harrogate, N. Yorks, HG1 3JL. The email address *help@bullying.co.uk* is available if further details are required. Individual leaflets can be downloaded.

Childline (0800 1111) is the free, national helpline for children in trouble or danger. The service is available for 24 hours, 365 days a year Children living away from home can also call 'The Line' a special helpline for children living away from home on *0800 884444* (Monday to Friday 15.30 to 21.30, Saturday and Sunday, 14.00 to 20.00.)

ChildLine (0800 400 222) operates a minicom service for children who are deaf or hearing impaired. This service operates Mon. to Fri. 9.30 to 21.30, Sat. and Sun. 9.30 to 20.00.

Parentline (080 88 00 22 22) provides a confidential telephone helpline for anyone in a parenting role. They offer a tension release and a source of information about parenting issues. The helpline workers are parents who have undergone training in order to help callers find answers to concerns ranging from bad behaviour, depression or parental access.

Contact a Family Helpline (0808 808 3555) provides an empathic listening service to parents following diagnosis of disability in a child. It provides information on all medical conditions affecting children, including the many rare disorders. It puts families in touch on a one-to-one basis; it also puts them in touch with local and national support groups. Available 10.00 to 16.00, Monday to Friday.

Saneline (0845 767 8000) is an out-of-hours telephone helpline offering practical information, crisis care and emotional support to anybody affected by mental health problems. The service is open from 12 noon until 2 a.m.

Drinkline (*0800 917 8282*) is a national alcohol helpline providing counselling, support, advice and information, which is available 9.00 to 23.00, Monday, Tuesday, Wednesday, Thursday and Friday.

Frank Campaign Helpline (*0800 776600*) provides information and advice about drugs and information on local services. The service can take calls in over 120 languages via a three way call with a translator. It is available 365 days a year, 24 hours a day. There is also a website providing information and an email service for users to send in questions which will be answered.

Gingerbread Advice Line (*0800 018 4318*) is available 11.00 to 16.00, Monday to Friday. It provides confidential advice and emotional support to all lone parent families by telephone.

Kidscape (*0845 120 5204*) helpline offers practical advice to children, parents, and carers on child safety, sexual abuse, abduction by strangers, child abduction, and bullying. Available 10.00 to 16.00, Monday to Friday.

The *Learning Disability Helpline* (*0808 808 111*) provides information and advice on learning disability issues to callers including people with learning disabilities, their families and carers, and professionals working in the field. Available 9.00 to 17.00.

Stillbirths and Neonatal Deaths Helpline (*020 7436 5881*) provides an opportunity for parents to express their grief with trained counsellors. Available 10.00 to 17.00, Monday to Friday.

Miscarriage Association Helpline (*01924 200799*) offers support and information to those affected by the loss of a baby in pregnancy. Available 9.00 to 16.00, Monday to Friday. (There is an answer-phone for outside office hours.)

Sexual Health Line (*0800 567123*) provides advice and information about HIV, AIDS and sexual health/local services. Calls to the helpline are confidential. Available 24 hours. The service is available 365 days a year.

■ NHS Helplines

NHS Direct (*0845 4647*) Available 24 hours, 7 days a week, NHS Direct provides advice and information about health and the NHS so that people are better able to care for themselves and their families. The service aims to provide clinical advice to support self-care and appropriate self-referral to NHS services. Nurses who take the calls provide advice that may include how to manage minor illnesses at home or when and how to get further help for more serious illness.

NHS Pregnancy Smoking Helpline (*0800 1699169*) Available 12 noon to 21.00 (7 days a week). Offers practical, helpful and friendly advice to pregnant woman wanting to give up smoking as well as details of local stop smoking services. A call back service is also offered, whereby the individual receives calls from a specialist counsellor for the duration of the pregnancy.

NHS Smoking Helpline (*0800 1690169*) Available 7.00 to 23.00, 7 days a week Offers practical, helpful and friendly advice to individuals wanting to give up smoking as well as details of local stop smoking services. Health professionals can order a range of literature from the helpline.

NHS Asian Tobacco Helpline offers practical advice in the appropriate mother tongue language (or English) to those South Asians wishing to give up smoking and/or chewing tobacco paan.

Telephone Directory of Helplines Over 900 national, regional and local telephone helplines throughout England, Wales, Scotland and Northern Ireland, can be found by a search facility provided to members of this organization.

Typical Development Summaries

These are adapted with permission from Herbert, 2003.

■ Prenatal Development

The Germinal Stage: The First 14 Days

The baby-to-be's very first journey following the fertilization that took place in one of the mother's two Fallopian tubes, is as a cluster of dividing cells moving down her oviduct and uterine lumen. Cell division begins 24–36 hours following conception. During the process of so-called cleavage divisions, all cells are identical. After approximately four days the multiplying cells separate into two distinct masses: the outer cells of the bilaminar disk forming a protective cocoon around the embryo, a cocoon that will create the rudiments of the all-important placenta – the embyro's life support system, and the shelter within which it will grow. The inner layers of cells called the embryonic disk will form a nucleus of cells to become the embryo.

Further differentiation takes place in the fallopian tube resulting in the blastocyst. As it approaches the uterus, small burr-like tendrils (villi) emerge from its outer surface and after entry into the womb they burrow into its lining (the endometrium). This process is known as implantation, and at around 10–14 days marks the end of the germinal period and the beginning of the embryonic stage of development.

The Embryonic Stage: The Third to the Eighth Week

From the third week following conception, the embryo enters a highly sensitive period of growth. The first trimester of human development is a period of morphogenesis in which a differentiated fetus will eventually emerge from a homogenous embryo. The major organs and basic tissues are laid down, and disturbances in the uterus can produce calamitous effects on their growth and development. After this phase of development it is difficult, if not impossible, to affect the morphology of the organism in any fundamental manner.

From roughly the beginning of the third week after conception the hitherto formless mass of cells becomes a distinct being. A perceptible sign of body formation is the development of a 3-layered (trilaminer) disk. A portion of the outer layer of cells folds into a neural tube that soon becomes the brain and spinal cord. The disk becomes attached to the uterine wall by the short, thick umbilical cord, and the placenta develops rapidly.

There is a rudimentary heart that begins to beat by the end of the fourth week. The eyes begin to form and the neural tube closes; if not, spina bifida is the result (see Chapter 5). The placenta, which is formed from the lining of the uterus and the chorion, provides for respiration and nourishment for the unborn baby, also for the elimination of its metabolic wastes. The umbilical cord connects the embryo to the placenta.

The mother's blood is divided by only a few cells from the fetus's blood, so that an exchange of nutrients and waste can take place in these blood spaces. Despite the intimacy of the mother as host, and the unborn child as temporary lodger, her blood, which carries the nourishment, stops on one side of the wall and the blood elements are broken down and strained through it. Nevertheless, there is an interchange of certain substances between the circulatory systems of mother and child by way of the placenta; they include vitamins, hormones, antigens, antibodies, blood proteins, oxygen, amino acids, drugs and viruses.

The Late Embryonic Stage

By five weeks after conception arm and leg buds form; by seven facial structures fuse (otherwise facial defects such as cleft palate occur); by eight weeks crown rump length is 3 cm (slightly over 1 in) and weight is 1 gm (about .03 oz). The major development of body organs and most structures is complete. Nerve cells that will form the brain will travel along pathways that are being laid down by glial cells which enable the neurons to move towards each other, connect and become active.

The Fetal Stage: The Ninth Week Until Birth

By the second trimester the pregnancy is well established. Most of the baby's external features that are observed at birth are now apparent. All of the structures which will be present when their baby is born in seven more months have already formed, at least in their beginning stages. Medically the unborn (organism) is no longer an embryo, but a fetus – an increasingly recognizable human being in the making. It seems somehow miraculous after this highly sensitive period of development just how much (and how often) things go right despite the potential hazards.

The fetus not only looks more human; it is possible by 12 weeks to discern its gender. It now contains the same number of neurons as an adult, and the nerves from the brain begin to be coated in myelin, a layer of protective fat. This is a crucial stage in their maturation as it facilitates the passage of messages to and from the brain.

The Final Months of the Third Trimester

These months find the baby growing bigger in his/her mother's abdomen; it is during this final period that the body parts and organ systems are enlarged and refined. Some of the milestones of fetal development are the announcing of his presence by kicking (by 16 weeks), sucking his thumb and displaying the beginning of hair growth (by 20 weeks). By the 7th month the fetus is able to breathe, cry, digest, and excrete, and is in a good position to survive premature birth. The final months of fetal development are primarily concerned with length and weight-gain.

Eventually, at around 266 days after conception the baby engages in his mother's pelvis relieving the pressure on her abdomen. No one can predict what will happen during labour; fortunately most births go without a hitch. The exceptions were described in Chapter 2.

■ Motor Development

By 12 months a child will stand unsupported. There are variations between infants in the timing of particular changes. For example, 50 per cent of children can walk unaided at 13 months, but a few can do this at 8 months, and others do not achieve this skill until 18 months. Typically, children begin to walk soon after 12 or 13 months of age. In the following period they progress from a hand-held walk to a speedy coordinated gait, or more accurately a sometimes unsteady toddle – hence the sobriquet 'toddler'. They go on to develop a form of 'advanced' locomotion, giving them the means to investigate their environment very actively.

The changes in motor ability that follow walking tend to be consolidation and refinements of existing abilities rather than the emergence of completely new skills. Toddlers' walking gradually increases in competence, and running becomes fluent and controlled. By 18 to 24 months the child runs stiffly, walks really well, climbs stairs with both feet on each step, unscrews the lid on a jar, stacks four to six blocks, turns pages one at a time, and picks things up without over-balancing. This is an impressive and by no means complete set of achievements, when one considers how few locomotor skills were available to the infant only two years earlier.

■ Language Development

Children need to learn four types of knowledge about language (Shaffer, 1993):

- *phonology*: the sound system of a language;
- *semantics*: the meanings conveyed by words and sentences;
- *syntax*: the collection of grammatical rules indicating how words may and may not be combined to construct sentences;
- *pragmatics*: the principles determining how language should be modified to suit the context in which it is being used (e.g. simplifying the speech used with a child as compared with an adult).

Children usually learn about language in the sequence described below, but with many individual developments with regard to the rate at which they learn.

- Between 4 and 6 months of age infants begin to babble, consisting of combinations of vowels and consonants, typically 'bababa' and 'dadada', which do not seem to have any meaning for the infants. The babbling displayed by babies up to the age of six months is somewhat similar in all parts of the world. It appears to be pre-programmed, as it is produced by congenitally deaf children who have no experience of hearing sounds produced by themselves or by others (see Chapter 12).
- Progression to the next stage occurs 'naturally' only in hearing infants. Throughout the following stages, children's *understanding* of language is far ahead of their ability to express themselves – not infrequently the source of frustration and outbursts of temper.

- Between 9 and 11 months the infant will begin to inhibit an activity in response to the word 'no', although he or she will not generally be using the word himself or herself.
- The first recognizable spoken word appears at about one year, and from this, single word labels are used for familiar objects and people.
- The single word stage lasts several months, speech being used increasingly for specific effects, and as more words are added, used with increasingly precise and adult-like meaning. Sentence development comprises the next stage.

The infant's *pre-linguistic communication* reaches a peak at about 16 to 20 months. Meaningful words appear towards the end of the first year or the beginning of the second year of life. At first they constitute a very small proportion of the infant's vocalization, but during the later part of the second year they become prominent

From a single word grows a variety of longer sentences. At approximately 18 months – when children have some 50 words in their speaking vocabularies – words begin to be combined in pairs to convey ideas, e.g. 'Dadad gone', and not long after there is a steady increase in sentence length and complexity. At age 2 the average length of sentences is one to seven words. At age 5 it has expanded to four to six words. Even those first two-word sentences show systematic regularity of word order, and from the very beginning express the basic grammatical relationships of subject, predicate and object.

Children from different nations with different languages express essentially the same range of meanings in their earliest sentences, including such basic semantic relations as identification, location, negation, attribution, agent-action and agent-object. By this stage infancy has come to an end but language development continues apace.

From 3 years, sentences are used to describe past and present happenings. The average adult length of sentences (6–7 words) is achieved by school-going age, reflecting important changes in the development of grammatical ability which appear to be closely linked with the development of cognitive and intellectual abilities. As these increase in capacity and sophistication, children can learn more complicated grammatical rules. By the age of 5 or 6 years, children can use several thousand words in complex adult-like sentences and are able to understand complex meanings. Improved verbal ability often facilitates cognitive functions such as memory, thinking, reasoning and problem solving. (Problems of speech and language were dealt with in Chapter 8.)

References

Adler, D. 1927: *Understanding Human Nature.* New York: Greenberg.

Adler, D. 1930: *The Education of Children.* New York: Greenberg.

Ainsworth, M.D.S., Behar, M., Waters, E. and Wall, S. 1978: *Patterns of Attachment: A Psychological Study of the Strange Situation.* Hillsdale, NJ: Lawrence Erlbaum.

Allport, G. 1937: *Personality: A Psychological Interpretation.* London: Constable.

Ambrosini, P.J. 2000: A review of pharmacotherapy of major depression in children and adolescents. *Psychiatric Services,* 51, 627–33.

American Psychiatric Association, 1987: *Diagnostic and Statistical Manual of Mental Disorders* (DSM-III-R: 3rd edn, rev.). Washington, DC: APA.

American Psychiatric Association, 1994: *The Diagnostic and Statistical Manual of Mental Disorders* (4th edn). Washington, DC: APA.

Apgar, V. 1953: A proposal for a new method of evaluation of the newborn infant. *Anesthesia and Analgesia,* 32, 260–7.

Appleby, L., Warner, R. et al. 1997: A controlled study of fluoxetine and cognitive behavioural counselling in the treatment of postnatal depression. *British Medical Journal,* 314, 932–6.

Attwood, T. 1993: *Asperger's Syndrome: A Guide for Parents and Professionals.* London: Jessica Kingsley.

Babiker, G. and Herbert, M. 1998: Critical issues in the assessment of child sexual abuse. *Clinical Child and Family Psychology Review,* 1, 231–52.

Baird, G., Cass, H. and Slonims, V. 2003: Diagnosis of autism. *British Medical Journal,* 327, 188–203.

Baird, G., Charman, T. et al. 2000: A screening instrument for autism at 18 months of age: A six year follow up (Baird, G. study). *Journal of the American Academy of Child and Adolescent Psychiatry,* 39, 694–702.

Baldwin, S. 1985: No silence please. Feature article in *The Times Educational Supplement,* 679 (8 November), 25.

Bandura, A. 1977: Self-efficacy: Toward a unifying theory of behavioural change. *Psychological Review*, 84, 191–215.

Barkley, R. 1996: *Taking Charge of ADHD*. New York: Guilford Press.

Barlow, J. 1997: *Systematic Review of the Effectiveness of Parent Training Programmes in Improving the Behaviour of 3–7 year old Children*. Oxford: Health Services Research Unit, University of Oxford.

Barlow, J., Coren, E. and Stewart-Brown, S. 2002: *Meta-Analysis of the Effectiveness of Parenting Programmes in Improving the Behaviour of 3–7 Year Old Children*. Oxford: Health Services Research Unit, University of Oxford.

Barnett, B. and Parker, G. 1998: The parentified child: Early competence or childhood deprivation? *Child Psychology and Psychiatry Review*, 3, 146–55.

Barrera, M., Rosenbaum, P. and Cunningham, C. 1986: Early home intervention with low weight infants and parents. *Child Development*, 51, 20–33.

Barrett, P.M., Dadds, M.R. and Rapee, R.M. 1996: Family treatment for childhood anxiety: A controlled trial. *Journal of Consulting and Clinical Psychology*, 64, 333–42.

Battro, A.M. 2001: *Half a Brain is Enough: The Story of Nico*. Cambridge: Cambridge University Press.

Benson, P.L., Galbraith, J. and Espenland, P. 1995: *What Kids Need to Succeed*. Minneapolis, MN: Free Spirit Publishing.

Berger, M., Yule, W. and Rutter, M. 1975: Attainment and adjustment in two geographical areas: The prevalence of specific reading retardation. *British Journal of Psychiatry*, 126, 510–19.

Besag, F.M.C. 1988: Cognitive deterioration in children with epilepsy. In M.R. Trimble and E.H. Reynolds (eds) *Epilepsy, Behaviour and Cognitive Function*. Chichester: John Wiley & Sons Ltd.

Bishop, D.V.M. 1992: The underlying nature of specific language impairment. *Journal of Child Psychology and Psychiatry*, 33, 3–66.

Bohman, M. 1996: Predisposition to criminality: Swedish adoption studies in retrospect. In G.R. Bock and J.A. Goode (eds) *Genetics of Criminal and Antisocial Behaviour*. Chichester: John Wiley and Sons, Ltd.

Bovicelli, L., Orsini, L.F. et al. 1982: Reproduction in Down syndrome. Obstetrics and Gynecology, 59, 135–75.

Bowlby, J. 1969: *Attachment and Loss*, Vol. 1: *Attachment*. New York: Basic Books.

Bowlby, J. 1973: *Attachment and Loss*, Vol. 2: *Separation, Anxiety and Anger*. New York: Basic Books.

Bowlby, J. 1988: *Attachment and Loss*, Vol. 3: *A Secure Base: Clinical Applications of Attachment Theory*. London: Routledge.

Brazelton, T.B. 1984: *The Neonatal Behavioural Assessment Scale*. Philadelphia, PA: Lippincott.

Brazelton, T.B. and Nugent, J.K. 1995: *The Neonatal Behavioural Assessment Scale* (3rd edn). London: MacKeith Press.

Brennan, J.D. et al. 1999: Current developments in the understanding of mental retardation, II: Psychopathology. *Journal of the Academy of Child and Adolescent Psychiatry*, 30, 861–72.

Brennan, P.A., Grekin, E.R. and Mednick, S.A. 1999: Maternal smoking during pregnancy and adult male criminal outcomes. *Archives of General Psychiatry*, 56, 215–24.

Brestan, E.V. and Eyberg, S.M. 1998: Effective psychosocial treatment of conduct-disordered children and adolescents: 29 years, 82 studies, 5275 children. *Journal of Clinical Child Psychology*, 27, 180–9.

Brockington, L. 1996: *Motherhood and Mental Health*. Oxford: Oxford University Press.

Bronfenbrenner, U. 1989: Ecological systems theory. In R. Vasta (ed.) *Annals of Child Development: Theories of Child Development: Revised Formulation and Current Issues*, Vol. 6. Greenwich, CT: JAI Press.

Browne, K. and Herbert, M. 1997: *Preventing Family Violence*. Chichester: John Wiley & Sons Ltd.

Butler, R. 1998: Annotation: Night wetting in children, psychological aspects. *Journal of Child Psychology and Psychiatry*, 39, 453–63.

Buys, M.L. (ed.) 1990: *Birth Defects Encyclopedia*. Dover, MA: Center for Birth Defects Information Services.

Carr, A. 2002a: *Avoiding Risky Sex in Adolescence* (*PACT 2* Series). Oxford: BPS Blackwell Publications.

Carr, A. (ed.) 2002b: *Prevention: What Works with Children and Adolescents?* London: Brunner-Routledge.

Carr, J. 1992: Longitudinal research in Down syndrome. *International Review of Research in Mental Retardation*, 18, 197–223.

Caspi, R., Moffitt, T.E. et al. 1996: Behavioral observations at age 3 years predict adult psychiatric disorders: Longitudinal evidence from a birth cohort. *Archives of General Psychiatry*, 53, 1033–9.

Caughy, M.O. 1996: Health and environmental effects on the academic readiness of school-age children. *Developmental Psychology*, 32, 515–22.

Chorpita, B.F. and Tim, L. 2002: Toward a large-scale implementation of empirically supported treatments for children. *Clinical Psychology: Science and Practice*, 9, 185–90.

Clark, P. and Rutter, M. 1981: Autistic children's responses to structure and to interpersonal demands. *Journal of Autism and Developmental Disorders*, 11, 201–17.

Claydon, G.S. and Agnarsson, U. 1991: *Constipation in Children*. Oxford: Oxford University Press.

Cline, S. and Schwartz, D. 1999: *Diverse Populations of Gifted Children*. New York: Merrill.

Cody, H. and Hynde, G.W. 1999: Neurological advances in child and adolescent mental health: The decade of the brain. *Journal of Child Psychology and Psychiatry Review*, 4, 103–8.

Cohen, S. and Williamson, G.M. 1991: Stress and infectious disease in humans. *Psychological Bulletin*, 109, 5–24.

Communities That Care, 1997: *A New Kind of Prevention Programme*. London: Communities That Care.

Cooke, D.J. and Philip, L. 2001: To treat or not to treat? An empirical perspective. In C.R. Hollin (ed.) *Handbook of Offender Assessment and Treatment*. Chichester: John Wiley.

Cooper, P.J. and Murray, L. 1997: The impact of psychological treatments of postpartum depression on maternal mood and infant development. In L. Murray and P.J. Cooper (eds) *Postpartum Depression and Child Development*. New York: Guilford, 201–20.

Cooper, P.J. and Murray, L. 2003: Controlled trial of the short- and long-term effect of psychological treatment of post-partum depression: Impact on maternal mood. *British Journal of Psychiatry*, 182, 412–19.

Coughan, B., Carr A. and Fitzgerald, M. 2000: Factors related to the adjustment of siblings following sudden infant death. In A. Carr (ed.) *Empirical Studies of Problems and Treatment Processes in Children and Adolescents Wales*. The Edwin Mellin Press.

Coughlan, B.J., Doyle, D.M. and Carr, A. 2002: Prevention of teenage smoking, alcohol use and drug abuse. In A. Carr (ed.) *Prevention: What Works with Children and Adolescents?* London: Brunner-Routledge.

Cowger, C. 1997: Assessing client strengths: Assessment for client empowerment. In D. Saleeby (ed.) *The Strength Perspective in Social Work Practice*. New York: Longman.

Cox, J.L., Holden, J.M. and Sagovsky, R. 1987: Detection of postnatal depression: Development of the 10-item Edinburgh postnatal depression scale. *British Journal of Psychiatry*, 150, 782–6.

Curry, J.F., March, J.S. and Hervey, A.S. 2004: Comorbidity of childhood and adolescent anxiety disorders: Prevalence and Implications. In T.H. Ollendick and J.S. March (eds) *Phobic and Anxiety Disorders in Children and Adolescents: A Clinician's Guide to Effective Psychosocial and Pharmacological Intervention*. Oxford: Oxford University Press.

Davis, H. 1998: *Counselling Parents of Children with Chronic Illness or Disability*. Leicester: BPS Books.

Davis, H., Day, C. and Bidmead, C. 2003: *Working in Partnership with Parents: The Parent Adviser Model*. London: The Psychological Corporation.

Davis, H. and Spurr, P. 1998: Parent counselling: An evaluation of a community child mental health service. *Journal of Child Psychology and Psychiatry*, 39, 365–76.

Dinkmeyer, D. and McKay, G. 1976: *Systematic Training for Effective Parenting*. Circle Pines, MN: American Guidance Service.

Doleys, D.M. 1977: Behavioral treatments for nocturnal enuresis in children: A review of the recent literature. *Psychological Bulletin*, 8, 30–54.

Doleys, D.M. 1978: Assessment and treatment of enuresis and encopresis in children. In M. Hersen, R.M. Eisler and P.M. Miller (eds) *Progress in Behavior Modification*, Vol. 6. New York: Academic Press.

Dreikurs, R. and Stolz, V. 1964: *Happy Children: A Challenge to Parents*. New York: Hawthorn.

Drillien, C. 1964: *The Growth and Development of the Prematurely Born Infant.* Edinburgh: E. & S. Livingston.

Dumas, J.E., Prinz, R.J. et al. 1999: The Early Alliance Prevention Trial: An integrative set of interventions to promote competence and reduce risk for conduct disorder, substance abuse, and school failure. *Clinical Child and Family Psychology Review*, 2, 37–53.

Du Plessis, A.J., Kaufman, W.E. and Kupsky, W.J. 1993: Intra-uterine onset myodonic encephalopathy associated with cerebral cortical dysgenesis. *Journal of Child Neurology*, 41, 53–61.

Dykens, E.M. 2000: Annotation: Psychopathology in children with intellectual disability. *Journal of Child Psychology and Psychiatry*, 41, 407–17.

Egan, G. 1986: *The Skilled Helper.* Monterey, CA: Brooks Cole.

Egeland, B., Carlson, E. and Sroufe, L.A. 1993: Resilience as process. *Development and Psychopathology*, 5, 517–28.

Egeland, B. and Erickson, M. 2003: Community programs for treating relationship problems. In A. Sameroff, S. McDonough and K. Rosenblum (eds) *Interventions for Early Relationship Problems.* New York: Guilford Publications, Inc.

Egeland, B., Yates, T., Appleyard, K. and van Dulmen, M. 2002: The long-term consequences of maltreatment in the early years: A developmental pathway model to antisocial behavior. *Children's Services: Social Policy, Research, and Practice*, 5, 249–60.

Emerson, E. 1995: *Challenging Behaviour: Analysis and Intervention in People with Severe Intellectual Disabilities* (2nd edn). Cambridge: Cambridge University Press.

Emerson, E. and Bromley, J. 1995: The form and function of challenging behaviour. *Journal of Intellectual Disability Research*, 39, 388–98.

Erikson, E. 1968: *Identity: Youth and Crisis.* New York: Norton.

Evans, D. 2003: *Placebo: The Belief Effect.* London: HarperCollins.

Evans, D. and Mellins, R.B. 1991: Educational programs for children with asthma. *Pediatrician*, 18, 317–23.

Farrington, D. 1995: The Twelfth Jack Tizard Memorial Lecture: The development of offending behaviour from childhood. *Journal of Child Psychology and Psychiatry*, 36, 929–64.

Fawcett, A.J. (ed.) 2001: *Dyslexia: Theory and Good Practice.* London: Whurr.

Fawcett, A.J., Nicolson, R.I. and Lee, R. 2001: *The Pre-School Screening Test.* London: The Psychological Corporation.

Fegan, L., Rauch, A. and McCarthy, W. 1993: Sexuality and People with Intellectual Disability, pp. 43–7. Baltimore, MD: Paul H. Brooks Publishing Co.

Ferster, C.B. and De Myer, M.K. 1962: A method for the experimental analysis of the behavior of autistic children. *American Journal of Orthopsychiatry*, 32, 89–98.

Field, M.T. and Sanchez, V.F. 1999: *Equal Treatment for People: Mental Retardation.* Cambridge, MA: Harvard University Press.

Field, T. 2000: *Touch Therapy.* London: Churchill Livingstone.

Field, T., Schanberg, S. et al. 1986: Tactile/kinaesthetic stimulation effects on preterm neonates. *Pediatrics*, 77, 654–8.

Fireman, G. and Koplewicz, H.S. 1992: Short-term treatment of children with encopresis. *Journal of Psychotherapy Practice and Research*, 1, 64–71.

Fonagy, P., Target, M. et al. 2002: *What Works for Whom? A Critical Review of Treatments for Children and Adolescents*. New York: Guilford Press.

Francis, G. and Gragg, R. 1996: *Obsessive Compulsive Disorder*. Thousand Oaks, CA: Sage.

Freud, A. 1958: *Adolescence: Psychoanalytic Study of the Child*. New York: International Universities Press.

Frith, U. and Hill, E.L. 2003: *Autism: Mind and Brain*. London: Royal Society.

Fryers, T. 1984: *The Epidemiology of Intellectual Impairment*. London: Academic Press.

Garmezy, N. and Masten, A.S. 1994: Chronic adversities. In M. Rutter, E. Taylor and L. Hersov (eds) *Child and Adolescent Psychiatry: Modern Approaches* (3rd edn). Oxford: Blackwell Scientific Publishers.

Garner, D.M. and Bemis, K.M. 1985: Cognitive therapy for anorexia nervosa. In D. Garner and P.E. Garfinkel (eds) *Handbook of Psychotherapy for Anorexia and Bulimia*. New York: Guilford Press.

Garraldo, M.E. 1996: Somatization in children. *Journal of Child Psychology and Psychiatry*, 37, 13–34.

Garrera, A.M., Freeman, J.B. et al. 2004: In H.T. Ollendick and J.S. March (eds) *Phobic and Anxiety Disorders in Children and Adolescents: A Clinician's Guide to Effective Psychosocial And Pharmacological Intervention*. Oxford: Oxford University Press.

Gerrard, N. 2000: Feature article. *Observer Review*, 15 October, 1–2.

Giannoulis, K., Beresford, E., Davis, H. et al. 2004: The role and value of a paediatric specialist neurodevelopmental diagnostic service: Parental perceptions. *Child and Adolescent Health*, 9, 977–83.

Ginsberg, G.S. and Walkup, J.T. 2004: Specific phobia. In T.H. Ollendick and J.S. March (eds) *Phobic and Anxiety Disorders in Children and Adolescents: A Clinician's Guide to Effective Psychosocial and Pharmacological Intervention*. Oxford: Oxford University Press.

Glick, B. and Goldstein, A.P. 1987: Aggression replacement training. *Journal of Counselling and Development*, 65, 356–67.

Goldberg, G.L. and Craig, C.L. 1983: Obstetric complications in adolescent pregnancies. *South African Medical Journal*, 64, 863–4.

Goldenberg, R.L. 1995: Small for gestational age infants. In B.P. Sachs et al. (eds) *Reproductive Health Care for Women and Babies*. New York: Oxford University Press.

Goldstein, S. (ed.) 1995: *Understanding and Managing Children's Classroom Behaviour*. New York: John Wiley.

Goodman, B.R. 1994: Brain disorders. In M. Rutter, E. Taylor and L. Hersov (eds) *Child and Adolescent Psychiatry* (3rd edn). Oxford: Blackwell Scientific Publications.

Goodman, B.R. 2002: Brain disorders. In M. Rutter and E. Taylor (eds) *Child and Adolescent Psychiatry* (4th edn). Oxford: Blackwell Scientific Publications.

Gordon, T. 1975: *Parent Effectiveness Training*. New York: Peter Wyden.

Graham, P. 1994: Prevention. In M. Rutter, E. Taylor and L. Hersov (eds) *Child and Adolescent Psychiatry: Modern Approaches* (3rd edn). Oxford: Blackwell Scientific Publications.

Grant, L. 1995: Sex and the adolescent. In S. Parker and B. Zwellerman (eds) *Behavioral and Developmental* Pediatrics. Boston: Little Brown & Co.

Greenberg, M., Kusche, C. and Mihalic, S. 1998: *Promoting Alternative Thinking Strategies: Blue Prints for Children* (Book 10). Boulder, CO: Center for the Study and Prevention of Violence, Institute of Behavioral Science, University of Colorado.

Guralnick, M.J. 1998: Effectiveness of early intervention for vulnerable children: A developmental perspective. *American Journal of Mental Retardation*, 102, 319–45.

Hagerman, R., Amery, C. and Kronister, A. 1991: Fragile X checklist. *American Journal of Medical Genetics*, 38, 283–7.

Hagerman, R.J. and Silverman, A.C. 1991: *Fragile X Syndrome: Diagnosis, Treatment, and Research*. Baltimore, MD: Johns Hopkins University Press.

Haka-Ikse, K. and Mian, M. 1993: Sexuality in children. Pediatrics Review, 14 (10) 401–7.

Harper, P.S. 1998: *Practical Genetic Counselling*. Oxford: Butterworth-Heinemann.

Hatton, C. 1998a: Epidemiology. In E. Emerson, J. Bromley and A. Caine (eds) *Clinical Psychology and People with Intellectual Disabilities*. Chichester: John Wiley & Sons Ltd.

Hatton, C. 1998b: Intellectual disability: Epidemiology and causes. In E. Emerson, J. Bromley and A. Caine (eds) *Clinical Psychology and People with Intellectual Disabilities*. Chichester: John Wiley & Sons Ltd.

Hawkins, J.D., Catalano, R.F. et al. 1992: Seattle Development Project: Effects of the first 4 years on protective factors and problem behaviours. In J. McCord and R. Tremblay (eds) *The Prevention of Anti-Social Behaviour in Children*. New York: Guilford Press.

Henggeler, S.W., Schoenwald, S.K. et al. 1998: *Multisystemic Treatment of Antisocial Behavior in Children and Adolescents*. New York: Guilford Press.

Herbert, M. 1964: The concept and testing of brain-damage in children: A review. *Journal of Child Psychology and Psychiatry*, 5, 197–216.

Herbert, M. 1965: Personality factors and bronchial asthma: A study of South African Indian children. *Journal of Psychosomatic Research*, 8, 353–7.

Herbert, M. 1967: Olfactory precipitants of bronchial asthma: *Journal of Psychosomatic Research*, 11, 195–202.

Herbert, M. 1987a: *Conduct Disorders of Childhood and Adolescence* (2nd edn). Chichester: John Wiley & Sons Ltd.

Herbert, M. 1987b: *Behavioural Treatment of Children with Problems: A Practice Manual* (2nd edn). London: Academic Press.

Herbert, M. 1993: *Working with Children and the Children Act*. Leicester: BPS Books (British Psychological Society).

Herbert, M. 1996a: *Toilet Training, Bedwetting and Soiling*. Leicester: BPS Books (British Psychological Society, *PACT I* Series).

Herbert, M. 1996b: *Coping with Children's Feeding Problems and Bedtime Battles.* Leicester: BPS Books (British Psychological Society, *PACT I* Series).

Herbert, M. 1998: *Clinical Child Psychology: Social Learning, Development and Behaviour* (2nd edn). Chichester: John Wiley & Sons Ltd.

Herbert, M. 2000: Assessment of child sexual abuse. *Behaviour Change,* 17, 15–27.

Herbert, M. 2003: *Typical and Atypical Development: From Conception to Adolescence.* Oxford: BPS-Blackwell.

Herbert, M. 2004: *Developmental Problems of Childhood and Adolescence: Treatment, Prevention and Rehabilitation.* Oxford: BPS-Blackwell.

Herbert, M. and Harper-Dorton, K. 2002: *Working with Children and Adolescents and their Families.* Oxford: BPS-Blackwell.

Herbert, M. and Kemp, M. 1969: The reliability of the brain. *Science Journal,* 5, 47–52.

Herbert, M., Sluckin, W.S. and Sluckin, A. 1982: Mother-to-infant bonding. *Journal of Child Psychology and Psychiatry,* 23, 202–21.

Herbert, M. and Wookey, J. 2004: *Managing Disruptive Behaviour: A Guide for Practitioners Working with Parents and Foster Parents.* Oxford: BPS-Blackwell.

Hermelin, B. and O'Connor, N. 1970a: *Psychological Experiments with Autistic Children.* Oxford: Pergamon Press.

Hermelin, B. and O'Connor, N. 1970b: Crossmodal transfer in normal, subnormal and autistic children. *Neuropsychologica,* 2, 229–32.

Heyne, D. and Rollings, S. (with King, N. and Tonge, B.) 2002: *School Refusal (PACT 2* Series). Oxford: BPS-Blackwell.

Heyne, D., King, N. and Tonge, B. 2004: School refusal. In T.H. Ollendick and J.S. March (eds) *Phobic and Anxiety Disorders in Children and Adolescents: A Clinician's Guide to Effective Psychosocial Intervention.* Oxford: Oxford University Press.

Houts, A.C., Berman, J.S. and Abramson, H. 1994: Effectiveness of psychological and pharmacological treatments for nocturnal enuresis. *Journal of Child Psychological and Psychiatry,* 39, 307–22.

Howlin, P. 1994 and 2002: Special educational attainment. In M. Rutter, E. Taylor and L. Hersov (eds) *Child Psychology and Psychiatry: Modern Approaches* (3rd edn). Oxford: Blackwell Scientific Publications.

Howlin, P. 1998: Practitioner review: Psychological and educational treatments for autism. *Journal of Child Psychology and Psychiatry,* 39, 307–22.

Howlin, P. and Rutter, M. 1987: *Treatment of Autistic Children.* New York: Wiley.

Howlin, P., Rutter, M., Berger, M., Hemsley, R., Hersov, L. and Yule, W. 1987: *Treatment of Autistic Children.* Chichester: John Wiley & Sons Ltd.

Hutchings, J., Gardner, F. and Lane, E. 2004: Making evidence-based interventions work. In C. Sutton, D. Utting and D. Farrington (eds) *Support from the Start* (DfES Publications Research Report S24, London: DfES.

Iwaniec, D., Herbert, M. and McNeish, S. 1988: Social work with failure-to-thrive children and their families: Part I, Psychosocial factors; Part II, Behavioural casework. *British Journal of Social Work,* 15, nos 3 (June) and 4 (August) respectively.

Iwaniec, D., Herbert, M. and Sluckin, A. 1988 (1st edn), 2002 (2nd edn): Helping emotionally abused child who fail to thrive. In K. Browne, C. Davies and P. Stratton (eds) *Early Prediction and Prevention of Child Abuse.* Chichester: John Wiley & Sons Ltd.

Jacobsen, B. and Kenney, D.E. 1980: Perinatal implications in adopted and non-adopted schizophrenics and their controls: Preliminary results. *Acta Psychiatrica*, Scandinavia, (suppl. 285) 337–46.

Johns, N. 1971: Family reactions to the birth of a child with a congenital abnormality. *Medical Journal of Australia*, 7, 277–82.

Johnson, D.L. and Walker, T. 1957: Primary prevention of behavior problems in Mexican American children. *American Journal of Community Psychology*, 15, 375–85.

Joseph, P.R. 1999: Selective mutism – the child doesn't speak at school. *Pediatrics*, 104 (2 pt. 1), 308–9.

Kazdin, A.E. 1990: Childhood depression. *Journal of Child Psychology and Psychiatry*, 31, 121–60.

Kazdin, A. 1997a: Practitioner review of psychosocial treatments for conduct disorders in children. *Journal of Clinical Psychology and Psychiatry*, 38, 161–78.

Kazdin, A. 1997b: A model for developing effective treatment: Progression and interplay of theory, research and practice. *Journal of Clinical Child Psychology*, 26, 114–29.

Kazdin, A.E. 1998: Psychosocial treatments for conduct disorder in children. In P. Nathan and J. Gorman (eds) *A Guide to Treatments that Work.* New York: Oxford University Press.

Kazdin, A.E. 2000: *Psychotherapy for Children and Adolescents: Directions for Research and Practice.* New York: Oxford University Press.

Kazdin, A. and Wassell, G. 1999: Barriers to treatment participation and therapeutic change among children referred for conduct disorders. *Journal of Clinical and Child Psychology*, 28, 160–72.

Kendall, P.C. and Gosch, E.A. 1994: Cognitive-behavioral interventions. In T.H. Ollendick, N.J. King and W. Yule (eds) *International Handbook of Phobic and Anxiety Disorders in Children and Adolescents.* New York: Plenum Press.

Kendall, P.C. and Hollon, S.D. (eds) 1994: *Cognitive-Behavioral Interventions: Theory Research and Procedures.* New York: Academic Press.

Kerr, B. 1991: *A Handbook for Counseling the Gifted and Talented.* Alexandria, VA: American Association for Counselling and Development.

Kiernan, C.C. 1983: The exploration of sign and symbol effects. In J.J. Hogg and P.J. Mittler (eds) *Advances in Mental Handicap Research*, Vol. 2: *Aspects of Competence in Mentally Handicapped.* Chichester: John Wiley & Sons Ltd.

Kim-Cohen, J. Moffitt, T.E., and Taylor, A. 2004: Genetic and environmental processes in young children's resilience and vulnerability to socioeconomic deprivation. *Child Development*, 75: 651–63.

King, N.J., Hamilton, D.I. and Ollendick, T.H. 1998: *Children's Phobias: A Behavioral Perspective.* Chichester: John Wiley & Sons Ltd.

King, N.J., Ollendick, T.H. and Tonge, B. 1995: *School Refusal: Assessment and Treatment.* Boston: Allyn & Bacon.

Kolvin, I. and Fundudis, T. 1981: Elective mute children: Psychological development and background factors. *Journal of Child Psychology and Psychiatry,* 22, 219–33.

Kopp, C.B. and Kaler, S.R. 1989: Risk in infancy. *American Psychologist,* 44, 224–30.

Kramer, M. et al. 2000: Report on the viability of preterm infants. *Journal of the American Medical Association,* 16 August.

Kratochwill, T. 1981: *Selective Mutism: Implications for Research and Treatment.* Hillsdale, NJ: Lawrence Erlbaum Associates.

Kreitman, N. 1993: Suicide and parasuicide. In R.E. Kendell and A.K. Zeally (eds) *Companion to Psychiatric Studies.* 5th edn. Edinburgh: Churchill and Livingstone.

Kumin, L.A. 1986: Survey of speech and language pathology services for Down syndrome: State of the art. *Applied Research in Mental Retardation,* 7, 491–9.

Kumin, L., Goodman, M. and Councill, C. 1991: Comprehensive communication intervention for school-aged children with Down syndrome. *Down Syndrome Quarterly,* 1, 1–8.

Kumin, L., Goodman, M. and Councill, C. 1996: Comprehensive communication intervention for infants and toddlers with Down syndrome. *Infant–Toddler Intervention,* 1, 275–96.

Ladd, G.W. 1984: Social skill training with children: Issues in research and practice. *Clinical Psychology Review,* 4, 317–37.

Lally, J.R., Mangione, P.L. and Honig, A.S. 1983: The Syracuse University Family Research Program. In D. Powell (ed.) *Parent Education as Early Childhood Intervention.* Norwood, NJ: Ablex.

Largo, R.H., Molinari, I. et al. 1986: Language development of term and preterm children during the first five years of life. *Developmental Medicine and Child Neurology,* 28, 33–5.

Lask, B. and Matthew, D. 1979: Childhood asthma: A controlled trial of family psychotherapy. *Archives of Disease in Childhood,* 54, 116–19.

Law, J., Boyle, J. et al. 1998: Screening for speech and language delay: A systematic review of the literature. *Health Technology Assessment,* 2, 1–81.

Law, J. and Garrett, Z. 2004: Speech and language therapy: Its potential role in CAMHS. *Child and Adolescent Mental Health,* 9, 50–5.

Leckman, J.F., Zhang, H., Vitale, A. et al. 1998: Course of tic severity in Tourette's syndrome: The first two decades. *Pediatrics,* 102, 14–19.

Lee, S.G. and Herbert, M. 1970: *Freud and Psychology.* Harmondsworth: Penguin.

Lehrer, P.M., Sangunaraj, D. and Hochron, S. 1992: Psychological approaches to the treatment of asthma. *Journal of Consulting and Clinical Psychology,* 60, 639–43.

Leib, S.A., Benfield, G. and Guidubaldi, J. 1980: Effects of early intervention and stimulation in the preterm infant. *Pediatrics,* 66, 83–90.

Leon, G.R. and Dinklage, D. 1989: Childhood obesity and anorexia nervosa. In T.H. Ollendick and M. Hersen (eds) *Handbook of Child Psychopathology*. New York: Plenum Press.

Levy, T. and Orlans, M. 1995: Intensive short-term therapy with attachment disordered children (unpublished manuscript).

Lewinsohn, P.M. and Clarke, G.N. 1999: Psychosocial treatments for adolescent depression. *Clinical Psychology Review*, 19, 320–42.

Lewinsohn, P.M., Clarke, G.N. et al. 1996: Cognitive-behavioural treatment for depressed adolescents. *Behavior Therapy*, 21, 385–401.

Lewis, V. 1987: *Development and Handicap*. Oxford: Basil Blackwell.

Lewis, V. 2002: *Development and Disability* (2nd edn). Oxford: Basil Blackwell.

Lilienfeld, S.O., Lynn, S.J., and Lohr, J.M. (eds) 2003: *Science and Pseudoscience in Clinical Psychology*. New York: The Guilford Press.

Lochman, J.E. 1992: Cognitive-behavioral interventions with aggressive boys: Three-year follow-up and preventive effects. *Journal of Clinical and Consulting Psychology*, 60, 426–32.

Lott, I. 1995: *The Neurology of Down Syndrome*. New York: National Down Syndrome Society.

Lovaas, O.I. 1987: Behavioral treatment and normal educational and intellectual functioning in young autistic children, *Journal of Clinical and Consulting Psychology*, 55, 3–9.

Lovaas, O.I. and Leaf, R.I. 1981: *Five Video Tapes for Teaching Developmentally Disabled Children*. Baltimore: University Park Press.

Luthar, S.S. 1991: Vulnerability and resilience: A study of high-risk adolescents, *Child Development*, 62, 600–16.

Lyon, G.R. and Cutting, I.E. 1998: Learning disabilities. In E.J. Mash and R.A. Barkley (eds) *Treatment of Childhood Disorders*. New York: Guilford Press.

Lyons-Ruth, K. and Jacobwitz, T.R. 1999: Attachment disorganisation. In J. Cassidy and P.R. Slater (eds) *Handbook of Attachment Theory, Research and Clinical Application*. New York: Guilford Press.

Lyons-Ruth, K., Zoll, A. et al. 1986: (presentation, European Down Syndrome Symposium, Valencia, Spain).

Maccoby, E.E. 1980: *Social Development: Psychological Growth and the Parent–Child Relationship*. San Diego, CA: Harcourt Brace Jovanovich.

MacKillop, J., Lisman, S.A., et al. 2003: Controversial treatments for alcoholism. In S.O. Lilienfeld., S.J. Lynn., and J.M. Lohr (eds) *Science and Pseudoscience in Clinical Psychology*. New York: The Guilford Press.

Mar, H. 1998: Psychological evaluation of children who are deaf-blind: An overview with recommendations for practice. *DB-Link The National Clearing-house on Children Who Are Deaf-Blind*.

March, J.S. and Mulle, K. 1998: *OCD in Children and Adolescents: A Cognitive Behavioral Treatment Manual*. New York: Guildford Press.

March, J.S., Mulle, K. and Herbel, B. 1994: Behavioral psychotherapy for children and adolescents with obsessive compulsive disorder: An open trial of a new protocol drugs package. *Journal of the American Academy of Child and Adolescent Psychiatry*, 33, 333–41.

March, J.S. and Ollendick, T.H. 2004: Integrated psychosocial and pharmacological treatment. In T.H. Ollendick and J.S. March (eds) 2004: *Phobic and Anxiety Disorders in Children and Adolescents: A Clinician's Guide to Effective Psychosocial and Pharmacological Intervention*. Oxford: Oxford University Press.

Marsscark, M. 1993: *Psychological Development of Deaf Children*. Oxford: Oxford University Press.

Mattis, S.G. and Ollendick, T.H. 2002: *Panic Disorder and Anxiety in Adolescence* (*PACTS 2* Series). Oxford: BPS Blackwell.

Maughan, B. and Yule, W. 1994: Reading and other learning difficulties. In M. Rutter, E. Taylor and L. Hersov (eds) *Child and Adolescent Psychiatry: Modern Approaches*. Oxford: Blackwell Scientific.

McBrien, D. 1998: Attention problems in Down syndrome: Is this ADHD? University of Iowa Hospital website.

McCord, W. and McCord, J. 1964: *The Psychopath*. London: Van Nostrand.

McEachin, J.J., Smith, T. and Lovaas, O.I. 1993: Long-term outcome for children with autism who received early intensive behavioral treatment, *American Journal on Mental Retardation*, 97, 359–72.

McGaw, S. 2004: Parenting exceptional children. In M. Hoghughi and N. Long (eds) *Handbook of Parenting: Theory and Research for Practice*. London: Sage.

McLaren, J. and Bryson, S. 1987: Review of recent epidemiological Studies of mental retardation: prevalence, associated disorders and etiology. *American Journal of Mental Retardation*, 92, 243–54.

Meyer, E., Coll, C. et al. 1994: Family-based intervention improves maternal psychological well-being and feeding interaction of preterm infants. *Pediatrics*, 93, 241–6.

Middle. C., Johnson, A. et al. 1996: Birthweight, health and development at the age of 7 years. *Child Care, Health and Development*, 22, 55–71.A.

Mitchell, T. and Carr, A. 2000: Anorexia and bulimia. In A. Carr (ed.) *What Works with Children and Adolescents?* London: Routledge.

Monat-Haller, R.K. 1992: *Understanding and Expressing Sexuality*. Baltimore. MD: Paul H. Brookes.

Moore, T. 1966: Difficulties of the ordinary child in adjusting to primary school. *Journal of Child Psychology and Psychiatry*, 7, 299.

Morrison, J. 1995: *DSM-IV Made Easy*. New York: The Guilford Press.

Murray, L. 1992: The impact of postnatal depression on child development. *Journal of Child Psychology and Psychiatry*, 33, 543–61.

Murray, L. and Cooper, P.J. 1997: Effects of postnatal depression on infant development. *Archive of Disease in Childhood*, 77, 99–107.

Murray, L., Fiori-Cowley, A., Hooper, R. and Cooper, P.J. 1996: The impact of postnatal depression and associated adversity on early mother–infant interactions and later infant outcome. *Child Development*, 67, 2512–26.

Nemeroff, R., Gipson, P. and Jensen, P. 2004: From efficacy to effectiveness: What we have learned in the last 10 years. In T.H. Ollendick and J.S. March (eds) *Phobic and Anxiety Disorders in Children and Adolescents: A Clinician's Guide to Effective Psychosocial And Pharmacological Intervention*. Oxford: Oxford University Press.

Nolan, M. and Carr, A. 2000: ADHD. In A. Carr (ed.) *What Works with Children and Adolescents?* London: Routledge.

O'Connor, T.G., Heron, J., Glover, V., ALSPAC Study Team, 2002: Antenatal anxiety predicts child behavioral/emotional problems independently of postnatal depression. *Journal of the American Academy of Child and Adolescent Psychiatry*, 41, 1470–89.

Offord, D.R. and Bennett, K. 2002: Prevention. In M. Rutter and E. Taylor (eds) *Child Psychology and Psychiatry* (4th edn). Oxford: Blackwell Scientific Publications.

O'Hara, M.W. 1997: The nature of postpartum depressive disorders. In L. Murray and P.J. Cooper (eds) *Postpartum Depression and Child Development*, pp. 3–31. New York: Guilford Press.

Ohtahara, S. 1984: Seizure disorders in infancy and childhood. *Brain Development*, 6, 509–19.

Olds, D.L., Hill, R. et al. 1998: Pre-natal and infant home visitation by nurses: A program of research. In B.S. Elliott (ed.) *Blueprint for Violence Prevention*. Boulder, CO: Colorado Center for the Study of Prevention of Violence, University of Colorado.

Ollendick, T.H. 1979: Behavioral treatment of anorexia nervosa: A five-year-old study. *Behavior Modification*, 3, 124–35.

Ollendick, T.H., Davis, T. and Muris, P. 2004: Treatment of specific phobias. In T.H. Ollendick and J.S. March (eds) *Phobic and Anxiety Disorders in Children and Adolescents: A Clinician's Guide to Effective Psychosocial And Pharmacological Intervention*. Oxford: Oxford University Press.

Ollendick, T.H. and King, N.J. 2004: Empirically supported treatments for children and adolescents: Advances toward evidence-based practice. In P.M. Barrett and T.H. Ollendick (eds) *Handbook of Interventions that Work with Children and Adolescents: Prevention and Treatment*. Chichester: Wiley.

Ollendick, T.H., King, N.J. and Yule, W. (eds) 1994: *International Handbook of Phobic and Anxiety Disorders in Children and Adolescents*. New York: Plenum Press.

Ollendick, T.H. and March, J.S. (eds) 2004: *Phobic and Anxiety Disorders in Children and Adolescents: A Clinician's Guide to Effective Psychosocial and Pharmacological Intervention*. Oxford: Oxford University Press.

Olweus, D., Limber, S. and Mihalic, S.F. 1999: *Bullying Prevention Program*, Book 9: *Blueprints for Violence Prevention*. Boulder, CO: Center for the Study and Prevention of Violence. Institute of Behavioral Science, University of Colorado.

O'Sullivan, A.M. and Carr, A. 2002: Prevention of developmental delay in low birthweight infants. In A. Carr (ed.) *What Works with Children and Adolescents?* London: Brunner-Routledge.

Parker, S., Zahr, A. et al. 1992: Outcomes after developmental intervention in the neonatal intensive care unit for mothers of preterm babies with low socio-economic status. *Journal of Pediatrics*, 129, 780–5.

Pattenden, S., Delk, H. and Vrijheid, M. 1999: Inequality in low birthweight parental social class, area deprivation, and 'lone mother' status. *Journal of Epidemiology and Community Health*, 52, 355–8.

Patterson, G.R. 1982: *Coercive Family Process.* Eugene, OR: Castalia.

Pharoah, P.O., Stevenson, C.J. et al. 1994: Prevention of behavior disorders in low birthweight infants. *Archive of Disease in Childhood*, 70, 271–4.

Powell, L.F. 1974: The effect of extra stimulation and maternal involvement on the development of low birthweight infants and on maternal behavior. *Child Development*, 45, 106–13.

Powers, A.R. and Elliott, R.N. (eds) 1993: *Deaf and Hard of Hearing Students with Mild Additional Disabilities.* Tuscaloosa, AL: The University of Alabama.

Prior, M., Smart, D. et al. 1999: Relationships between learning difficulties and psychological problems in preadolescent children from a longitudinal sample. *Journal of the American Academy of Child and Adolescent Psychiatry*, 38, 429–36.

Puckering, C. 2004: Parenting in social and economic adversity. In M. Hoghughi and N. Long (eds) *Handbook of Parenting: Theory and Research for Practice.* London: Sage.

Pueschel, S.M. 1986: Masturbation during adolescence: *Down syndrome. Paper and abstracts for* Professional, 9, 1.

Rahi, J. et al. 2003: Institute of Child Health, *The Lancet*, 24 October.

Rani, A.S., Jyothem, A., Reddy, P.P. and Reddy, O.S. 1990: Reproduction in Down syndrome. International Journal of Gynecology and Obstetrics, 31, 1–86.

Rauch, P. and Jellinek, M. 2002: Paediatric consultation. In M. Rutter and E. Taylor (eds) *Child and Adolescent Psychiatry.* Oxford: Blackwell Scientific Publications.

Rauh, V., Achenbach, T. et al. 1988: Minimizing adverse effects of low birth weight: Four year results of an early intervention program. *Child Development*, 59, 544–53.

Raynor, P. and Rudolf, M.C.J. 1996: What do we know about children who fail to thrive? *Child Care, Health and Development*, 22, 241–50.

Reason, R. 2001: Educational practice and dyslexia. *The Psychologist*, 14, 298–301.

Reed, G.F. 1968: Elective mutism in children: A reappraisal. *Journal of Child Psychology and Psychiatry*, 4, 99–107.

Robertson, M.M. 2004: Gilles de la Tourette. *The Psychologist*, 17, 76–9.

Rogers, C.R. 1960: *On Becoming a Person.* Boston: Houghton Mifflin.

Rosenblith, J. 1992: *In the Beginning: Development from Conception to Age Two* (2nd edn). Newbury Park, CA: Sage.

Ross, R.R. and Fabiano, E.A. 1985: *Time to Think: A Cognitive Model of Delinquency and Offender Rehabilitation.* Johnson City. In: Institute of Social Sciences and Arts.

Rutter, M. 1985: The treatment of autistic children. *Journal of Child Psychology and Psychiatry*, 26, 193–214.

Rutter, M. 1995: Clinical implications of attachment theory, retrospect and prospect. *Journal of Child Psychology and Psychiatry*, 36, 549–71.

Rutter, M. 2003: Commentary: Nature–nurture interplay in emotional disorders. *Journal of Child Psychology and Psychiatry*, 44, 20–34.

Rutter, M., Maughan, B., Mortimore, P., Ousten, J. and Smith, A. 1979: *Fifteen Thousand Hours: Secondary Schools and their Effects on Children.* Cambridge, MA: Harvard University Press.

Rutter, M., Silberg, J., O'Connor, T. and Simonoff, E. 1999a: Genetics and psychiatry: I Advances in quantitative and molecular genetics (pp. 3–18); II Empirical research findings (pp. 19–36). *Journal of Child Psychology and Psychiatry*, 40.

Rutter, M., Silberg, J., O'Connor, T. and Simonoff, E. 1999b: Genetics and child psychiatry: II Empirical research findings. *Journal of Child Psychology and Psychiatry*, 40, 19–55.

Rutter, M., Thorpe, K., Greenwood, R., Northstone, K. and Golding, J. 2003: Twins as a natural experiment to study the causes of mild language delay, I: Design; twin–singleton differences in language, and obstetric risks. *Journal of Child Psychology and Psychiatry*, 44, 326.

Rutter, M., Tizard, J. and Whitmore, K. (eds) 1970: *Education, Health and Behaviour.* Harlow: Longman. (Reprinted 1981, Krieger, Melbourne, FC.)

Samra, B. 1999: Supporting parents through parenting programmes. In H. Enzig and S. Wolfendale (eds) *Parenting Education and Support.* London: David Fulton Publishers.

Sanders, M. 2003: *Triple P Positive Parenting Program.* University of Queensland.

Schopler, E., Reichler, R.J. and Renner, B.R. 1999: *A Childhood Autism Rating Scale.* Los Angeles: Western Psychological Services.

Schwab, W.E. 1992: Sexuality and community living. In I.T. Lott and E.E. McCoy (eds) Down Syndrome: Advances in Medical Care. New York: Wiley-Liss.

Scott, S. 2002: Parent training programmes. In M. Rutter and E. Taylor (eds) *Child and Adolescent Psychiatry.* Oxford: Blackwell Scientific Publications.

Scott, S., Knapp, M., Henderson, J. and Maughan, B. 2001: Financial costs of social exclusion: Follow up study of children into adulthood. *British Medical Journal,* 323 (7306), 191–3.

Seeley, S., Murray, L., Cooper, P.J. 1996: Postnatal depression: The outcome for mothers and babies of health visitor intervention. *Health Visitor,* 69, 135–8.

Seitz, V., Rosenbaum, L.K. and Apfel, N. 1985: Effects of family support intervention: A ten year followup. *Child Development,* 56, 376–91.

Seligman, D., Goza, A.P. and Ollendick, T.H. 2004: Treatment of depression in children and adolescents. In P.M. Barrott and T.H. Ollendick (eds) *Handbook of Interventions that Work with Children and Adolescents: Prevention and Treatment.* Chichester: John Wiley.

Shaffer, D.R. 1999: *Developmental Psychology: Childhood and Adolescence*. Pacific Grove, CA: Brooks/Cole.

Simeonsson, R.L. and Rosenthal, S.L. (eds) 2001: *Psychological and Developmental Assessment: Children with Disabilities and Chronic Conditions*. New York: Guilford Press.

Skuse, D. 1989: Emotional abuse and delay in growth. In R. Meadow (ed.) *Handbook of Child Abuse*. London: British Medical Association.

Sluckin, A., Foreman, N. and Herbert, M. 1990: Behavioural treatment programmes and selectivity of speaking at follow-up to a sample of 25 selective mutes. *Australian Psychologist*, 26, 132–7.

Sluckin, W., Herbert, M. and Sluckin, A. 1983: *Maternal Bonding*. Oxford: Basil Blackwell.

Smith, C. 1996: *Developing Parenting Programmes*. London: National Children's Bureau.

Snowling, M.J. 2000: *Dyslexia*. Oxford: Blackwell.

Standart, S. and Le Couteur, A. 2003: The quiet child: A literature review of selective mutism. *Child and Adolescent Mental Health*, 8, 154–60.

Stevenson, J. and Goodman, R. 2001: Association between behaviour at age 3 years and adult criminality. *British Journal of Psychiatry*, 179, 197–202.

Stone, K.M. 1994: HIV, other STDs, and barriers. In C.M. Mauck, M. Coredero, H.L. Gabelnick, J.M. Spieler and R. Rivera (eds) *Barrier Contraceptives: Current Status and Future Prospects*. New York: Wiley-Liss.

Streissguth, A.P. 1997: *Fetal Alcohol Syndrome: A Guide for Families and Communities*. Baltimore: Paul H. Brookes Publishing Co.

Streissguth, A.P., Barr, H.M., Kogan, J. and Bookstein, F.L. 1996: Understanding the occurrence of secondary disabilities in clients with fetal alcohol syndrome (FAS) and fetal alcohol effects (FAE): Final report to the Centers for Disease Control and Prevention (CDC), August 1996, Seattle: University of Washington, Fetal Alcohol and Drug Unit, Tech. Rep. No. 96–06.

Streissguth, A.P. and Kanter, J. (eds) 1997: *The Challenge of Fetal Alcohol Syndrome: Overcoming Secondary Disabilities*. Seattle: University of Washington Press.

Sutton, C. 2000: *Child and Adolescent Behaviour Problems*. Leicester: BPS Books, (British Psychological Society).

Sutton, C. and Herbert, M. 1992: *Child Care and the Family*. Windsor: NFER-Nelson.

Sutton, C., Utting, D. and Farrington, D. 2004: *Support from the Start*. DfES Publications Research Report S24. London: DfES.

Sykes, D.H., Hay, A. et al.1997: Low birthweight prematures: Preventive intervention and maternal attitude. *Child Psychology Psychiatry and Human Development*, 17, 152–65.

Target, M. and Fonagy, P. 1996: The psychological treatment of child and adolescent psychiatric disorders. In A. Roth and P. Fonagy (eds) *What Works for Whom?* London: Guilford Press.

Taylor, E. and Rutter, M. 2002: Psychiatric diagnosis. In M. Rutter and E. Taylor (eds) *Child and Adolescent Psychiatry* (4th edn). Oxford: Blackwell Scientific Publishing.

Terman, L.M. and Oden, M. 1947: *The Gifted Child Grows Up: Gender Status of Genius.* CA: Stanford University Press.

Thorpe, K., Rutter, M. and Greenwood, R. 2003: Twins as a natural experiment to study the causes of mild language delay, II: Family interaction risk factors. *Journal of Child Psychology and Psychiatry,* 44, 342–55.

Tourette Syndrome Association International Consortium for Genetics, 1999: A complete genome scan in sib-pairs affected with Gilles de la Tourette syndrome. *American Journal of Human Genetics,* 65, 1428–61.

Touyz, S.W. 1995: A recipe for the psychological treatments of eating disorders. In presentation by M. Maj, K. Halmi et al., Psychosexual behavior, sexuality, and management issues in individuals with Down syndrome, European Down Syndrome Symposium, Mallorca, Spain.

Van Londen, A., Van Londen, B. and Monique, W. 1995: Relapse rate and subsequent parental reaction after successful treatment of children suffering from nocturnal enuresis: A 2 1/2 year follow-up of bibliotherapy. *Behaviour Research and Therapy,* 33, 309–11.

Vatten, L. 2003: Norwegian University of Science and Technology in Trondheim (reported in *The Times,* Friday, 14 November).

Vine, S. 1999: Feature article. (p. 24, *The Times,* 23 October 2003).

Wadhwa, P.D., Sandman, C.A. et al. 1993: The association between prenatal stress and infant birth weight and gestational age at birth: A prospective investigation. *American Journal of Obstetrics and Gynecology,* 160, 858–65.

Wakschlag, L.S., Lahey, B.B. and Loeber, R. 1997: Maternal smoking during pregnancy and the risk of conduct disorder in boys. *Archives of General Psychiatry,* 54, 670–6.

Waldron, H.B. and Kern-Jones, S. 2004: Treatment of substance abuse disorders in children and adolescence. In P.M. Barrett and T.H. Ollendick (eds) *Handbook of Interventions that Work with Children and Adolescents: Prevention and Treatment.* Chilchester: John Wiley.

Walker, C.E. 1995: Elimination disorders: Enuresis and encopresis. In M.C. Roberts (ed.) *Handbook of Pediatric Psychology* (2nd edn). New York: Guilford Press.

Walker-Hirsch, L. and Champagne, M.P. 1992: Circles III: safer ways. In A.C. Crocker, H.J. Cohen and L.T.A. Kastner (eds) *HIV Infection and Developmental Disabilities.* Baltimore, MD: Paul H. Brookes Co.

Warren, S.T. and Nelson, D.L. 1994: Advances in molecular analysis of fragile X syndrome. *Journal of the American Medical Association,* 271, 536–42.

Webster-Stratton, C. 1991: Annotation: Strategies for working with families of conduct-disordered children. *Journal of Child Psychology and Psychiatry,* 32, 1047–62.

Webster-Stratton, C. and Dahl, R.W. 1995: Conduct disorder. In M. Hersen and A.T. Ammerman (eds) *Advanced Abnormal Child Psychiatry.* Hillsdale, NJ: Lawrence Erlbaum Associates.

Webster-Stratton, C. and Herbert, M. 1993: What really happens in parent training? *Behavior Modification,* 17, 407–56.

Webster-Stratton, C. and Herbert, M. 1994: *Troubled Families – Problem Children: Working with Parents, a Collaborative Process.* Chichester: John Wiley & Sons Ltd.

Wellings, K., Field, J. et al. 1995: *Sexual Behaviour in Britain.* Harmondsworth: Penguin.

Werner, E. and Smith, R.S. 1982: *Vulnerable but Invincible: A Longitudinal Study of Resilient Children and Youth.* New York: McGraw-Hill.

Wishart, T.G. 1991: Taking the initiative on learning: A developmental investigation of infants with Down syndrome. *Journal of Intellectual Disability Research,* 37, 339–403.

Wolf, L.C., Noh, S., Fisman, S.N. et al. 1989: Psychological effects of parenting stress on parents of autistic children. *Journal of Autism and Developmental Disorders,* 19, 157–66.

Wood, N.S., Marlow, N., Costeloe, K., et al. 2000: Neurologic and developmental disability after extremely preterm birth study group. *New England Journal of Medicine,* Aug 10; 343(6): 378–84 (the EPICURE project).

World Health Organisation (WHO) 1992: *The ICD-10 Classification of Mental and Behavioural Disorders: Clinical Descriptions and Diagnostic Guidelines.* Geneva: WHO.

World Health Organization (WHO) 2002: Multi-axial Classification of Child and Adolescent Psychiatric Disorders: *ICD-10 Classification of Mental and Behavioural Disorders in Children and Adolescents.* Cambridge: Cambridge University Press.

Yoshikawa, H. 1994a: The future of children on social outcomes and delinquency. *Psychological Bulletin* (Special Issue: 'Long Term Effects of Early Childhood Programs'), 115, 24–54.

Yoshikawa, H. 1994b: Prevention as cumulative protection: Effects of early family support and education on chronic delinquency and its risks. *Psychological Bulletin,* 115, 28–54.

Yoshikawa, H. 2000: Community prevention and intervention: Prevention with young children. In A.E. Kazdin (ed.) *Encyclopedia of Psychology.* Washington, DC: American Psychological Association.

Yoshikawa, H. and Knitzer, J. 1997: *Lessons from the Field: Head Start Mental Health Strategies to Meet Changing Needs.* New York: National Center for Children in Poverty and American Orthopsychiatric Association.

Author Index

Subject Index